VOLUME NINETY SIX

ADVANCES IN
COMPUTERS
Dataflow Processing

VOLUME NINETY SIX

Advances in
COMPUTERS
Dataflow Processing

Edited by

ALI R. HURSON
Missouri University of Science and Technology,
Rolla, MO, USA

VELJKO MILUTINOVIC
School of Electrical Engineering,
University of Belgrade,
Belgrade, Serbia

AMSTERDAM • BOSTON • HEIDELBERG • LONDON
NEW YORK • OXFORD • PARIS • SAN DIEGO
SAN FRANCISCO • SINGAPORE • SYDNEY • TOKYO
Academic Press is an imprint of Elsevier

Academic Press is an imprint of Elsevier
225 Wyman Street, Waltham, MA 02451, USA
525 B Street, Suite 1800, San Diego, CA 92101-4495, USA
125 London Wall, London, EC2Y 5AS, UK
The Boulevard, Langford Lane, Kidlington, Oxford OX5 1GB, UK

First edition 2015

Notices
Knowledge and best practice in this field are constantly changing. As new research and experience broaden our understanding, changes in research methods, professional practices, or medical treatment may become necessary.

Practitioners and researchers must always rely on their own experience and knowledge in evaluating and using any information, methods, compounds, or experiments described herein. In using such information or methods they should be mindful of their own safety and the safety of others, including parties for whom they have a professional responsibility.

To the fullest extent of the law, neither the Publisher nor the authors, contributors, or editors, assume any liability for any injury and/or damage to persons or property as a matter of products liability, negligence or otherwise, or from any use or operation of any methods, products, instructions, or ideas contained in the material herein.

ISBN: 978-0-12-802134-7
ISSN: 0065-2458

For information on all Academic Press publications
visit our web site at store.elsevier.com

CONTENTS

PREFACE

Traditionally, *Advances in Computers*, the oldest series to chronicle the rapid evolution of computing, annually publishes several volumes, each typically comprised of four to eight chapters, describing new developments in the theory and applications of computing. The theme of this 96th volume is inspired by the advances in computer architecture. Within the spectrum of computer architecture, this volume concentrates on dataflow processing, heterogeneous and reconfigurable architecture, and caching. The volume is a collection of five chapters that were solicited from authorities in the field, each of whom brings to bear a unique perspective on the topic.

In Chapter 1 "An Overview of Selected Heterogeneous and Reconfigurable Architectures," Stojanović *et al.* introduce and articulate the motivations behind heterogeneous and reconfigurable architectures. A classical classification of heterogeneous architectures and the extended Flynn's taxonomy are discussed. The authors then introduce a new classification based on the computational model, i.e., control flow and dataflow model of computations. Several commercially available heterogeneous platforms (CBEA, ClearSpeed, SGI RASC, Convey, Maxeler MaxNodes, NVidia GPU, and AMD ATI GPU) are studied and comparatively analyzed. Finally, three systems, namely, Intel Core i7-870 CPU with 4 cores, NVidia C2070 GPU, and Maxeler MAX3 card as typical representative of CPU, GPU, and Dataflow computing model have been experimentally studied and compared against each other.

In Chapter 2 "Concurrency, Synchronization, and Speculation—The Dataflow Way," Kavi *et al.* survey the evolution of dataflow processing. Dataflow model of computation is introduced and its advantages in terms of concurrency, synchronization, and speculation relative to control flow computation are addressed. The chapter then studies several data flow languages, historical architectures, and recent architectures. Finally, the so-called scheduled dataflow architecture which applies dataflow execution model at the thread level as a case study is discussed in detail.

Application targeting reconfigurable architecture (see Chapter 1 "An Overview of Selected Heterogeneous and Reconfigurable Architectures") can exploit inherent fine-grained parallelism and predictable low latency features on the underlying platform to achieve high throughput per watt. However, traditional techniques for designing FPGA (Field Programmable

Gate Array)-based reconfigurability are time consuming and hence have limited commercial attraction. To overcome this handicap, Maxeler Technology has developed a dataflow-based platform based on earlier static synchronous dataflow architecture (see Chapter 2 "Concurrency, Synchronization, and Speculation—The Dataflow Way") enhanced by data streaming. In Chapter 3 "Dataflow Computing in Extreme Performance Conditions," Oriato et al. discuss about the Maxeler dataflow engine and show its practicality in a case study for a complex atmospheric simulation. It is shown that in comparison to the conventional technologies, a performance improvement by two orders of magnitude is possible.

Chapter 4 "Sorting Networks on Maxeler Dataflow Supercomputing Systems" by Kos et al. is intended to show the application of dataflow paradigm in general, and Maxeler dataflow computer in particular, in handling a popular and classical problem, i.e., sorting. The chapter gives a short survey on sorting algorithms. Several classes of sorting algorithms, i.e., sequential sorting algorithms, parallel sorting algorithms, and sorting networks, along with their comparative analysis are discussed. The chapter then focuses on sorting networks and discusses its suitability for dataflow paradigm and its implementation on the Maxeler platform. Experimental results are detailed and analyzed.

Finally, in Chapter 5 "Dual Data Cache Systems: Architecture and Analysis," Sustran et al. open up the discussion about dual data cache systems in which the data cache is split into two subsystems based on the data access patterns. The advantages of dual cache systems are articulated and a classification of the proposed schemes as advanced in the literature is introduced. The proposed approaches are studied in detail and critically based on speed, complexity, and power consumption analyzed. The so-called Split Temporal/Special Data Cache (STS) design is extensively studied and analyzed.

We hope that you find these chapters of interest, and useful in your teaching, research, and other professional activities. We welcome feedback on the volume, and suggestions for topics for future volumes.

ALI R. HURSON
Rolla, MO, USA
and
VELJKO MILUTINOVIC
Belgrade, Serbia

## CHAPTER ONE

An Overview of Selected Heterogeneous and Reconfigurable Architectures

Saša Stojanović, Dragan Bojić, Miroslav Bojović
School of Electrical Engineering, University of Belgrade, Belgrade, Serbia

Contents

Abstract

Node level heterogeneous architectures are gaining popularity because of their excellent performance exhibited in real world applications from various domains. The main advantages of these architectures are better price-performance and power–performance ratios compared to traditional symmetric CPU architectures. This article presents an overview of most interesting node level heterogeneous architectures, focusing on some common architectures, such as the NVIDIA and the ATI graphics processing units, the Cell Broadband Engine Architecture, the ClearSpeed processor, the field programmable gate array accelerator solutions from Maxeler MaxNodes, the SGI systems (RASC), and the Convey Hybrid-Core Computer. The presentation encompasses hardware resources and available software development tools for each of the mentioned architectures with both qualitative and quantitative comparisons. Toward the conclusion, the authors express their viewpoint on the future of heterogeneous computing.

Advances in Computers, Volume 96
ISSN 0065-2458
http://dx.doi.org/10.1016/bs.adcom.2014.11.003
1

ABBREVIATIONS

ALU arithmetic logic unit
CBEA cell broadband engine architecture
CF control flow
CG coarse grain
CMP chip multiprocessor
CPU central processing unit
CUDA compute unified device architecture
DF data flow
DMA direct memory access
DSP digital signal processing
ECC error correction code
EDF explicit data flow
FG fine grain
FPGA field programmable gate array
FPU floating point unit
FSB front side bus
GDB the gnu debugger
GNU the GNU Project of the Free Software Foundation
GP-GPU general purpose graphics processing unit
GPU graphics processing unit
HET heterogeneous architectures
HOM homogeneous architectures
HPC high performance computing
IDF implicit data flow
ILP instruction level parallelisms
LC loosely coupled systems
MESM multiple execution modes, single machine model
MEMM multiple execution modes, multiple machine models
MFC memory flow controller
MIMD multiple instructions multiple data
MPI message passing interface
MPMD multiple program multiple data
MTAP multithreaded array processor
NUMA nonuniform memory access
PCIe peripheral component interface express
PE processing element
PPE power processing element
RASC Reconfigurable Application-Specific Computing
RC reconfigurable computing
SDK software development kit
SESM single execution mode, single machine model
SEMM single execution mode, multiple machine models
SIMD single instruction, multiple data
SM streaming multiprocessor
SMP symmetrical multiprocessing
SMT simultaneous multithreading

SPE synergistic processing element
SPMD single program multiple data
TC tightly coupled systems

1. INTRODUCTION

Heterogeneous architectures (HET) have been present in the open literature for a long time now, incorporating a huge set of highly diverse architectures. A common property of all HETs is a nonuniform execution model along different nodes of architecture. Older classifications of computer architectures into four different classes are based on two criteria [1,2]. The first criterion classifies architectures according to the number of execution modes, while the other one uses the number of machine models. The following classes are defined: SESM (single execution mode, single machine model), SEMM (single execution mode, multiple machine models), MESM (multiple execution modes, single machine model), and MEMM (multiple execution modes, multiple machine models), respectively. The last two classes represent "fully" HET.

Some more recent contributions use an extended Flynn's taxonomy, where the MIMD class of architectures (Multiple Instructions Multiple Data) is further divided into two subclasses: SPMD (Single Program Multiple Data) and MPMD (Multiple Programs Multiple Data) [3]. The first subclass is composed of architectures in which processing elements (PEs) group executes the same program, but on different data. The second subclass is composed of architectures that are capable to execute in a parallel way different programs on its PEs, where each PE executes its own program that can be different from all of the other programs.

Some of HET include a reconfigurable hardware. The reconfigurable hardware is implemented using field programmable gate array (FPGA) chips and attached into a system as an accelerator. Modern advances in technology have made this approach feasible and implementable in practice [4]. As electrical energy consumption becomes one of the main concerns in the modern computers' design, energy efficiency of reconfigurable hardware has led to significant increase of attractiveness of HET with a reconfigurable hardware [5].

In this comparative study, we scrutinize commercially available systems (as opposed to academic projects). Each one of the solutions presented here is a proven, more or less commercially successful representative of a particular computing style. An examination of their comparative advantages and disadvantages serves to envision future trends for such systems. We focus on a single node, noting that systems can be formed by connecting together multiple nodes of the same type. In this context, the term "node" refers to the smallest unit of hardware that is capable of working as a standalone system.

It is important to point out that the data presented in this chapter, like in any other survey, have been obtained from available sources provided either by authors or by vendors' web sites, both of which have introduced the surveyed concepts/systems that are being surveyed. Thus, the data obtained from different sources were generated under different conditions, and therefore, any direct performance comparison may always be questionable. In these circumstances, it is best to compare the number of systems sold and the experiences of those who utilize the presented systems/concepts, in order to solve their critical problems on a daily basis.

2. PROBLEM STATEMENT

The continuous performance improvement of microprocessor technology is not likely to press ahead in the future. The positive trend observed in the past occurred due to two main factors: an increase in clock speed and improvements in instruction level parallelism (ILP).

Over the past years, the speed has been increased by a constant growth of the clock frequency, while the capacity has been boosted by the transistor size reduction. The increased capacity has enabled the implementation of sophisticated algorithms for exploitation of ILP in a way that is transparent to the programmer. Consequently, existing applications have been capable of taking advantage of ILP without the need for modifications. Nowadays, it has become more and more difficult to maintain the same increase in speed due to several reasons. The first one is that, on the average, there is a limited amount of available ILP parallelism in an application program. Moreover, executing a set of instructions in parallel requires a check, for each pair of instructions disregarding them being independent of each other. Hence, the chip area required to support parallel execution is proportional to the square of a number of instructions executed in parallel. Due to the above, further enhancements of the ILP design (including the increase of the instruction width and the number of instructions issued concurrently) are not followed anymore by an increased system performance [6].

In addition to this, more recently, electrical energy consumption has become one of the main concerns in high performance computing. In order to solve this problem, the research community and industry have started using a large amount of available chip area to implement several processors, thus creating the so-called chip multicore processing systems. It has been observed that some computational problems pose huge levels of intrinsic parallelism, and for those problems, it is more efficient to exploit thread level parallelism, rather than ILP. In case of thread level parallelism, the required chip area is linearly dependant on the number of instructions that can be executed in parallel, instead of quadratic, as is the case with ILP.

The next step in decreasing electrical energy consumption is through reconfigurability of hardware intended for calculations. Reconfigurable computing (RC) implies a hardware that can be reconfigured to implement application-specific functions. The basic concept of RC was proposed in the 1960s, but has only recently become feasible for commercially successful systems. Reconfigurable computers consist of a flexible hardware fabric and one or more (heterogeneous and/or customized) processors. These systems customize the internal structure of the platform to suit the application, leading to faster runtime, more energy-efficient processing, and better device utilization [7]. Dynamically reconfigurable systems go even further; their internal structure may even adapt to the workload, at runtime.

3. EXISTING SOLUTIONS AND THEIR CRITICISM

In this section, we give a short overview of seven existing hardware platforms that are based on HET, or more precisely: Cell Broadband Engine Architecture (CBEA), ClearSpeed, SGI RASC, Convey, Maxeler MaxNodes, NVIDIA GPU, and AMD ATI GPU computing. In general, the reviewed platforms are well-established commercial solutions and give good results under the conditions of interest for their operating environments and problem-solving domains. Nevertheless, each one of them has certain comparative advantages and disadvantages.

This section starts with an overview for each selected platform based on the following criteria: (a) The seven Ws of the solution (who, where, when, whom, why, what, how, or a subset thereof) and (b) Essential elements of the approach, in terms of the architecture and the programming model. It continues with a classification of the platforms in the domain of contemporary computing architectures. Finally, aforementioned platforms are critically set against each other regarding their current state.

3.1. Presentation of Existing Solutions

We shall now present details of several commercially available systems. The NVIDIA Fermi GPU and the AMD ATI Cypress GPU are examples of heterogeneous systems in which a central processing unit (CPU) is accompanied by a highly multithreaded single instruction, multiple data (SIMD) accelerator. The CBEA and ClearSpeed are representatives of heterogeneous multicore chips with one or two highly sophisticated processors and several simpler processing cores intended for acceleration of parallel portions of program. Finally, the Maxeler Dataflow Engines (MaxNodes), the SGI RASC, and the Convey coprocessor belong to the domain of symmetric multicore processors enhanced by reconfigurable hardware accelerators.

3.1.1 NVIDIA Fermi GPU

The graphics processing unit (GPU), first invented by NVIDIA in 1999, is the most pervasive parallel processor to date [8]. It is a symmetric multicore processor that is exclusively accessed and controlled by the CPU, making the two a heterogeneous system. The GPU operates asynchronously from the CPU, enabling concurrent execution and memory transfer. Today's GPUs greatly get ahead of CPUs in arithmetic throughput and memory bandwidth, making them the ideal processor to accelerate a variety of data-parallel applications.

The Fermi-based GPU (see Fig. 1), implemented with 3.0 billion transistors, features up to 512 compute unified device architecture (CUDA) cores. A CUDA core executes a floating point or integer instruction per clock for a thread. The 512 CUDA cores are organized in 16 streaming multiprocessors (SMs). Each SM includes 32 cores for single precision floating point operations, 16 load store units (LD/ST), 4 special function units (SFUs), and 64 KB of local memory. The local memory can be configured to split 16 K/48 K or 48 K/16 K between L1 cache and shared memory. LD/ST unit can calculate source and destination addresses for a thread per clock cycle. Each SFU unit calculates one transcendental function (such as sin, cosine, reciprocal, square root) per clock. Each CUDA core has a fully pipelined integer arithmetic logic unit (ALU) and a floating point unit (FPU). The GPU has six 64-bit memory partitions, for a 384-bit memory interface, supporting up to a total of 6 GB of GDDR5 DRAM memory. The GPU also contains host interface connecting the GPU to

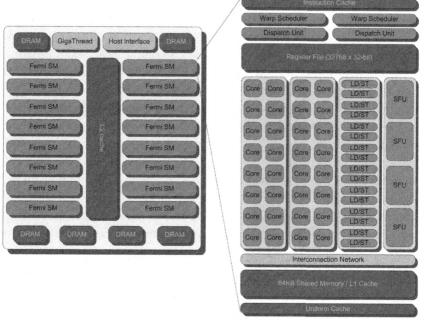

Figure 1 The Fermi architecture: Fermi SM, Fermi streaming multiprocessor, LD/ST, load/store unit; SFU, special function unit.

the CPU via peripheral component interface express (PCIe). The GigaThread global scheduler distributes thread blocks to SM thread schedulers [8].

The CUDA is the hardware and software architecture that enables NVIDIA GPUs to execute programs written in C, C++, Fortran, OpenCL, DirectCompute, and other languages. A CUDA program calls parallel kernels. A kernel executes in parallel across a set of parallel threads. The programmer or compiler organizes these threads in thread blocks and thread blocks grids. The GPU instantiates a kernel program on a grid of parallel thread blocks [8].

Each thread within a thread block executes an instance of the kernel and has a thread ID within its thread block, program counter, registers, per-thread private memory, inputs, and output results. A thread block is a set of concurrently executing threads that can cooperate among themselves through barrier synchronization and shared memory. A thread block has a block ID within its grid. A grid is a thread blocks' array that executes the same kernel, reads inputs from global memory, writes results to global memory, and synchronizes between dependent kernel calls [8].

In the CUDA parallel programming model (shown in Fig. 2), each thread has a per-thread private memory space used for register spills, function calls, and C automatic array variables. Each thread block has a per-block shared memory space used for interthread communication, and for sharing of parallel algorithms data and results. Grids of thread blocks share results in Global Memory space after kernel-wide global synchronization [8].

The CUDA's hierarchy of threads maps to a hierarchy of processors on the GPU: a GPU executes one or more kernel grids, a SM executes one or more thread blocks, and CUDA cores and other execution units in the SM execute threads. To improve performance by memory locality, the SM executes threads in groups of 32 threads called a warp [8]. Up to two warps are scheduled to execute on each SM, using two groups of 16 cores, 16 LD/ST units or 4 SFUs. 32 instructions from one or two warps are executed in any two of four available groups of execution resources. It takes two cycles to

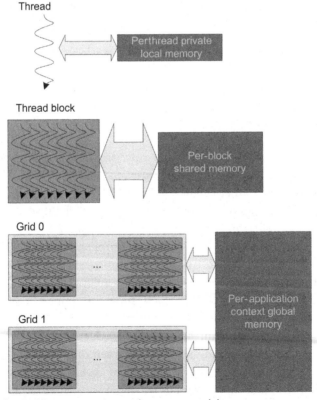

Figure 2 The CUDA programming and memory models.

dispatch one instruction from each thread of a warp to any group of 16 cores or to 16 LD/ST units. To dispatch one instruction per thread from a warp to SFU units, eight clocks are required. In this way, each SM can execute 32 logic or arithmetic instructions per clock cycle in case of integer and single precision floating point numbers. In case of double precision floating point numbers, an operation is performed by two coupled cores, and hence only 16 arithmetic instructions can be executed per clock cycle.

3.1.2 AMD ATI

The first ATI's GP-GPU appeared in 2004. Code name Cypress represents the most successful AMD ATI's GPU architecture of today.

The Cypress-based GPU (Fig. 3), implemented with 2.15 billion transistors contains 320 cores with 1600 PEs (ALU), which are organized as 20 SIMD engines. Each is made of 16 units, what AMD calls thread processors. These processors, as the primary execution units, are superscalar and five ALUs wide. The fifth ALU (SFU) is a superset of the others, capable of handling more advanced operations like transcendentals (e.g., sin, cosine, arc tan, sqrt, pow, etc.). The execution units are pipelined with eight cycles of latency, but each SIMD engine can execute two hardware thread groups, or "wavefronts" in AMD parlance, in interleaved fashion, so the effective wavefront latency is four cycles. In every cycle, an execution unit can issue

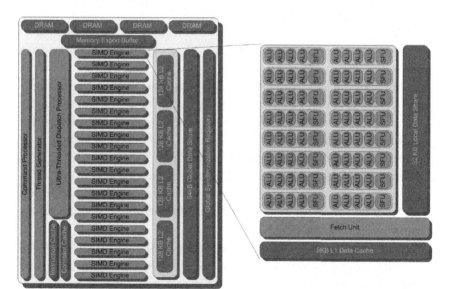

Figure 3 The Cypress architecture.

four single precision operation, or two single precision multiply add operation, or two double precision operations, or one double precision multiply add operation, and one more single precision operation or some transcendental function. Every SIMD engine is equipped with 32 KB of local memory with 8 KB L1 cache. There is also a global shared memory of 64 KB, and four banks of L2 cache, 64 KB each. Processor has four 64-bit interfaces to the external memory, which gives the total bandwidth of 156.3 GB/s [9,10].

AMD GPUs are supported by Open Computing Language (OpenCL), an industry open-standard application programmer interface (API). OpenCL is cross-platform parallel programming framework for different kinds of modern processors. It is very similar to NVIDIA's CUDA, but more flexible and portable between different platforms. Flexibility of OpenCL lays in flexibility of compute kernel specification. Compute kernels can be thought of either as data-parallel, which is well matched to the architecture of GPUs, or as task-parallel, which is well matched to the architecture of CPUs. Moreover, programs written in OpenCL can execute on reconfigurable architectures, which is a solution offered by Altera.

A compute kernel represents the basic unit of executable code which is similar to a C function. Such kernels are executed inside of threads. The execution can proceed either in-order or out-of-order depending on the parameters passed to the system when queuing up the kernel for execution. Status of outstanding execution requests can be checked through events that can be used to communicate between different devices.

In terms of organization, the execution domain of a kernel is defined by an N-dimensional computation domain. This lets the system know size of a problem the user would like the kernel to be applied to. An element in the execution domain is a work-item. Work-items are grouped into work-group that represents a domain whereby work-items can communicate and synchronize. A work-group is executed on compute unit enabling each work-item to access the local memory shared inside of work-group.

OpenCL defines a multilevel memory model with memory ranging from private memory visible only to the individual compute element in the device to global memory that is visible to all compute units on the device. Depending on the actual memory subsystem, different memory spaces are allowed to be collapsed together.

OpenCL 1.0 defines four memory spaces: private, local, constant, and global. Figure 4 shows a diagram of the memory hierarchy defined by OpenCL. Private memory is memory that can only be used by a single work-item executed on a compute element. This is similar to registers in

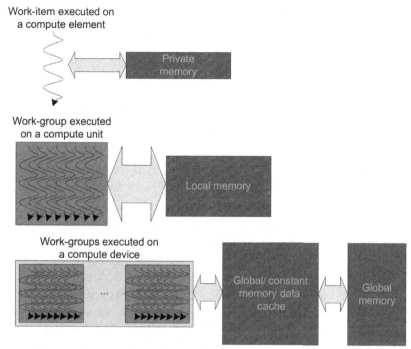

Figure 4 Memory hierarchy in OpenCL.

a single compute element or a single CPU core. Local memory is memory that can be used by the work-items in a work-group executed on a compute unit. This is similar to the local data share that is available on the current generation of AMD GPUs. Constant memory is memory that can be used to store constant data for read-only access by all of the compute units in the device during the execution of a kernel. The host processor is responsible for allocating and initializing the memory objects that reside in this memory space. This is similar to the constant caches that are available on AMD GPUs. Finally, global memory is memory that can be used by all the compute units on the compute device. This is similar to the off-chip GPU memory that is available on AMD GPUs [11].

An example of kernel for OpenCL framework that calculates the sum of two vectors placed in global memory is shown in Fig. 5. The kernel represents a code of work-items (threads) used for calculation of the sum. It is assumed that the dimension of vectors is equal to the number of work-items used for calculation of the sum. The calculation is distributed between work-items in a way that each work-item is responsible for addition of single

```
__kernel void vec_add (__global const float *a,
                       __global const float *b,
                       __global float *c)
{
    int gid = get_global_id(0);
    c[gid] = a[gid] + b[gid];
}
```

Figure 5 The OpenCL example kernel: vector addition.

dimension of vectors. Each work-item accepts three pointers for global memory of the device. The first two of them point to vectors that will be added, while the third one points to a buffer in global memory where the resulting vector will be placed. In order to process a corresponding element, each work-item fetches its unique global id that is then used to access elements of vectors.

A brief relationship between two frameworks used for programming of GPUs, CUDA and OpenCL, is given in Table 1. From the portability viewpoint, OpenCL represents more promising approach. However, from the performance viewpoint, CUDA offers slightly better performance due to the more mature and custom tailored framework of NVIDIA devices [12,13]. From a viewpoint of terminology and concepts used in CUDA and OpenCL, there is almost one to one correspondence between these two frameworks. Moreover, tools are developed to automatically port code from CUDA to OpenCL framework [14].

Table 2 gives a comparative summary of presented GPU systems. It specifies technology related parameters (feature size, transistor count, and clock frequency), declared peak performances (for single and double precision floating point numbers), and programming-related information (programming language and short description of programming model). It also summarizes advantages and disadvantages of presented systems.

3.1.3 Cell Broadband Engine Architecture

The CBEA, developed by Sony, Toshiba, and IBM, was conceived as the next-generation chip architecture for multimedia and compute-intensive processing [15,16]. It was first used in the Sony PlayStation 3 game console. Currently, IBM offers the PowerXCell 8i processor based on the CBEA, which is used in Roadrunner, the world's first petaflop supercomputer.

Figure 6 shows the major components of a Cell/B.E. processor: The main PE (the power processing element, PPE), the parallel processing

Table 1 Brief Overview of Relationship Between CUDA and OpenCL Frameworks

	CUDA	OpenCL
Supported hardware platforms	NVIDIA GPU devices	GPU devices (AMD and NVIDIA), multicore CPUs (Intel, IBM, and Samsung), and accelerators (Altera FPGA based)
Performance	Slightly better than OpenCL on NVIDIA GPU, orders of magnitude better than Intel multicore CPUs	Orders of magnitude better than Intel multicore CPUs
Terminology	CUDA thread	Work-item
	CUDA thread block	Work-group
	CUDA kernel grid	Kernel execution instance
	CUDA core	Compute element
	CUDA streaming multiprocessor	Compute unit
	CUDA-enabled GPU	Compute device
Memory	Local memory	Private memory
	Shared memory	Local memory
	Global memory	Global memory

Table 2 Summary of GPU-Based Systems

	NVIDIA GPU	AMD GPU
Programming model	Same function is executed over large number of cores, each processing its own data	
Advantages	• High computation capacity • High memory bandwidth • Widespread technology	• High computation capacity • High memory bandwidth • Widespread technology
Disadvantages	• Moderate memory capacity • High power consumption • Fixed precision for floating point numbers	• Moderate memory capacity • High power consumption • Fixed precision for floating point numbers • Achieves good performances only in case when there are enough instructions to utilize VLIW

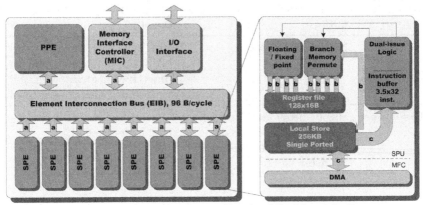

PPE, Power Processor Element; SPE, Synergistic Processor Element; a – 8 B/cycle in each direction;
b, 16 B/cycle in one direction; c, 128 B/cycle in one direction

Figure 6 The Cell B.E. architecture.

accelerators (synergistic processor elements, SPEs), the on-chip interconnect (a bidirectional data ring known as the element interconnect bus), the memory interface controller, and the I/O interface.

The PPE contains a 64-bit PowerPC processor unit (PPU), two dedicated separate 32-KB level 1 cache for instructions and data, and a unified 512-KB level 2 cache for instructions and data. The PPU supports two-way simultaneous multithreading (SMT). The PPE can complete two double precision operations per clock cycle, resulting in a peak performance of 6.4 GFLOPS at 3.2 GHz.

Each SPE is composed of a synergistic processing unit (SPU) and memory flow controller (MFC). The SPU is an accelerator core based on a SIMD reduced instruction set computer processor. The SPU operation semantics are similar to those of the PowerPC SIMD extensions. The SPU has a unified 128-entry 128-bit wide SIMD register file to store operands of all data types and it can directly address a local store of 256 KB for instruction and data references.

The SPE's local store is explicitly managed by software—that is, the compiler or programmer—by way of MFC block transfers between system memory and the local store, as shown in Fig. 7. The MFC can issue up to 16 simultaneous direct memory access (DMA) operations of up to 16 KB each between the local store and system memory. Unlike traditional caches hierarchy found in modern processors, this organization lets the system prefetch large memory operands into on-chip memory in parallel during program execution, avoiding the performance degradation due to the

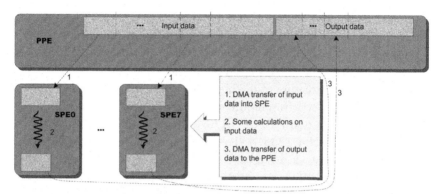

Figure 7 Each SPE independently computes a part on the input dataset. The results are assembled on the main processing unit, PPE.

frequent cache misses commonly associated with the caches. This local memory hierarchy is very important, especially in conditions when execution rate of a SPE is significantly higher than the rate at which data can be fetched into the SPE.

In the Cell/B.E., the peak SPE-to-main-memory bandwidth is 25.6 GB/s, which is one of the highest memory-to-CPU bandwidth designs. With double buffering to overlap communication and computation, the Cell/B.E. has a compute-to-memory bandwidth ratio of 8 ops per byte of data fetched from the system memory (204.8 GFLOPS/25.6 GB).

To compile code for the Cell/B.E., one can use either the IBM xlc or the GNU (the GNU Project of the Free Software Foundation) gcc (ppu-gcc and spu-gcc) compilers [17]. In addition to the original thread-based programming model for developing Cell/B.E. applications, developers have ported several other programming models to this architecture, including OpenMP, message passing interface, Google's MapReduce, the data-parallel RapidMind model, and the data-driven Cell Superscalar (CellSs) model [3].

3.1.4 ClearSpeed

The ClearSpeed Technology focuses on alleviating power, heat, and density challenges of high-performance systems. Their latest processor CSX700 is high-performance solution with very low power consumption, mainly due to low clock frequency and advanced clock gating [18]. It is at the heart of ClearSpeed's e720 accelerator card that brings the power of ClearSpeed's processor to the HP blade server. Thanks to compact size of card and low power consumption of processor it can fit into type II mezzanine slot without requiring any additional cooling or power supply [19]. Low power consumption means lower heating and has positive effects on the reliability of system. Further reliability improvement is done by inclusion of error correction code (ECC) bits with each memory.

Figure 8 shows structure of the processor. It is a dual core SIMD architecture, where each core is multithreaded array processor (MTAP). Along with cores, there are two DDR2 DRAM interfaces that supports 8 GB of RAM each, two on-chip 128 KB SRAM memory, PCIe x16 host interface, and system services block. Inside of core, there are one main multithreaded processor and one SIMD processing unit. Main processor supports 8 hardware threads and uses 128 8-bit semaphores for synchronization of threads. Processor has two caches, instruction and data cache. Both caches are organized as four-way set-associative caches. Instruction cache has 512 lines of four instructions, while data cache has 256 lines of 16B each. Execution unit has ALU, double precision FPU, and several register files, 128B each.

The SIMD processing unit has 96 PEs that give a lot of processing power to the ClearSpeed's processor. Poly controller accepts instructions from the main processor, and organizes execution on PEs. Each PE is equipped with 128B

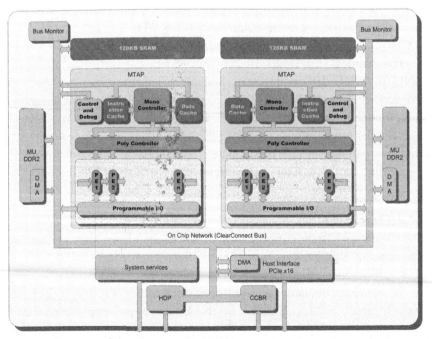

Figure 8 Structure of the ClearSpeed's CSX700 processor.

register file, one FPU for single and double precision operations with dual issue pipelined add and multiply, a 6 KB of PE's SRAM, 16-bit multiply and accumulate with a 64-bit accumulator, and support for integer and floating point divide and square root operations. The PE's SRAMs provide high memory bandwidth for the purpose of parallel execution on PEs. The PEs have a possibility to communicate directly to the memory or I/O through configurable programmed I/O channel. Channel is 128-bit wide; can transfer 8, 16, 32, or 64 bit per PE; and can use hardware semaphore for synchronization. The code is fetched by the main processor, and depending on the instruction type, executed by main processor or by the SIMD processing unit.

Accelerator can be used in two ways. The first one is plug and play where ClearSpeed supported library intercepts call and determine whether that call can be accelerated or not. If the answer to the previous question is positive, library makes further steps in order to utilize accelerator without any programmer's help. The other one is a native code development where programmer recognizes parts of code that can be speeded up and used ClearSpeed software development kit (SDK) to translate them into the code for accelerator. The SDK includes: (a) a suite of tools including an industry standard source-level debugger based on GDB (the GNU Project Debugger) and an ANSI C-based cross-compiler for ClearSpeed's CSX family of processors, (b) an extensive set of standard C libraries based on the newlib open source library together with a set of libraries to support architecture-specific features, (c) the ClearSpeed Vector Math Library and ClearSpeed Random Number Generator Library, and (d) documentation for the software development tools and languages.

Table 3 gives a comparative summary of presented on-chip heterogeneous multicore systems. It specifies technology related parameters (feature size, transistor count, and clock frequency), declared peak performances (for single and double precision floating point numbers), and programming-related information (programming language and short description of programming model). It also summarizes advantages and disadvantages of presented systems.

3.1.5 Maxeler Dataflow Engines

Maxeler Technologies in Palo Alto and London is a fast expanding high performance computing (HPC) company with roots at Stanford, Bell Labs, in the United States, and Imperial College, London, in the United Kingdom. Maxeler Technologies' core competence is in delivering substantially increased performance for HPC applications through the rewriting of applications for Dataflow Engines (see in this chapter and "Concurrency,

Table 3 Summary of On-Chip Heterogeneous Multicore Systems

	Cell B.E.	ClearSpeed
Technology	65 nm	90 nm
Transistor count	234 millions	256 millions
Clock frequency	3.2 GHz	250 MHz
Single precision performance	230.4 GFLOPS	96 GFLOPS
Double precision performance	21.3 GFLOPS	96 GFLOPS
Programming language	Extended C/C++ and OpenCL	C with parallel programming extensions and standard libraries
Programming model	Concurrent communicating threads without shared memory	Parallelism is expressed through data type; same code is executed on different part of data
Advantages	• Large memory capacity	• Large memory capacity • Low power consumption • Good performance–power consumption ratio
Disadvantages	• Moderate computation capacity • Moderate memory bandwidth • High power consumption • Hard to achieve good performance due to memory managed by programmer	• Modest computation capacity • Modest memory bandwidth

Synchronization, and Speculation—The Dataflow Way"). The complete applications can be accelerated by orders of magnitude over conventional CPU implementations by means of mapping compute-intensive algorithms directly into parallel hardware, tightly coupled to a conventional CPU through a high-speed I/O bus. By exploiting massive parallelism at the bit-level, Maxeler MaxNode solutions deliver performance far in excess of CPUs at approximately a 10th of the clock frequency and power consumption.

Figure 9 sketches the architecture of a Maxeler hardware acceleration system which equips one or more Dataflow Engines attached to a set of memories and connected to a host CPU via PCI Express channels [20,21]. MaxRing interconnects (not shown in Fig. 9) establish high bandwidth communication channels between the Dataflow Engines on the accelerator. Accelerating an application involves analyzing the entire application, adapting program structure and partitioning the execution flow and data layout between CPUs and accelerators. The program of the Dataflow Engines comprises arithmetic data paths for the computations (the kernels) and modules orchestrating the data I/O for these kernels (the manager).

The Maxeler Kernel Compiler generates configuration of hardware, which configured forms the Dataflow Engines used as accelerators to the CPU. Therefore, the program describes computations structurally (computing in space) rather than specifying a sequence of processor instructions (computing in time). The main unit of processing is a kernel, which is a streaming core with a data flow (DF) described by a unidirectional graph.

An example of a kernel is given for algorithm that calculates three-point moving average over N values with two-point averages at the boundaries. The algorithm is described in Fig. 10.

Figure 11 depicts the kernel graph for the moving average which splits into a data part (right-hand side) and a control part (left-hand side). The

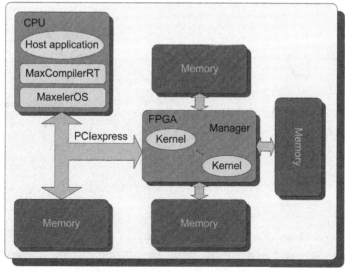

Figure 9 The Maxeler accelerator architecture.

Kernel Compiler is effectively a Java software library and as such, kernel graphs are created by writing a Java program and executing it.

Kernel graphs are directly mapped to hardware. Subsequently, data streams through the arithmetic nodes. Efficient streaming kernels strongly emphasize the regularity of the DF, making the actual computations look

$$
y_i = \begin{cases} (x_i + x_{i+1})/2 & \text{if } i = 0 \\ (x_{i-1} + x_i)/2 & \text{if } i = N-1 \\ (x_{i-1} + x_i + x_{i+1})/2 & \text{otherwise} \end{cases}
$$

Figure 10 Algorithm for moving average over *N* values.

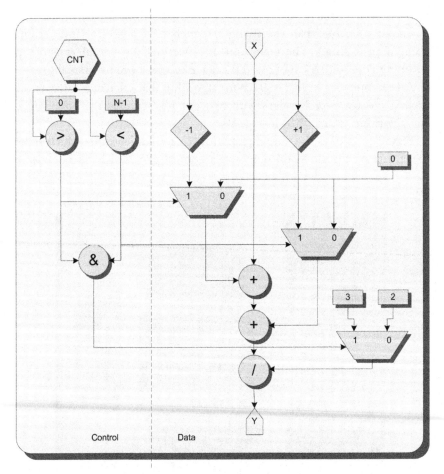

Figure 11 Kernel graph for the moving average example.

like a side effect of streaming. These kernels are suitable for deeply pipelined DF implementation, which is crucial for achieving good performance. One highly valuable property of this accelerator is local memory access pattern, which is available on the accelerator card. As each part of loop body is executed on each clock, each access inside of loop body will be made once per a clock. As parts of loop body that are executed at the same time are from different iterations (because of pipelined implementation of the loop body), data accessed at the same time will be usually from different loop iterations. The essence is that required bandwidth to/from memory will be constant during the most of time. There are only two short time periods when required bandwidth is smaller than previously described (the time needed to fill in pipeline at the beginning of processing and the time needed to flush pipeline at the end of processing).

3.1.6 SGI's Reconfigurable Application-Specific Computing

SGI was founded as a spinoff of the Stanford University's research in accelerating a specific application, three-dimensional graphics. The SGI pioneered acceleration of graphics through hardware setting records and by providing technological capabilities that were impossible without specialized computational elements [22].

Altix is a family of SGI's SMP (symmetrical multiprocessing) solutions. Its distinguishing feature is that each processor has both fast access local memory and slower access to local memories of other processors in the system. Processors' data exchange is achieved via nonuniform memory access link (NUMALink) bus. The NUMALink bus enables data exchange between processors to be relatively fast. The NUMALink interconnect is a hierarchical system bus. It allows for global addressing and scalability of SMP systems. The maximum NUMALink data transfer is 6.4 GB/s. The integral component of the Altix system can be the Reconfigurable Application-Specific Computing (RASC) module. It is the SGI's technology that is enabling users to develop application-specific hardware using reconfigurable logic elements.

The SGI RASC is tightly integrated with NUMALink. From the hardware perspective, FPGA is no longer a coprocessor (COP) mode in this model. As shown in Fig. 12, with the NUMALink FPGA has access to global shared memory and there is no need to load and unload data. The RASC is coupled with two Virtex4LX200 FPGA chips. Each one offers 200 K of reconfigurable logic cells. Additionally there are two blocks of 64 MB QDR RAM memory. This memory acts like a second level cache for FPGA. The first-level cache is implemented inside the Virtex4LX200 structure and is called BlockRAM. Bidirectional data interface implemented for FPGA has a 128-bit width and is clocked with frequency of 200 MHz [23].

The RASC hardware module is concentrated around an application-specific integrated circuit (ASIC) called TIO. The TIO attaches to the Altix system NUMALink interconnect directly, instead of being driven from a compute node using the XIO channel. One TIO supports two PCI-X busses, an AGP-8X bus (not shown in Fig. 13), and the Scalable System Port that is used to connect the FPGA to the rest of the Altix system for the RASC program. The RASC module contains a card with the COP FPGA device, as shown in Fig. 13.

In order to accelerate an application using SGI RASC, the first step is to identify computationally intensive parts of C program (Fig. 14). The identified parts are then ported to SGI RASC by generating bitstream using Core Services and language of choice. The last step is to replace the identified parts of the program with calls to RASC abstraction layer (rasclib). The abstraction layer supports two languages: C and Fortran90. The adapted program can be run and debugged using GNU Debugger.

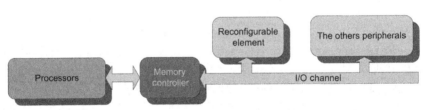

Figure 12 RASC architecture.

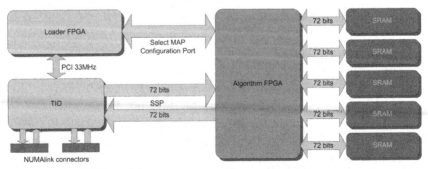

Figure 13 The RASC module structure.

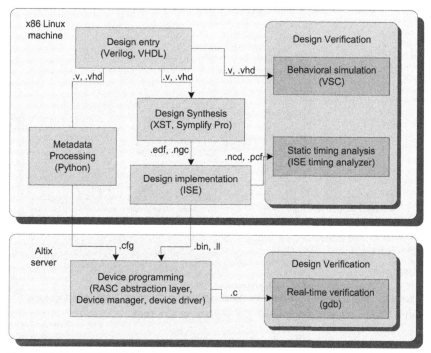

Figure 14 The RASC FPGA programming process.

3.1.7 Convey's Reconfigurable COP

The Convey Hybrid-Core is the FPGA-based accelerator board coupled to the processor as a COP [24]. This system, appeared in 2008, brings a new programming model, where personalities are used as an extension of the instruction set of the processor. There are predefined sets of personalities for problems in several industries, including: oil and gas, computer-aided engineering, bioinformatics, and financial services.

A structure of the system is shown in Fig. 15. The main component is a board with four Xilinx Virtex 5 LX330 chips intended for calculations. There are two additional FPGAs that implements interface to the host. The board is tightly coupled with processor and has access to the processor's RAM memory. The board also has its local memory, with significantly greater throughput. A cache-coherent shared virtual memory system is provided allowing the data access in the CPU's memory and the accelerator device memory across the whole system. Though, logically, memory is seen as uniform, because different memories are being used, the system is implemented as cache-coherent nonuniform memory access (ccNUMA) [25]. For the best

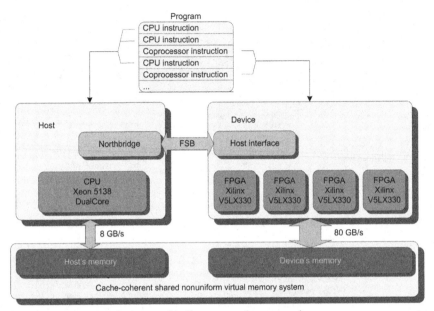

Figure 15 Structure of system with Convey accelerator card.

performance, a programmer has to carry out appropriate data placement. FPGAs have on-chip memory, known as BlockRAM, but this memory is not directly visible to the programmer.

The programming model of this system offers solution to overcome complexity of programming FPGA-based accelerators [26]. The solution is in a form of the predesigned hardware, as Convey calls it, personality. Operations that are often in the domain of interest, and that are time consuming, are implemented in the hardware. According to a particular program that will be executed, FPGAs are configured with personalities. Which personalities will be used is decided in compile time by setting compiler flags. Compiler is in some degree able to automatically recognize parts of code that can be accelerated with specified personalities, and to compile those parts, so they can be also executed on FPGAs (generated code can be executed on machine without FPGAs). Because of limited abilities of compiler, it is possible that programmer annotates source code written in C, C++, or Fortran with pragma directives. All of this is possible because compiler gives to the programmer unique view of all memory, host's memory and accelerator's memory. From programmer's point of view, this significantly simplifies programming, but because of nonuniform memory access (NUMA) nature of the system it can significantly reduce performance. To deal with this drawback, programmer has to think where to put which data, and to specify that in a form of pragma directives. Pragma directives are also used for compiler optimizations. Code intended for execution on FPGA has some other limitations. It cannot call non-COP code including system calls, and it cannot do input/output operations.

Compiler comes with some predefined personalities that are single precision and double precision floating point operations, defining a soft-core for vector COP. For someone who needs more, there is Convey's personality development kit for developing new customized personalities, but that requires significant additional knowledge and effort.

Table 4 gives a comparative summary of presented reconfigurable systems. It specifies technology related parameters (feature size and clock frequency), declared peak performances (for single and double precision floating point numbers), and programming-related information (programming language and short description of programming model). It also summarizes advantages and disadvantages of presented systems.

3.2. Classification of Presented Solutions

In addition to the widespread classification according to Flynn's taxonomy, computers can be classified based on the flow type. The basic division is into control flow (CF) and DF "supercomputers." In essence, the CF supercomputers compile the source code down to the machine code and execute the machine code using one of several possible execution paradigms; the DF supercomputers compile the source code down to gate transfer level, which brings a better speed/watt at the expense of a more complex programming paradigm.

CF "supercomputers" span over a wide range of different architectures. These architectures can be composed of cores that all belong to the same architectural type or of cores that belong to several different architectural types. Based on this, CF architectures can be further classified into two additional subclasses: homogeneous architectures (HOM, e.g., Intel processors) and HET (e.g., NVIDIA GPU, AMD ATI GPU, IBM CELL, and ClearSpeed).

HOM are outside of the scope of this article, and will not be further discussed. Heterogeneous CF architectures are most often composed of one or several large and highly sophisticated cores and a large number of simpler and smaller cores. Depending on how these two groups of cores are coupled, the HET subclass can be partitioned into two subclasses: Loosely coupled

Table 4 Summary of Reconfigurable Systems

	SGI RASC	Maxeler MAX3	Convey HC-1
Technology	90 nm	40 nm	65 nm
Clock frequency	200 MHz	100–300 MHz	n/a
Single precision performance	47 GFLOPS	450 GFLOPS	80 GFLOPS
Double precision performance	19.2 GFLOPS	160 GFLOPS	n/a
Programming language	VHDL and Verilog	Maxeler Java and VHDL	Prebuilt libraries and VHDL
Programming model	Data are streamed through configured hardware		
Advantages	• Adaptable processing unit	• Extra large memory capacity • Excellent performance–power consumption ratio • Adaptable processing unit	• Large memory capacity • High memory bandwidth • Easy to use predefined functions from library • Adaptable processing unit
Disadvantages	• Pure computation capacity • Small memory capacity • Moderate memory bandwidth • Pure performance–power consumption ratio • Extremely complex programming	• Moderate computation capacity for double precision floating point number • Moderate memory bandwidth • Complex programming	• Modest computation capacity • Moderate performance–power consumption ratio • Difficult to define new hardware accelerator

systems (LC, e.g., NVIDIA GPU and AMD ATI GPU), where cores are implemented on two or more chips interconnected on printed boards, and tightly coupled systems (TC, e.g., IBM CELL and ClearSpead), where all cores are on the same chip.

DF is the other class of "supercomputers," where systems are composed of the CPU and a flexible hardware accelerator based on the DF concept. The main component that enables flexibility is FPGA, in which a set of processors and a set of custom hardware accelerators are implemented and made to communicate with each other using a network. The system can be made adaptable by modifying the computation infrastructure. This can be done at compile time using full device reconfiguration or at runtime by means of partial device reconfiguration.

The essential difference of various systems with DF accelerators is due to the fact that some use explicit DF paradigm, while the others use implicit DF concept. Therefore, one possible classification criterion is explicit data flow (EDF, e.g., MaxNode) versus implicit data flow (IDF, e.g., Convey and SGI RASC).

Systems that use IDF computation can be further differentiated by the model granularity that is presented to the programmer. The first group can be seen as COPs, where each COP has a set of instructions for execution (coarse grain (CG) implicit data flow, e.g., Convey). The other group can be regarded as a chip area on which a set of operational units is implemented and used in arbitrary combinations (fine grain (FG) implicit data flow, e.g., SGI RASC).

Our classification is given in Fig. 16, together with specifications of classification criteria, outcomes generated by applying these criteria, and the representative examples discussed in this chapter.

Other interesting issues in CF supercomputers, not encompassed by the presented classification, are discussed next. Among the CF machines, two basic paradigms exist for parallel computation on multiprocessors. The first paradigm is *message passing interface (MPI)*, usually available where communication among processors happens in a network. The second paradigm, the *shared memory* or *SMP* is where communications are performed via the shared memory. On heterogeneous multiprocessors, any one of these paradigms can be used.

In most of the existing research efforts, the purpose is to have an efficient mapping of a set of threads onto a set of processors. Two possibilities have been presented that address this purpose: SMT [27–29] and *chip multiprocessor (CMP)* [6,30–33]. An SMT is based on a superscalar processor with a set of units for parallel execution of instructions. Given a set of threads, resources

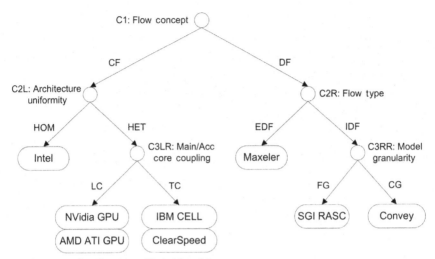

Figure 16 A classification of hybrid architectures.

are dynamically allocated by extracting several independent instructions to be executed in parallel. Threads that need long memory access are preempted to avoid idle states of processors. This paradigm can also be used with both MPI and SMP.

Instead of using only one superscalar core to execute instructions in parallel, the CMPs use many processor cores to compute threads in parallel. Each processor has small first-level local instruction and data caches. A second level cache is available for all the processors on a chip. The CMPs target applications consist of a set of independent computations that can be easily mapped to threads.

Existence of independent computations is usually the case in database or web server applications where transactions do not rely on each other. In CMPs, threads having long memory access are preempted to allow others to use the processor [4].

DF supercomputers can be classified according to communication to its host machine. Some use front side bus (FSB), while others use standard peripheral buses, e.g., PCIe or custom-made bus, e.g., nonuniform memory access link (NUMA Link from SGI RASC supercomputer).

4. SUMMARY OF PRESENTED SOLUTIONS

We have presented several commercially available solutions for high performance computing. We have provided an overview of both hardware and software for each one. This section gives a comparison of selected architectures in terms of capacity, performance, and programming considerations.

4.1. Computation and Memory Capacity

The selected architectures' comparison in terms of computation and memory capacities is given in the Table 5 [3,9,25,34,18,35–37,10]. When interpreting the data presented in the table, it should kept in mind that not all solutions belong to the same generation of technology. Year of issue can be used as an orientation to which generation a particular solution belongs to. This is important because the generation has a significant impact on the system speed, concealing the true relationship between two different architectures. Furthermore, most of the quoted sources present peak performances as the major (often times the only one) performance data, while the reality says that the only useful performance measures are those related to sustained performances. Some studies show that the sustained performance is usually several times lower than the peak performance. One such study shows that presented GPUs with peak performance measured in TFLOPS are able to sustain only several hundreds of GFLOPS [10]. Also, the shown differences between CPU and GPU performances have been brought in question [38]. The latter one shows that Convey HC-1 performs less than 10 GFLOPS (80 GFLOPS in peak performance) on most of the used kernels (parts of larger real world program that are time consuming, e.g., dense matrix-vector multiplication), and that real bandwidth to the memory is less than half of the presented peak bandwidth [25]. One respected exception is the Maxeler machine, and its data related to the sustained performance in the context of oil drilling. In addition to peak performance, other important parameters for assessing parallel algorithms' performance potential are both bandwidth of shared memory access and interconnection network speed.

The architectures presented so far have their own strengths and weaknesses, which make differences between them. The main problem of all these solutions is difficulty of programming them, particularly bearing in mind that programs have to be tuned for the target architecture, in order to obtain the best of it. The level of difficulty of programming these systems, as well as the performance that will be achieved differs significantly from application to application.

Based on data published by manufacturers and presented in Table 5, the best performing architectures for single precision floating point operations are GPUs. Often, they achieve better performance several times than the

Table 5 Computation and Memory Capacity

Intel Core i7-870 CPU

Computation Capacity				Memory Capacity			
				L1 Cache		Memory	
# cores	Clock Frequency	Peak Performance	Power	Size	Bandwidth	Size	Bandwidth
4	2.93 GHz	46.8 GFLOPS	95 W	256 KB	n/a	16 GB	21 GB/s

Cell/B.E.

Computation Capacity				Memory Capacity					
				CPU Cache		Local Store			
# cores	Clock Frequency	Peak Performance	Power	Size	Bandwidth	Size	Bandwidth	Memory Size	Bandwidth
1 + 8 hetero	3.2 GHz	230.4 GFLOPS	135 W	512 KB	44 GB/s	8*256 KB	204.8 GB/s	16 GB	25 GB/s

ClearSpeed CSX700

Computation Capacity				Memory Capacity					
				CPU Cache	Local Store		Memory		
# cores	Clock Frequency	Peak Performance	Power	Size	Size	Bandwidth	Size	Bandwidth	Bandwidth to Host
2 + 192 hetero	250 MHz	96 GFLOPS	11.4 W	24 KB	2*128 KB	192 GB/s	2*8 GB	2*4 GB/s	4 GB/s

SGI RASC Accelerator Board (2× Virtex4 LX200) Max 120 W

Computation Capacity

# LUTs	# FFs	# DSP48E	Clock Frequency	Peak Performance
200448 × 2	200448 × 2	96 × 2	200 MHz	47 GFLOPS

Memory Capacity

Block RAMs			On Board Memory		
Power	#	Size	Size	Bandwidth	Bandwidth to Host
120 W	336	0.7 MB	40 MB	16 GB/s	6.4 GB/s

Maxeler MAX3 FPGA Acceleration Card

Computation Capacity

# LUTs	# FFs	# DSP48E	Clock Frequency	Peak Performance
297600	595200	2016	100–300 MHz	450 GFLOPS

Memory Capacity

Block RAMs			On Board Memory		
Power	#	Size	Size	Bandwidth	Bandwidth to Host
55 W	2128	4.68 MB	1519 GB/s	48 GB	38.4 GB/s	8 GB/s

Convey Coprocessor HC-1

Computation Capacity

# LUTs	# FFs	# DSP48E	Clock Frequency	Peak Performance
4*207360	4*207360	4*192	n/a	80 GFLOPS

Memory Capacity

Block RAMs			On Board Memory		
Power	#	Size	Bandwidth	Size	Bandwidth	Bandwidth to Host
100 W	4*288	4*1.25 MB	n/a	16 GB	80 GB/s	1066 MT/s

Continued

Table 5 Computation and Memory Capacity—cont'd

NVIDIA C2070

Computation Capacity					Memory Capacity				
					Shared Memory		On Board Memory		
# Multiprocessors	# Cores	Clock Frequency	Peak Performance	Power	Size	Bandwidth	Size	Bandwidth	Bandwidth to Host
14	448	1.15 GHz	1.03 TFLOPs	238 W	672 KB	n/a	6 GB	144 GB/s	8 GB/s

AMD ATI HD5870

Computation Capacity					Memory Capacity				
					Shared Memory		On Board Memory		
# Multiprocessors	# Cores	Clock Frequency	Peak Performance	Power	Size	Bandwidth	Size	Bandwidth	Bandwidth to Host
20	1600	850 MHz	2.72 TFLOPs	188 W	640 KB	2176 GB/s	6 GB	153.6 GB/s	8 GB/s

Abbreviations: LUT, look-up table; FF, flip-flop; DSP48E, digital signal processing element of Xilinx devices; #. number of.

others. A prerequisite for this performance benefit is reflected in the fact that the same operation can be done on a large amount of data in parallel. Algorithms with a lot of synchronization and communication are not suitable for these architectures, especially if the communication pattern is irregular [38]. If a decision is based on price and performance per watt ratio (as specified by vendors), then GPUs are a preferred solution as well.

ClearSpeed, which has been made exclusively for acceleration of high performance calculations, seems very similar to the GPU, except that it has only two SIMD processors several times wider than the ones in the GPU. It is one order of magnitude slower, mainly due to a low clock frequency. On the other hand, lower frequency means a significantly lower electrical energy consumption and better performance per watt ratio.

Despite the fact that CBEA appeared more than 7 years ago, it is still comparable to the state-of-the-art CPUs. It presents a very flexible architecture with eight independent cores. Each core can execute a different program. It has fast communication and synchronization, with over 200 GB/s bandwidth of the interconnect bus, which make CBEA a very flexible solution. Double precision calculations can also be carried out very efficiently. When compared to GPUs, more difficult programming is the price to pay.

The performance of FPGA-based solutions cannot be easily measured using the number of floating point operations done per unit of time, as FPGAs do not have predefined FPUs. Implementing floating point requires use of a significant amount of available logic, while generated logic is much slower than that of CPUs and GPUs. The FPGA-based solutions are much better suited for algorithms based on fixed point, integer, or logical operations. FPGA can significantly outperform competitions for those applications. An additional benefit of FPGAs utilization is the ability to implement custom precision floating point, completely independent of the IEEE-754 standard. The peak performance potential of the chip is not a good guide to overall achieved performance for Maxeler FPGA solutions in particular, since the inherent flexibility of the architecture often enables devising good solutions for a wide range of applications where more rigid solutions (even with higher peak performance) struggle.

4.2. Programming Considerations

According to the far-reaching opinion, the major obstacle for heterogeneous and reconfigurable architectures utilization is the lack of programming environment at higher levels of abstraction. Such an environment will remove some burden for the programmer who, in that case, would not be expected to take into account every detail of the target architecture and will be provided with a much faster development cycle. It will also simplify the existing software migration to these new architectures.

The main obstacle in offering a high-level programming (e.g., C and Java), lies in the semantic gap between this model and the explicitly concurrent models used to program hardware devices. Common hardware description languages, such as VHDL or Verilog use an execution model based on communicating sequential processes (CSP) [20] and are thus far detached from the imperative models.

Approaches to solve a semantic gap problem cover a wide spectrum of solutions, ranging from the easier approach where the input language already offers a concurrent execution model close to the hardware CSP model to the harder approach of automatic uncovering of concurrency from traditional imperative languages [39]. Compilation of programs from the imperative paradigm to hardware has to automatically extract as much concurrency as possible in order to bridge this semantic gap. A popular alternative approach is relying on library implementations in which the concurrent execution notions have been crystallized by library developers, as well as openly publicized in APIs. Programming systems, such as Maxeler MaxCompiler [21], address this by allowing the programmer to describe their application in a high-level language (Java) but in an explicitly parallel way. Aforementioned approach unlocks a great potential for domain-specific languages adoption intended for underlying parallel architectures. One such example can already be found in MATLAB, a highly popular domain-specific language aimed at image/signal processing and control application.

Current FPGA compilation flows are too rigid since programmers must endure long compilation cycles, for the definition of a suitable RC implementation. A possible avenue for mitigating the issues pertaining to long compilation cycles would include the utilization of dynamic just-in-time and incremental compilation techniques. A first, quick translation to possibly not very efficient mappings, using only the regions of the input code exercised, would allow the execution to proceed as quickly as possible. As the execution would progress, a run-time system would trigger a recompilation of the more frequently exercised structures for recompilation, this time with the benefit reflected in the knowledge of key specific program values.

5. PERFORMANCE COMPARISON OF PRESENTED SOLUTIONS

Among presented solutions, three models of parallel processing are mainly used, these being: (a) the multicore CPU execution (MC) model (Intel, CBEA, and ClearSpeed); (b) the GPU execution (GP) model (NVIDIA and AMD ATI); (c) DF execution model (MaxNodes, SGI RASC, and Convey). The first two models implement a larger number of cores for parallel processing. The difference is found in cores' number and complexity. The multicore CPU model uses a small number of highly sophisticated cores, while the GPU model uses a large number of simple cores, often tightly coupled. The DF model empowers standard CPU with reconfigurable hardware through which DF in order to be processed. All three models are compared analytically and experimentally in the next two subsections.

5.1. Analytical Comparison

Analytical comparison has been conducted by using an example program that processes Ni input datasets (Ni is a problem dependent constant) in the same way and produces Ni results, in which case No operations are applied on each input dataset to produce a corresponding result. The example assumes that each result can be produced independently of all others. In traditional sequential programming model, the example can be described as a single loop, where loop body contains No operations and is repeated Ni times.

In all three models, the speedup is achieved by exploiting loop level and ILP. The loop level parallelism is mainly exploited by implementing more than one core and distributing different iterations of the same loop to different cores. Accordingly, execution time is reduced to Ncores times, where Ncores refer to the number of cores in the processor. The ILP is mainly exploited by pipelining processing units. In CPU and GPU models, each operation of processing unit is pipelined, with fixed depth of only up to several tens of pipeline phases (more likely no more than 20 phases). On the other hand, reconfigurable architectures (DF model) are adapted to the problem by implementing pipelined processing structure in a configurable hardware (by interconnecting appropriate operational components) corresponding to whole loop body. The number of pipeline phases depends on the size of the loop body and can reach several thousands. In this way, the implemented hardware exploits available ILP and also loop level parallelism as well; a pipeline executes many iterations of the loop in parallel, but each one in different phase.

The consequences of aforementioned facts are shown in Fig. 17. In CPU and GPU models, depicted in Fig. 17A and B, loop can start executing in as many iterations as the number of available cores (each vertical line in the figure represents execution of an iteration of the loop). The next group of loop body iterations cannot start until a group of Ncores iterations, that has previously started, finishes. As the execution time of an iteration linearly depends on No (the number of operations in the loop body), the total execution time for loop in CPU and GPU models is proportional to the product of No and Ni. In the DF model, each core is used to calculate the whole iteration of the loop body through a large number of clock cycles, which is proportional to the No. However, a DF core is capable of starting a new iteration on each clock cycle. Similarly, after the time period needed for execution of a single iteration, the results are produced on each clock. As a consequence, the total execution time is the sum of two values.

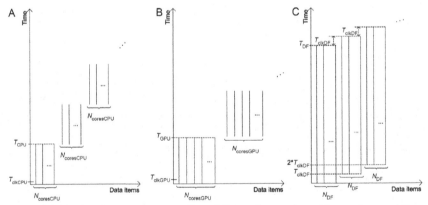

Figure 17 Graphical representation of capabilities of execution units on three architectural platforms: (A) The multicore CPU execution (MC) model (Intel, CBEA, and ClearSpeed): $N_{coresCPU}$, number of available cores; T_{clkCPU}, clock period; T_{CPU}, execution time of one loop iteration; C_{CPU}, clocks per instruction. (B) The GPU execution (GP) model (NVIDIA and AMD ATI): $N_{coresGPU}$, number of available cores; T_{clkGPU}, clock period; T_{GPU}, execution time of one iteration, C_{GPU}, clocks per instruction. (C) Data flow (DF) execution model (MaxNodes, SGI RASC, Convey): N_{DF}, number of implemented data flows; T_{clkDF}, clock period; T_{DF}, latency of data flow pipeline; C_{DF}, clocks per instruction (each instruction is implemented as a piece of pipelined hardware and all instructions are chained to form a set of data flow paths from the input to the output). The x-axis depicts the number of input data items, and the y-axis depicts the execution time.

Namely, the first value, which refers to the time needed for the iteration execution, is proportional to No. The second value, which refers to the time needed to produce results, is proportional to Ni. In case of large input dataset, the second part of execution time is dominant. However, in the DF model, the total execution time almost remains unchanged (i.e., does not depends on Ni) for problems with larger loop body, while in the first two approaches the total execution time increases proportionally to loop body size increase.

In Fig. 17, we assume that the loop iterations are not data dependent. In reality, some amount of data dependency typically does exist, which does not jeopardize the quality of the conclusion to follow; this is because in any parallel application, some amount of parallelism always does exist, which is the main prerequisite for the conclusion to follow. In cases (A) and (B), processing of each input data is faster than in the case (C), but in the case (C) much more input data can be processed in parallel. In other words, the first result latency in the case (C) is significantly higher than in cases (A) and (B), but after that latency, the rate at which the results are generated does not depend on number of operations on each data item (C).

The execution times of Fig. 17 are derived from the following equations:

$$(A) \quad T_{\text{CPU}} = No^* C_{\text{CPU}}^* T_{\text{clkCPU}}$$
$$t_{\text{CPU}} = Ni^* T_{\text{CPU}} / N_{\text{coresCPU}}$$
$$= Ni^* No^* C_{\text{CPU}}^* T_{\text{clkCPU}} / N_{\text{coresCPU}},$$

$$(B) \quad T_{\text{GPU}} = No^* C_{\text{GPU}}^* T_{\text{clkGPU}}$$
$$t_{\text{GPU}} = Ni^* T_{\text{GPU}} / N_{\text{coresGPU}}$$
$$= Ni^* No^* C_{\text{GPU}}^* T_{\text{clkGPU}} / N_{\text{coresGPU}},$$

$$(C) \quad T_{\text{DF}} = No^* C_{\text{DF}}^* T_{\text{clkDF}}$$
$$t_{\text{DF}} = T_{\text{DF}} + (Ni - N_{\text{DF}})^* T_{\text{clkDF}} / N_{\text{DF}}$$
$$= No^* C_{\text{DF}}^* T_{\text{clkDF}} + (Ni - N_{\text{DF}})^* T_{\text{clkDF}} / N_{\text{DF}}$$

Meanings of the variables in the above equations are given in the caption of Fig. 17. For CPU and GPU models, enlarging the operations' number per data item by some factor increases execution time by the same factor (because No multiplies rest of expressions (A) and (B)). However, enlarging the operations' number per data item in data flow architectures (C) causes only the latency to the first result to increase. After the first result has been produced, the rate at which remaining results are produced remains unchanged in DF model. In other words, enlarging the operations' number per input dataset in cases (A) and (B), leads to a decrease in the rate at which results are produced, while in the case (C) this rate remains unchanged.

Aforementioned equations are correct until bandwidth between memory and processing chip (CPU, GPU, or DF) is large enough, and until there are enough space on DF to implement a complete loop body. When processing loop body requires more bandwidth between processing chip and memory than it is available, the processing time becomes determined by available bandwidth. In this case, data flow architecture can benefit because it requires constant bandwidth (required bandwidth does not change over time due to the fact that each part of loop is executed once during each clock cycle, bud different phases for different iterations). Contrary to DF, the required bandwidth for CPU and GPU can arbitrarily change over time depending on which part of loop body is currently being executed. It could possibly slow down CPU and GPU due to the fact that the communication channel remains unused during some period of time, while it is saturated during the rest of time. Moreover, reconfigurable architectures pass temporary results between pipeline phases using on-chip memory instead of using caches. Hence, it is expected that HET based on data flow accelerators could better utilize available bandwidth between processing chip and memory.

5.2. Experimental Comparison

The following three systems (Intel Core i7-870 CPU with 4 cores, NVIDIA C2070 GPU, and Maxeler MAX3 card) have been selected as the typical representatives of CPU, GPU, and DF computing models, respectively. The performances and power consumption of those three systems have been compared. Table 6 shows results of two benchmark programs' execution: Multidimensional European Option pricer and Bond Option pricer [40,41]. Results for DF have been obtained for an implementation with reduced numeric precision that is big enough to produce valid results. Calculating with original precision (that is double precision floating point) in case of Multidimensional European Option pricer extends DF execution time to 34.5 s that is 4.2 times faster than CPU, but 3 times slower than GPU.

The possibility to select the reduced numeric precision made DF the most promising model for applications the results of which do not differ from the results obtained using high-precision (e.g. double precision) floating point numbers. Moreover, DF is the most energy efficient. For the same amount of work GPU spends 3.2–3.8 times more energy, while CPU spends

Table 6 Declared and Measured Performance Data for Three Representative Systems

	Intel Core i7-870	NVIDIA C2070	Maxeler MAX3
Declared data [42–44]			
1. Working frequency (MHz)	2930	1150	150
2. Declared performance (GFLOPS)	46.8	1030	450
3. Declared normalized speedup	1	22	9.6
Measured on bond option [40]			
4. Execution time (s)	476	58	50.3[a]
5. Normalized measured speedup	1	8.2	9.5
6. Measured power consumption of the system (W)	183	240[b]	87[b]
7. Normalized energy for the system	19.9	3.2	1
Measured on 3D European option [41]			
8. Execution time (s)	145	11.5	9.6[a]
9. Normalized measured speedup	1	12.7	15.1
10. Measured power consumption of the system (W)	149	271[b]	85[b]
11. Normalized energy for the system	26.5	3.8	1

[a]Shown results are for reduced precision that is large enough to give the same result as SP or DP floating point.
[b]Power consumption of the whole system: CPU + GPU card or CPU + MAX3 card.

even over 20 times more energy than DF. In the case of Multi-dimension Bond Option, the consumed energy on DF architecture that works with double precision floating point numbers is nearly the same as on CPU. However, in systems with high demand for calculations, it is very likely that more than one DF accelerator card is installed. In that case, a ratio between energy consumed by accelerator cards and the rest of the system is much more important than the energy consumed by whole system. The consumed energy ratio changes in favor of a DF approach by subtracting the idle power consumption from the system, without any accelerator card from systems' power consumptions with accelerator cards.

The main reason why the current data flow systems struggle in case of double precision numbers lies in the fact that resources found in FPGAs are not optimized for arithmetic on double precision floating point numbers.

An example is implementation of floating point multiplier, which for the sake of precision has been reduced to 17 bits of mantissa, and it requires only one digital signal processing (DSP) element, while a multiplier intended for double precision numbers requires 10 DSP elements. Consequently, the number of multipliers that can be implemented on chip for double precision numbers is 10 times smaller than the number of multipliers for reduced precision numbers.

In accordance with the presented results and taking into consideration the analysis from Section 5.1, each architectural model performs better than the other models for a specific problem type. On the one hand, a highly sophisticated multicore CPU achieves the best results for sequential problems and problems with thread level parallelism, in which case available parallelism is in the form of small number of different mostly sequential threads that cannot be parallelized itself. On the other hand, GPU is the best performing approach for problems with large amount of data parallelism, for which double precision floating point numbers are mandatory. Otherwise, the best performing architectural style is data flow based, particularly with technology improvements that will lead to a faster clock and larger system capacity.

6. CONCLUSION

In our opinion, heterogeneous computing has a great future. As we have discussed in Section 4, there are several obstacles that represent stumbling blocks to a more widespread use of heterogeneous computing. One of them is the existing software migration to these new architectures. One approach to this problem is to offer libraries that will be used by existing software in order to get benefits from these new architectures.

Looking at the future directions of GPU technology development, it seems that some new hardware resources, e.g., new high-speed reconfigurable interconnections like those in FPGAs, will be incorporated in GPU. Software environment has also improved: The CUDA 4.0 offers a shared address space, where the whole memory can be accessed by both CPU and GPU. Earlier versions of CUDA were limited to the use of the C language subset, but the newer ones support full C++.

The future of the CBEA cannot be seen clearly. Although the CBEA has independent cores and uses the local memory together with DMA, its programming complexity makes this architecture less attractive. However, in our opinion, as power becomes one of the most limiting factors, some features of CBEA will be taken into account again in new generation of processors [45].

Due to the fast growth rate in the capacity of FPGAs, the price reduction and reduced electrical energy consumption, the FPGA-based solutions represent a very promising approach [46]. It is widespread opinion that FPGAs will be further improved by increasing the clock frequency and by adding new hardware resources, such as floating point support. Adding new resources will make FPGAs suitable for much wider range of applications. These solutions are more difficult to program while achieving a better performance because of the hardware design need. Programming issue comprises: Generation bit stream methodology for the FPGA, debugging application support, and application–system interface. Performance issue includes data movement optimizations (partitioning) between microprocessors and FPGAs, and partitioning between multiple CPU + FPGA pairs, driving the scalability of the system topology. There are several approaches that offer solution for these problems. The best performing approach is Maxeler DF programming model which offers modeling of DF machine on high level of abstraction instead of directly designing hardware. Some other solutions offer a more preferred programming model where programmer sees only the library calls, but with one order of magnitude lower achieved performance.

For certain data-intensive applications, more cores do not mean better performance, according to Sandia's simulation [47]: "After about 8 cores, there's no improvement, and further it even decreases." Therefore, it is difficult to envision efficient use of hundreds of traditional CPU cores [48]. The use of hundreds of accelerator cores in conjunction with a handful of traditional CPU cores, on the other hand, appears to be a sustainable roadmap.

Currently, there is no one-size-fits-all approach for different computing domains, including general purpose computing. The seven presented architectures are intended for different problem domains, and none of them seem to be universal.

The GPU provides a mass-appeal via highly parallel and accessible accelerator technology where communication and synchronization are avoided. On the other hand, FPGA-based solutions are very suitable for applications relying on very large datasets and complex computations, in which case even the utilization of reduced precision numbers gives correct result.

ACKNOWLEDGMENTS

This work has been partially funded by the Ministry of Education and Science of the Republic of Serbia (III44009, TR32047, and III44006).

REFERENCES

[1] I. Ekmecic, I. Tartalja, V. Milutinovic, A survey of heterogeneous computing: concepts and systems, Proc. IEEE 84 (8) (1996) 1127–1144.

[2] I. Ekmecic, I. Tartalja, V. Milutinovic, EM/sup 3/: a taxonomy of heterogeneous computing systems, Computer 28 (12) (1995) 68–70.

[3] A. Brodtkorb, C. Dyken, T. Hagen, J. Hjelmervik, O. Storaasli, State-of-the-art in heterogeneous computing, Sci. Program. 18 (1) (2010) 1–33.

[4] C. Bobda, Introduction to Reconfigurable Computing: Architectures, Algorithms and Applications, Springer, Dordrecht, The Netherlands, 2007.

[5] K. Compton, S. Hauck, Reconfigurable computing: a survey of systems and software, ACM Comput. Surv. 34 (2) (2002) 171–210.

[6] K. Olukotun, L. Hammond, The future of microprocessors, ACM Queue 3 (7) (2005) 26–29.

[7] C. Schryver, H. Marxen, S. Weithoffer, N. Wehn, High-performance hardware acceleration of asset simulations, High-Performance Computing Using FPGAs, Springer, New York, 2013, pp. 3–32.

[8] NVIDIA, NVIDIA's Next Generation CUDA Compute Architecture: FERMI, NVIDIA, 2009. Online: http://www.nvidia.com/content/PDF/fermi_white_papers/NVIDIAFermiComputeArchitecture Whitepaper.pdf, accessed November 24 2013.

[9] AMD ATI, ATI Radeon™ HD 5870 Graphics Specification, AMD ATI, 2011. Online: http://www.amd.com/us/products/desktop/graphics/ati-radeon-hd-5000/hd-5870/Pages/ati-radeon-hd-5870-overview.aspx#2, accessed November 24 2013.

[10] Y. Zhang, L. Peng, B. Li, J.-K. Peir, J. Chen, Architecture comparisons between NVIDIA and ATI GPUs: computation parallelism and data communications, in: IEEE International Symposium on Workload Characterization (IISWC), 6–8 November, 2011, pp. 205–215.

[11] A. Munshi, B. Gaster, G.T. Mattson, J. Fung, D. Ginsburg, OpenCL Programming Guide, first ed., Addison-Wesley Professional, Boston, MA, 2011.

[12] K. Komatsu, S. Katsuto, A. Yusuke, K. Kentaro, T. Hiroyuki, K. Hiroaki, Evaluating performance and portability of OpenCL programs, in: The Fifth International Workshop on Automatic Performance Tuning, USA, October, 2010.

[13] P. Du, R. Weber, P. Luszczek, S. Tomov, G. Peterson, J. Dongarra, From CUDA to OpenCL: towards a performance-portable solution for multi-platform GPU programming, Parallel Comput. 38 (8) (2012) 391–407.

[14] M.J. Harvey, G. De Fabritiis, Swan: a tool for porting CUDA programs to OpenCL, Comput. Phys. Commun. 182 (4) (2011) 1093–1099.

[15] G. Shi, V. Kindratenko, F. Pratas, P. Trancoso, M. Gschwind, Application acceleration with the cell broadband engine, Comput. Sci. Eng. 12 (1) (2010) 76–81.

[16] Sony Corporation, Cell Broadband Engine Architecture, Sony Corporation, 2006. Online: http://cell.scei.co.jp/pdf/CBE_Architecture_v101.pdf, accessed November 24 2013.

[17] J.M. Perez, P. Bellens, R.M. Badia, J. Labarta, CellSs: making it easier to program the cell broadband engine processor, IBM J. Res. Dev. 51 (5) (2007) 593–604.

[18] Clearspeed Technology Ltd., CSX700 Floating Point Processor Datasheet, Clearspeed Technology Ltd., 2011. Online: http://www.clearspeed.com/products/documents/CSX700_Datasheet_Rev1E.pdf, accessed November 24 2013.

[19] Clearspeed Technology Ltd., Advance e720 Accelerator Card User Guide, Clearspeed Technology Ltd., 2010. Online: http://support.clearspeed.com/resources/documentation/Advance_e720_User_Guide_Rev1.D.pdf, accessed: November 24 2013.

[20] H. Fu, W. Osborne, R. Clapp, O. Mencer, W. Luk, Accelerating seismic computations using customized number representations on FPGAs, EURASIP J. Embedded Syst. 2009 (2009) 13.

[21] Maxeler Technologies, MaxCompiler White Paper, Maxeler Technologies, 2011. Online: http://www.maxeler.com/media/documents/MaxelerWhitePaperProgramming. pdf, accessed: November 24 2013.

[22] SGI, Reconfigurable Application-Specific Computing User's Guide, SGI, Inc, doc. No 007-4718-007, 2008. Online: http://techpubs.sgi.com/library/tpl/cgi-bin/summary. cgi?coll=linux&db=bks&docnumber=007-4718-007, accessed: November 24 2013.

[23] E. Jamro, M. Janiszewski, K. Machaczek, P. Russek, K. Wiatr, M. Wielgosz, Computation acceleration on SGI RASC: FPGA based reconfigurable computing hardware, Comput. Sci. 9 (2008) 21–34.

[24] J.D. Bakos, High-performance heterogeneous computing with the convey HC-1, Comput. Sci. Eng. 12 (6) (2010) 80–87.

[25] W. Augustin, V. Heuveline, J.-P. Weiss, Convey HC-1 hybrid core computer—the potential of FPGAs in numerical simulation, in: Proceedings of the 2nd International Workshop on New Frontiers in High-performance and Hardware-Aware Computing (HipHaC'11), San Antonio, Texas, USA, 2011, pp. 1–8.

[26] Convey Computer Corporation, Compilers for Convey Hybrid-Core Computers, Convey Computer Corporation, 2009. Online: http://www.conveycomputer.com/ files/3913/5085/4426/Compiler_Data_Sheet.pdf, accessed: November 24 2013.

[27] S.J. Eggers, J.S. Emer, H.M. Leby, J.L. Lo, R.L. Stamm, D.M. Tullsen, Simultaneous multithreading: a platform for next-generation processors, IEEE Micro 17 (5) (1997) 12–19.

[28] M. Gulati, N. Bagherzadeh, Performance study of a multithreaded superscalar microprocessor, in: Proceedings of the Second International Symposium on High-Performance Computer Architecture, 3–7 February, 1996, pp. 291–301.

[29] H. Hirata, K. Kimura, S. Nagamine, Y. Mochizuki, A. Nishimura, Y. Nakase, T. Nishizawa, An elementary processor architecture with simultaneous instruction issuing from multiple threads, in: Proceedings on the 19th Annual International Symposium on Computer Architecture, 1992, pp. 136–145.

[30] L.A. Barroso, K. Gharachorloo, R. McNamara, A. Nowatzyk, S. Qadeer, B. Sano, S. Smith, R. Stets, B. Verghese, Piranha: a scalable architecture based on single-chip multiprocessing, in: Proceedings of the 27th International Symposium on Computer Architecture, 10–14 June, 2000, pp. 282–298.

[31] L. Geppert, Sun's big splash [Niagara microprocessor chip], IEEE Spectr. 42 (1) (2005) 56–60.

[32] L. Hammond, B.A. Hubbert, M. Siu, M.K. Prabhu, M. Chen, K. Olukolun, The Stanford hydra CMP, IEEE Micro 20 (2) (2000) 71–84.

[33] P. Kongetira, K. Aingaran, K. Olukotun, The hydra chip, IEEE Micro Mag. 25 (2) (2005) 21–29.

[34] T. Chen, R. Raghavan, J.N. Dale, E. Iwata, Cell broadband engine architecture and its first implementation—a performance view, IBM J. Res. Dev. 51 (5) (2007) 559–572.

[35] H. Fu, Accelerating scientific computing through GPUs and FPGAs, in: Stanford Center for Computational Earth & Environmental Science (CEES) Workshop, 2010.

[36] T. Ilsche, G. Juckeland, First experiences with SGI RASC, Technical University Dresden, 2008. Online: http://www.juckeland.net/wp-content/uploads/sgirep.pdf, accessed: November 24 2013.

[37] D. Strenski, J. Simkins, R. Walke, R. Wittig, Evaluating FPGAs for floating-point performance, in: Second International Workshop on High-Performance Reconfigurable Computing Technology and Applications, HPRCTA 2008, 16 November, 2008, pp. 1–6.

[38] V.W. Lee, C. Kim, J. Chhugani, M. Deisher, D. Kim, A.D. Nguyen, N. Satish, M. Smelyanskiy, S. Chennupaty, P. Hammarlund, R. Singhal, P. Dubey, Debunking the 100X GPU vs. CPU myth: an evaluation of throughput computing on CPU and GPU, SIGARCH Comput. Archit. News 38 (3) (2010) 451–460.

[39] A. Papakonstantinou, K. Gururaj, J.A. Stratton, C. Deming, J. Cong, W.-M.W. Hwu, FCUDA: enabling efficient compilation of CUDA kernels onto FPGAs, in: SASP '09. IEEE 7th Symposium on Application Specific Processors, 27–28 July, 2009, pp. 35–42.

[40] Q. Jin, D. Dong, A.H.T. Tse, G.C.T. Chow, D.B. Thomas, W. Luk, S. Weston, Multi-level customisation framework for curve based Monte Carlo financial simulations, Lect. Notes Comput. Sci 7199 (2012) 187–201.

[41] A.H.T. Tse, G.C.T. Chow, Q. Jin, D.B. Thomas, W. Luk, Optimising performance of quadrature methods with reduced precision, Lect. Notes Comput. Sci 7199 (2012) 251–263.

[42] P. Gepner, V. Gamayunov, D.L. Fraser, The 2nd generation Intel Core processor. Architectural features supporting HPC, in: 10th International Symposium on Parallel and Distributed Computing (ISPDC), 6–8 July, 2011, pp. 17–24.

[43] NVIDIA, Tesla C2050 and C2070 GPU computing processor, NVIDIA, July 2010. Online: http://www.nvidia.com/docs/IO/43395/NV_DS_Tesla_C2050_C2070_jul10_lores.pdf, accessed: November 24 2013.

[44] P. Sundararajan, High Performance Computing Using FPGAs, Xilinx, Sep. 2010. Online: http://www.xilinx.com/support/documentation/white_papers/wp375_HPC_Using_FPGAs.pdf, accessed: November 24 2013.

[45] I. Ouda, K. Schleupen, Application Note: FPGA to IBM Power Processor Interface Setup, IBM Research Report RC24596, July 2008. Online: http://domino.watson.ibm.com/library/CyberDig.nsf/1e4115aea78b6e7c85256b360066f0d4/0019083255e3732c8525747a0068a14d?OpenDocument&Highlight=0, Schleupen, accessed: November 24 2013.

[46] D.H. Jones, A. Powell, C. Bouganis, P.Y.K. Cheung, GPU versus FPGA for high productivity computing, in: 2010 International Conference on Field Programmable Logic and Applications (FPL), August 31–September 2, 2010, pp. 119–124.

[47] S.K. Moore, Multicore is bad news for supercomputers, IEEE Spectr. 45 (11) (2008) 15.

[48] K. Pedretti, S. Kelly, M. Levenhagen, Summary of Multi-Core Hardware and Programming Model Investigations, Sandia Technical Report, SAND2008-3205, May 2008. Online: http://www.cs.sandia.gov/~ktpedre/papers/multicore-tech.pdf, accessed: November 24 2013.

ABOUT THE AUTHORS

Saša Stojanović, Ph.D. student, received his BS and MS EE at School of Electrical Engineering, University of Belgrade in 2001. He is a teaching assistant at School of Electrical Engineering, University of Belgrade. Saša's interest spans dataflow programming, automatic parallelism extraction, code transformation, and low level code analysis.

Dragan Bojić received a Ph.D. degree in Electrical Engineering and Computer Science from the University of Belgrade in 2001. He is an assistant professor at the School of Electrical Engineering, University of Belgrade. His research interests include software engineering techniques and tools, and e-learning.

Miroslav Bojović received a Ph.D. in Computer Engineering from the University of Belgrade, in 1988. He is an associate professor at the Faculty of Electrical Engineering, University of Belgrade, where he teaches database managements systems. Previously, he was with the Pupin Institute, Belgrade and UCLA, Los Angeles. His research interests include database management systems, distributed information systems, fault tolerant computing, software engineering, and internet technologies.

CHAPTER TWO

Concurrency, Synchronization, and Speculation—The Dataflow Way

Krishna Kavi*, Charles Shelor*, Domenico Pace†

*Department of Computer Science and Engineering, University of North Texas Denton, Texas, USA
†Information Technology and Services Accenture, Turin, Italy

Contents

Advances in Computers, Volume 96
ISSN 0065-2458
http://dx.doi.org/10.1016/bs.adcom.2014.10.004

47

Abstract

This chapter provides a brief overview of dataflow, including concepts, languages, historical architectures, and recent architectures. It is to serve as an introduction to and summary of the development of the dataflow paradigm during the past 45 years. Dataflow has inherent advantages in concurrency, synchronization, and speculation over control flow or imperative implementations. However, dataflow has its own set of challenges to efficient implementations. This chapter addresses the advantages and challenges of dataflow to set a context for the remainder of this issue.

ABBREVIATIONS

ABI address buffer identifier
AQ acknowledgment queue of D^2NOW
CU computing unit in Codelet
D^2NOW data-driven network of workstations
DDM data-driven multithreading model
DFE dataflow engine in Maxeler
D-TSU distributed thread scheduling unit in Teraflux
DU data cache unit in TRIPS
EDGE explicit data graph execution in TRIPS
EP execution pipeline of SDF
EPN epoch number of SDF
ETS explicit token store
EU execution unit in TRIPS
EXC execution continuation of SDF
FP frame pointer
GM graph memory of D^2NOW
GU global control unit in TRIPS
IP instruction pointer
IU instruction cache unit in TRIPS
L-TSU local thread scheduling unit in Teraflux
NIU network interface unit of D^2NOW
PE processing element of WaveScalar
PLC preload continuation of SDF
PSC poststore continuation of SDF
RIP retry instruction pointer of SDF

RQ ready queue of D^2NOW
RS register set identifier
RU register unit in TRIPS
SC synchronization count in SDF
SDF scheduled dataflow
SISAL streams and Iteration in a Single Assignment Language
SM synchronization memory of D^2NOW
SP synchronization pipeline of SDF
SU scheduling unit in Codelet
SU scheduling unit of SDF
TLS thread-level speculation
TP threaded procedure in Codelet
TRIPS Tera-op Reliable Intelligently adaptive Processing System
TSU thread synchronization unit of D^2NOW
VAL value-based programming language
WTC waiting continuation of SDF

1. INTRODUCTION

Achieving high performance is possible when multiple activities (or multiple instructions) can be executed concurrently. The concurrency must not incur large overheads if it is to be effective. A second issue that must be addressed while executing concurrent activities is synchronization and/or coordination of the activities. These actions often lead to sequentialization of parallel activities, thus defeating the potential performance gains of concurrent execution. Thus, effective use of synchronization and coordination are essential to achieving high performance. One way to achieve this goal is through speculative execution, whereby it is speculated that concurrent activities do not need synchronization or coordination or predict the nature of the coordination. Successful speculation will reduce sequential portions of parallel programs; but misprediction may add to execution times and power consumption since the speculatively executed activities must be undone and the activity must be restarted with correct synchronization.

The dataflow model of computation presents a natural choice for achieving concurrency, synchronization, and speculations. In the basic form, activities in a dataflow model are enabled when they receive all the necessary inputs; no other triggers are needed. Thus, all enabled activities can be executed concurrently if functional units are available. And the only synchronization among computations is the flow of data. In a broader sense, coordination or predicate results can be viewed as data that enable or coordinate dataflow activities. The functional nature of dataflow (eliminating side effects that plague imperative programming models) makes it easier to use speculation or greedy execution; unnecessary or unwanted computations can be simply discarded without any need for complex recovery on mis-speculations.

In this chapter, we introduce well-understood dataflow models of computation in Section 2. We review programming languages that adhere to dataflow principles in Section 3. We present historical attempts at developing architectures implementing the dataflow models along with a discussion of the limitations of dataflow encountered by these architectures in Section 4. We present some recent variations of the dataflow paradigm that could potentially lead to efficient architectures in Section 5. As a case study in Section 6, we provide how one such architecture, scheduled dataflow (SDF), implements concurrency, synchronization, and speculation. Finally, we include our conclusions and prognosis on the future of the model as a viable alternative to control-flow systems in Section 7.

2. DATAFLOW CONCEPTS

2.1. Dataflow Formalism

The dataflow model of computation is based on the use of graphs to represent computations and flow of information among the computations. The signal processing community uses a visual dataflow model to specify computations. Some examples of environments used by this community include Signal [1, 2], Lustre [3], and Ptolemy [4]. In this chapter, our focus is on general-purpose programming and general-purpose computer architectures. Hence, we will not review programming models, languages, or environments for specific or restricted domains; however, Lee [5] provides a good survey on such languages and models.

One of the earliest dataflow models is called Kahn [6] process networks. A program in this model consists of channels, processes, and links connecting these processes. Figure 1 shows an example program and the corresponding graphical representation of the process network. In principle, channels can be viewed as arrays or lists (sequence of values). It is also possible to associate firing semantics with a process to define necessary input sequences and non-determinism. We again refer the reader to the survey by Lee [5]. A process takes the required sequences of inputs from its input channels and creates sequences on output channels. To facilitate continuous execution and

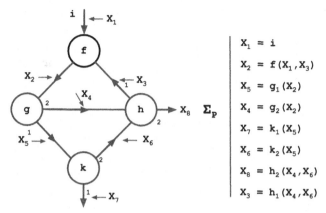

$$X_1 = i$$
$$X_2 = f(X_1, X_3)$$
$$X_5 = g_1(X_2)$$
$$X_4 = g_2(X_2)$$
$$X_7 = k_1(X_5)$$
$$X_6 = k_2(X_5)$$
$$X_8 = h_2(X_4, X_6)$$
$$X_3 = h_1(X_4, X_6)$$

Figure 1 Kahn process networks example.

concurrency, one can view the sequences of data on channels as partially ordered. A set of inputs may contain multiple, partially ordered inputs, where the lack of ordering among subsequences allows for concurrency.

There have been several formalisms that have extended Kahn process networks. We use specific notations to describe a process network, which resemble the most common view of dataflow graphs to graphically represent computations. We use the notations from Ref. [7] in the rest of this section.

A dataflow graph is a directed graph in which the elements are called links and actors [8]. In this model, actors (nodes) describe operations, while links receive data from a single actor and transmit values to one or more actors by way of arcs; arcs can be considered as channels of communication, while links can be viewed as placeholders or buffers

$$G = < A \cup L, E >,$$

where $A = \{a1, a2, ..., an\}$ is the set of actors; $L = \{l1, l2, ..., lm\}$ is the set of links and $E \subseteq (A \times L) \cup (L \times A)$ is the set of edges connecting links and actors.

In its basic form, activities (or nodes) are enabled for execution when all input arcs contain tokens and no output arcs contain tokens. However, if we consider arcs as (potentially infinite) buffers, as in Kahn's process networks, the condition related to output arcs can be removed. The values in these buffers can be viewed as partially ordered sequences allowing for multiple invocations of activities. This concept is the basis of tagged-token dataflow architectures.

The model described above, without semantic interpretation of activities, has been shown to be isomorphic to free choice Petri nets [9]. In addition, it was used as a model for concurrent processes with semantics of actors defined using predicate logic and using partial ordering of values at links [10, 11]. The model was then used to derive conditions to assure liveness and safety properties of concurrent processes. By attaching semantics with nodes (or activities), or describing the computation performed by the nodes using some programming notation, dataflow graphs can be used for parallel programming. A hardware schematic can also be viewed as a dataflow graph where the schematic components are dataflow nodes and the signals on the schematic are the dataflow arcs bringing the outputs of generating nodes to the inputs of receiving nodes.

To be useful as a general purpose programming model, we need to permit conditional operations (such as if...then...else constructs). Thus, we can view actors, graphically represented using nodes, as belonging to one of three types: activities, predicates, and gates (or conditional execution). Activities represent computations that consume data on input arcs and produce data on output arcs. Predicates consume input data and produce Boolean (true or false) outputs. Gates require two types of inputs: a Boolean input and data inputs. Gates use the value of the Boolean input to decide how to process inputs or generate outputs. Control arcs (which enter or leave control links) have tokens of type Boolean (true or false). Data arcs (which enter or leave data links) have tokens of any data type (e.g., integer, real, or character). In Section 3.1, we introduce how complex data structures such as arrays and structures can be handled in dataflow languages and architectures.

2.2. Generalized Firing Semantic Sets (FSS)

The basic firing rule adopted by most dataflow researchers requires that all input arcs contain tokens and that no tokens be present on the output arcs. This provides an adequate sequencing control mechanism when the nodes in dataflow graphs represent primitive operations. However, if the nodes are complex procedures, or dataflow subgraphs, more generalized firing control for both input and output links is required. The rules can indicate which subset of input links of an actor must contain values and which subset of output links of the actor must not contain any values for enabling the actor for execution. The ability to enable actions using only subsets of inputs provides flexible scheduling of activities; for example, a node which represents a function or a thread may be allowed to initiate execution with a minimum set of required inputs, while additional input are delivered later (but before they are actually needed).

2.3. Graphical Notations

For the purpose of this chapter, we simplify the formalism and notations. We use the graphical representations shown in Fig. 2 for activities, predicates, and gates. Using these notations, we can think of writing dataflow programs. The first program shown in Fig. 3 is a single computation that does not use conditional statements.

The second example which is shown in Fig. 4 represents how the conditional programming constructs (a loop in this example) can be represented in dataflow. The graph computes the following:

$$\text{sum} = \sum_{i=1}^{N} f(i).$$

As stated previously, an actor in a dataflow graph can actually represent a function or a module so that we can construct more complex programs using simpler programs as subgraphs.

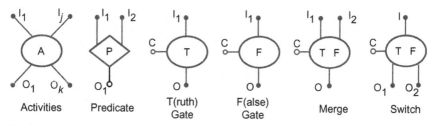

Figure 2 Some graphical notations of dataflow actors.

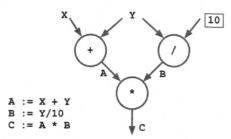

```
A := X + Y
B := Y/10
C := A * B
```

Figure 3 A simple dataflow program example.

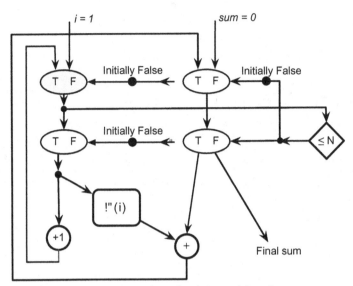

Figure 4 A dataflow program example with a loop and function.

The dataflow model of computation is neither based on memory structures that require inherent state transitions nor does it depend on history sensitivity. Thus, it eliminates some of the inherent von Neumann pitfalls described by Backus [12]. We now describe how the dataflow model is natural for representing concurrency, synchronization, and speculation. Several extensions to basic dataflow have been proposed so that dataflow techniques can be used in a variety of applications, including the use of producer–consumer synchronization, locks, and barriers. However, in this section, we rely on the dataflow formalism already introduced here.

2.4. Concurrency

An activity in dataflow is enabled when the necessary inputs are available on input arcs; no other trigger is needed. Thus, all activities that are enabled can execute concurrently provided sufficient computational units are available. This should be contrasted with von Neumann (or control-flow) model, which sequences activities, typically using a program counter. In the simple dataflow program shown in Fig. 3, both the addition and division operations can be executed concurrently. Likewise, in the second example in Fig. 4, the subgraph representing $f(i)$ can be invoked concurrently for all values of

$$1 \leq i \leq N.$$

In addition to this concurrency, using flexible firing rules mentioned previously, activities represented by subgraphs (i.e., functions are threads) can be enabled upon receiving a subset of inputs, thus creating an additional level of concurrency, similar to pipelining used in conventional systems.

2.5. Synchronization

The only synchronization among activities in dataflow is the data dependency. Thus, dataflow only includes true (or Read After Write, RAW) dependency. This is because the dataflow model of computation is neither based on memory structures that require inherent state transitions nor does it depend on history sensitivity: only values have meaning in dataflow and not storage locations. This eliminates side effects and false dependencies caused by the use of storage that can be modified several times during a program execution. Imperative languages that do use variables for storing data values cause anti (or Write After Read, WAR) and output (Write After Write, WAW) dependencies. These false dependencies force strict order on the execution of activities based on the order in which variables are accessed and modified. The correctness of a program requires that any read access to a variable must return the most recently written value, in the order in which the activities are sequenced (or program order). These false dependencies require complex compile time analyses and/or complex hardware.

2.6. Speculation or Greedy Execution

As stated above, use of variables that can be modified require ordering of statements. In addition, in most modern imperative languages, variables may be modified indirectly using pointers. These aspects of imperative programs make it very difficult to determine which activities (or functions, threads) can be executed concurrently, particularly when the dependencies cannot be determined statically. When speculation is used with control-flow models, it is necessary to buffer values generated by activities that are enabled speculatively. These values must then be discarded and the effects of the speculative computation must be undone when the speculation fails.

Since the dataflow model does not use variables, but only values, activities can be executed speculatively or aggressively without waiting to completely determine data dependencies (even true dependencies). The output of these speculatively executed activities may be wrong, but they cause no side effects, and thus can be safely discarded, and an instance of the activity with correct inputs can be initiated. In principle, it is possible to complete all possible speculative instances of activities and discard all mis-speculated computations, provided sufficient resources are available. For example, the function $f(i)$ in Fig. 4 can be invoked greedily for all values of i, and the results from invocations for $i > N$ can be discarded.

3. DATAFLOW LANGUAGES

In this section, we discuss dataflow languages and structures used to implement complex types within dataflow languages. An example is presented to show how dataflow languages can be used for typical problems.

A language that implements the dataflow paradigm must have the following features:

- freedom from side effects;
- locality of effects;
- data dependencies equivalent to scheduling;
- single assignment of named values;
- efficient representation of data structures, recursion, and iteration;

Since scheduling is determined from data dependencies, it is important that the value of variables does not change between their definition and their use. The only way to guarantee this behavior is to disallow the reassignment of variables once their value has been assigned. Therefore, variables in dataflow languages must obey the *single-assignment rule* [13]. This means that they are considered as named values rather than variables. The implication of the single-assignment rule is that the compiler can represent each value as one or more arcs in the resultant dataflow graph, going from the instruction that assigns the value to each instruction that uses that value. An important consequence of the single-assignment rule is that the order of statements in a dataflow language is not important. As long as there are no data loops in the program, the definition of each value can be placed in any order in the program.

Freedom from side effects is also essential if data dependencies are to determine scheduling. Most languages that avoid side effects disallow global variables and scope rules. To ensure the validity of data dependencies, a dataflow program does not permit a function to modify its own input arguments. In addition, since there are no variables or storage locations containing data, the concept of using a pointer to access a storage location is foreign to dataflow. This also eliminates side effects caused by aliasing. This approach leads to some issues when the program manipulates data structures like arrays.

3.1. Dataflow Structures

One of the key points in the implementation of an efficient dataflow system is that of data structures. As described in Section 2, the dataflow execution model specifies that all data are represented by values that once created cannot be modified. If a node wants to modify a value, it creates a new token, containing new data which is identical to the original data, except for the element that had to be modified. While this data model is perfectly adherent to the theoretical dataflow execution model and for dataflow graphs that deal only with primitive data types, this approach is clearly unsatisfactory for graphs that use more complex data structures, especially in the era of object-oriented programming. The following sections briefly describe some data structure models.

3.1.1 Direct Access Method

This scheme treats each array element as an individual (scalar) data token, which eliminates the concept of an array or structures. A *tag* could be used to associate the value with a specific array. Although this method is simple, it requires that entire data structures be passed from one node to the next or to be duplicated among different nodes.

3.1.2 Indirect Access Method

In an indirect access scheme, arrays are stored in special (separate) memory units and their elements are accessed through explicit *read* and *write* operations. Arrays can be appended with new values, and arrays (and elements of arrays) are accessed using pointers. Modified elements can be made inaccessible by using reference counts with pointers (when the count becomes zero the elements become inaccessible). The main disadvantages of this method are as follows:

- $O(\log n)$ to access successive elements of an array;
- append operations are executed sequentially, and this results in only one element of an array being modified at a time which limits concurrency;
- a garbage collector is needed to manage elements whose count reaches zero.

3.1.3 Dennis's Method

Dennis's method [14] was the first method to provide realistic data structures in a dataflow context by proposing that the tokens in the dataflow program hold not the data itself, but rather a pointer to the data. This schema uses a memory heap in the form of a finite, acyclic, directed graph where each node represents either an elementary value or a structured value which behaves like an indexed array. Each element of a structured value is, in turn, a node that represents either an elementary value or a structured value. The pointers in the data tokens refer to one of this node and a reference count is maintained. A node which is no longer referred to, either directly or indirectly, in the graph is removed by an implicit garbage collector. This method behaves in the following way:

- whenever an elementary value is modified, a new node is simply added to the heap;
- whenever a structured value is modified, and there is more than one reference to the value, a new root node is added to the heap, pointing to the same values as the original initial root node, with the exception of the one value that was to have been modified for which a new node is created.

Figure 5 shows the effects of Dennis's method on the modification of an array. The second element (b) is modified; this leads to the creation of a new value (e). Since the element belongs to a structured value (and assuming reference count > 1), a new root (B) is created that refers to the array [a, e, c]. Meanwhile, value A remains unmodified, preserving the functional semantics of the model. This method prevents copying a large amount of complex values. It also permits the sharing of identical data elements which saves memory. However, this method is not the best for all situations. For example, consider a dataflow program that has two main sections. The first creates a 100-element array and populates it, one element at a time. The second takes the array and reads the elements, one at a time. In this case, the second part cannot begin to execute until the first completes its execution, even if it could read element 1 while the first part is populating element 2 and so on. A program that could potentially take as few as 101 time units to execute takes 200 time units. These situations led to the development of *I-structures*.

3.1.4 I-Structures

Arvind proposed I-structures for accessing large data structures in a dataflow paradigm [15]. This method allows more flexible access to the data structures

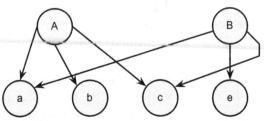

Figure 5 Dennis method for array access.

than Dennis's method. A data structure is created in memory, but its constituent fields are left blank. Each field can either store a value or be *"undefined."* A value can only be stored in a field that is currently undefined: I-structures adhere to the single-assignment rule. Any attempt to read from an undefined field is deferred until that value becomes available (that is, until a value is assigned to the field). By following this set of rules, a data structure can be used by the rest of the program as soon as it is created, while the population process continues. Meanwhile, consumers can begin to read from the structure. This method has a *producer–consumer* behavior. SDF [16] uses this approach for memory management.

3.1.5 Hybrid Scheme

The idea behind the hybrid scheme [17] is to associate a template, called the *structure template*, with each array. Each array is represented by a structure template and a vector of array elements. A template is divided into the following fields:

- reference count field, used to keep track of the number of hybrid structures created and destroyed during program execution;
- two pointers to two different arrays;
- location field, a string of 1's and 0's where the length of the string equals the number of elements in the array. Each location bit determines in which vector (*left* or *right*) the desired element resides;
- status bit (S), which is used when accessing array elements.

Whenever an array is defined, a hybrid structure is created: the elements of the array are stored sequentially in its vector and the reference count is set to 1; the status bit is initialized to 0; and the left pointer is linked to the vector. Since no modifications have been made, this hybrid structure is considered to represent the original array. If we want to modify only one element, this method generates a new template structure with its right pointer pointing to a vector containing only the modified element and its left pointer pointing to the original structure template. In cases where an array is entirely updated, the sharing is no longer needed and the dependence between original and modified arrays can be removed.

3.2. Id: Irvine Dataflow Language

Id is a dataflow language developed at the University of California–Irvine [18] and was designed to provide a high-level programming language for the dynamic dataflow architecture proposed by Arvind. Id is a block-structured expression-oriented single-assignment language. An interpreter was designed to execute Id programs on dynamic dataflow architectures.

Data types in Id are associated with values and variables are implicitly typed by the values they carry. Composite data types include both arrays and (record) structures; and elements can be accessed using either integer indices or string values defining the name of the element (for example, t["height"]). Structures are defined with two operators: *Select* and *Append*. *Select* is used to get the value of an element, while *Append* is used to define a new structure by copying the elements of the original structure and adding new values defined by the *Append* operation. Id programs consist of side-effect free expressions. These expressions (or subexpressions) can be executed in any order or concurrently based on the availability of input data. Loops in Id can be easily understood from the following example, which computes

$$\text{sum} = \sum_{i=1}^{N} f(i).$$

```
(initial i ← 1; sum ← 0;
    while i ≤ N do
        new i ← i + 1;
        new sum ← sum + f(i);
    return sum)
```

Id also uses the concept of a *new* operation to define a new value associated with an expression. It should be noted that a variable is not assigned a new value (like in conventional languages), but a new value is generated. Variables are used only for the convenience of writing programs. It is also convenient to remember that expressions in a loop can form recurrence expressions.

Procedures and functions in Id are pure functions and represent value(s) returned by the application of the function on the input values. Recursive procedures can be defined by associating names with procedure declarations as shown in the following:

```
y ← procedure f(n)
    (if n=0 then 1 else n * f(n-1))
```

The procedure *y* now defines factorial recursively, and the procedure is invoked as y(3).

The matrix multiply routine for Id is shown in Fig. 6. The inputs *a* and *b* are the input matrices and *l*, *m*, and *n* are inputs giving the size of the matrices. Where *a* is *l* by *m* and *b* is *m* by *n*. The result matrix will be *l* by *n*. A new matrix is created with the *initial* statement, setting *c* to the null value, Λ. The

```
procedure (a, b, l, m, n)
   (initial c ← Λ
   for i from 1 to l do
      new c[i] ← (initial d ← Λ
         for j from 1 to n do
            new d[j] ← (initial s ← 0
               for k from 1 to m do
                  new s ← s + a[i,k] * b[k,j]
               return s)
         return d)
   return c)
```
Figure 6 Matrix multiply in Id.

for statement computes the rows of *c*. The *new c[i]* creates a new matrix *c* from the previous matrix *c* by appending row *i* to form the new matrix. This row is created as a vector *d* that is initially given a null value Λ. New elements are appended to *d* as they are computed in the third *for* statement. The *for* statement nesting is similar to conventional imperative languages. The difference shows in the use of the *new* nomenclature to indicate a new and separate value named *s*, *d*, or *c*, rather than overwriting a value in an address *s*, *d*, or *c*. The inner expression from (*initial s* to *return s*) is generating and returning a scalar value to its calling expression. The intermediate expression from (*initial d* to *return d*) is collecting a scalar from each evaluation of the inner expression and appending it to the vector *d*. The outer expression from (*initial c* to *return c*) is collecting row vectors from the intermediate expression and appending them to the matrix *c*. No variable is ever overwritten, each value is created and then used in the creation of the next value.

No translators for converting Id programs to conventional (control-flow) architectures were developed; therefore, Id was used mostly by those with access to dynamic dataflow processors and Id interpreters.

3.3. VAL

VAL is a high-level programming language developed at MIT [19] and can be viewed as a textual representation of dataflow graphs. VAL relies on pure functional language semantics to exploit implicit concurrency. Since dataflow languages use single-assignment semantics, implementation and use of arrays present unique challenges. Array bounds are not part of the type declarations in VAL. Operations are provided to find the range of indices for the declared array. Array construction in VAL is also unusual to improve concurrency in handling arrays. It should be noted that to maintain the single-assignment feature of functional languages, traditional language syntax for accumulating values needs some changes as shown by the *eval plus a[i]* semantics in the second example below. To fully express such concurrencies, VAL provides parallel expressions in the form of *forall*. Consider the following examples:

```
forall i in [array_liml(a), array_limh(a)]
    a[i] := f(i);
forall i in [array_liml(a), array_limh(a)]
    eval plus a[i];
```

If one applies imperative semantics, both examples proceed sequentially. In the first case, the elements of the array *a* are constructed sequentially by calling the function *f(i)* with different values of the index *i*. In the second example, we compute a single value representing the sum of the elements of the array *a*, representing the sequential accumulation of the result. In VAL, the construction of the array elements in the first example can proceed in parallel since all functions in VAL are side-effect free. Likewise, the accumulation in the second example also exploits some concurrency since VAL translates such accumulations into a binary tree evaluation.

In addition to loops, VAL provides sequencing operations, *if-then-else* and *tagcase* expressions. When dealing with *oneof* data type, *tagcase* provides a means of interrogating values with the discriminating unions.

VAL does not provide good support for input/output nor recursion. These language restrictions provided a straightforward translation of programs to dataflow architectures, particularly static dataflow machines. The dynamic features of VAL can be translated easily if the machine supported dynamic graphs, such as the dynamic dataflow architectures.

A matrix multiplication to compute $C = A * B$ is shown in VAL in Fig. 7. The use of *forall* indicates there are no interactions among the *iteration* values for *i* and *j*. This allows expansion of the *forall* to be parallelized. The *array_liml* and *array_limh* built-in functions extract the lower and higher

```
forall i in [array_liml(A), array_limh(A)],        % range of A rows
    j in [array_liml(B[array_liml(B)]),
        array_limh(B[array_liml(B)])]              % range of B cols
    construct
        forall k in [array_liml(B), array_limh(B)]   % range of B rows
            eval plus A[i,k] * B[k,j]               % accumulate products
        endall
endall
```
Figure 7 Matrix multiply in VAL.

bounds of the array, respectively. Thus, *i* takes on all of the values of the indices for the rows of *A*. VAL does not have two-dimensional arrays, but uses nesting to have an array of arrays. Thus, *j* takes on all of the values of the indices of the array that is the first row of *B*, which are the indices of the columns of *B*. The *construct* function of VAL creates a new array with a range of *i* where each of those elements is an array with a range of *j* of the base type of the *A* and *B* arrays.

Nested within the *construct* clause is another *forall* giving *k* the range of the rows of *B* (which should match the columns of *A*). Where the *construct* created a matrix, the *eval* function of VAL creates a single value by combining the elements accessed by the *k* indices. In this instance, the *plus* indicates adding all of the products across the values of *k*. Other *eval* or reduction operators include *times, min, max, or*, and *and*. Notice that matrix *C* is not explicitly declared or named. Basically, the new matrix exists after the second *endall*. If this code fragment was in a function, it would return the new matrix to the calling program. Alternately, this code could have been used in the *declaration* section of a *let* block where *C :=* would precede the code and would receive the generated matrix as a named value.

3.4. Streams and Iteration in a Single Assignment Language

SISAL (Streams and Iteration in a Single Assignment Language) is perhaps the best-known dataflow language, mostly because of the support provided by the designers [20]. SISAL was heavily influenced by the VAL language.

The SISAL compiler generates optimized C code as its intermediate representation and thus could be run on any platform with a C compiler. The SISAL translator and runtime support software are available for UNIX and other platforms from http://sisal.sourceforge.net/. SISAL programs consist of one or more separately compilable units, which include a single program, plus any number of modules, and interfaces as needed. A module is similar to a program but is not a starting point of execution. It pairs with an interface to export some of its types and function names. SISAL supports scalar data types and structures (records, unions, arrays, and streams). A stream is a sequence of values produced in order by one expression and consumed in the same order by one or more other expressions. SISAL permits the creation of new values through the *new* notation. As can be seen in Fig. 8, each iteration of a loop assigns a value to a new instance of the iteration control variable *i* using the (*new i*) semantics to respect the single-assignment rule. This

```
for i := 1;
while (i < 5) do
    new i := i + 2;
    j := i + new i;
    returns product (i+j)
end for
```

Figure 8 SISAL stream.

program implicitly constructs a stream of values inside the loop and returns the product of the elements of the stream. The values of the stream are the values of $(i + j)$: 7, 13. Thus, 91 is returned by the loop. The example also illustrates that both the original value of *i* and the value of *new i* are available at the same time. One way of viewing an SISAL *for* statement is that multiple instances of the loop body are created and run in parallel with separate values for *i*.

Another important characteristic of the SISAL language is the optimization in the reduction operation using binary tree evaluations. SISAL has predefined reduction operations to evaluate sum, product, min, and max of a set of values. SISAL's popularity is also due to the concept of modules and interfaces. The interface shows the function templates that are visible publicly and the module defines the implementation of the functions, providing the language with a data abstraction capability.

The ubiquitous matrix multiplication function is easily implemented in SISAL [21]. The interface to the matrix multiplication function is described as

```
interface MatrixRoutines;
    type TwoDim = array [..,..] of type;
    function MatMul(A, B: TwoDim returns TwoDim);
end interface;
```

The first line within the interface specification defines a new type named *TwoDim* which is an array of two dimensions where the ..,.. indicates there are two unspecified dimensions within the array and each element is of *type*, meaning that any primitive SISAL type can form an array. This *parameterized* function declaration is valid for integers of any size, reals, and double precision numbers. The specification requires that the elements of *A*, the elements of *B*, and the elements of the returned array are all of the same type. The second line defines the calling sequence for the matrix multiply function. It accepts values for *A* and *B*, both of which are two-dimensional arrays and returns a two-dimensional array as a result. The implementation of the matrix multiply is given as

```
function MatMul(A, B: TwoDim returns TwoDim);
   if size(A, 2) ≅ size(B, 1) then error[TwoDim]
   else array[i in 1..size(A,1), j in 1..size(B, 2):
       sum(A[i,..] * B[..,j])]
   endif
end function
```

The first line of the function body determines if the matrices are compatible for multiplication by requiring the size of the second dimension of A to be equal to the first dimension of B. One of the features of SISAL is that every type has an error representation. New values can be immediately tested for an error, or the value can continue to be processed, while the error status is propagated through subsequent steps, allowing the locations of error processing to be controlled by the programmer. The second line creates a new two-dimensional array whose first dimension is the size of the first dimension of A and whose second dimension is the size of the second dimension of B. The third line of the function body uses the SISAL sum operator to accumulate all of the $A[i,k] * B[k,j]$ products as the ".." nomenclature means all elements within that dimension. Notice that there are no *for* statements in the code; all *distributions* are implied and no ordering is specified. SISAL uses the concept of distribution rather than iteration. This allows the multiplication of the elements to be distributed to as many multipliers as the hardware can provide and to accumulate the products to form each new array element through a tree reduction process.

Most operations on arrays, vectors, and streams in SISAL can be performed using just the dimension extents. However, some operations, such as Gaussian elimination, operate on varying subsets of one of the dimensions based on another dimension. A *for* statement is used in these instances, but is implemented as parallel, distributed loop bodies each with its local value for the *iteration variable*.

4. HISTORICAL DATAFLOW ARCHITECTURES

In this section, we explore how a processor architecture can be designed to implement the dataflow paradigm of execution. This section describes some early attempts at dataflow architectures. In Section 4.5, we explain why these early attempts were not commercially successful. More recent designs and implementations of dataflow architectures are discussed in Section 5.

4.1. Dataflow Instructions

The dataflow graph shown in Fig. 9 computes two simple arithmetic expressions $(X + Y) * (A + B)$ and $(X - Y)/(A + B)$. We can write an assembly language program for this dataflow graph using a control-flow architecture as shown in Fig. 10 using MIPS-like instructions. Now consider how the same graph can be represented using a hypothetical dataflow instruction set as shown in Fig. 11.

We used the same order for both versions of the code to make the dataflow version correlate to the MIPS version. In the dataflow version, the order of execution will depend on the arrival times of the data and is not constrained to the list order of the instructions. In the control-flow instructions, each instruction is provided with operand locations for its inputs and outputs. For example, the instruction $ADD\ R11,\ R2,\ R3$ uses values currently stored in registers R2 and R3 as inputs and stores the result of the operation in register R11. In contrast, the dataflow instruction $ADD\ 8R,\ 9R$ is not provided with input operands, but only the identification of the destination instruction receives its results, namely instructions 8 and 9

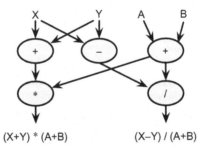

$$(X+Y) * (A+B) \qquad\qquad (X-Y) / (A+B)$$

Figure 9 A simple dataflow program.

1.	LOAD	R2,A	; load A into R2
2.	LOAD	R3,B	; load B into R3
3.	ADD	R11,R2,R3	; R11 = A + B
4.	LOAD	R4,X	; load X into R4
5.	LOAD	R5,Y	; load Y into R5
6.	ADD	R10,R4,R5	; R10 = X + Y
7.	SUB	R12,R4,R5	; R12 = X − Y
8.	MULT	R14,R10,R11	; R14 = (X+Y)*(A+B)
9.	DIV	R15,R12,R11	; R15 = (X−Y)/(A+B)
10.	STORE	VAL1,R14	; store first result to VAL1
11.	STORE	VAL2,R15	; store second result to VAL2

Figure 10 MIPS-like instructions.

```
 1. INPUT     3L      ; get A, send to instr 3, left input
 2. INPUT     3R      ; get B, send to instr 3, right input
 3. ADD       8R,9R   ; A + B, send to instrs 8, right and 9, right
 4. INPUT     6L,7L   ; get X, send to instrs 6, left and 7, left
 5. INPUT     6R,7R   ; get Y, send to instrs 6, right and 7, right
 6. ADD       8L      ; X+Y, send to instr 8, left
 7. SUB       9L      ; X - Y, send to instr 9, left
 8. MULT      10L     ; (X+Y)*(A+B), send to instr 10, left
 9. DIV       11L     ; (X-Y)/(A+B), send to instr 11, left
10. OUTPUT    VAL1    ; output first result to destination
11. OUTPUT    VAL2    ; output second result to destination
```

Figure 11 Pure dataflow instructions.

(the designation L and R with a destination are used to distinguish between left and right inputs at the destination). Thus, the ADD instruction waits for its input data to arrive (in this example from instructions 1 and 2). The arrival of these inputs enables the instruction, and when completed, the instruction sends the result to instructions 8 and 9.

A second difference to notice between the control-flow and dataflow instructions is that in the traditional control-flow architectures, instructions are executed in the order they appear. For example, instruction 7 is executed only after instruction 6 completes: a program counter keeps track of the next instruction that should be enabled for execution. In the dataflow version, no such sequence is implied. Since both instructions 6 and 7 receive their inputs at the same time (from instructions 4 and 5), they can be executed concurrently.

The goal of this example is to illustrate how we can think of designing dataflow instructions: instructions facilitate the flow of data (or results) from one instruction to another. Since in the purest form of dataflow, there are no variables or storage used, we introduced instructions such as INPUT and OUTPUT for receiving inputs or sending outputs to other modules which are outside the graph shown. In practical implementations, we will use storage for data but make sure that the data are defined only once (or apply the single-assignment principle).

The various dataflow architectures differ in how to pass data among instructions, where to save inputs to an instruction while waiting for other inputs, if an instruction can be activated multiple times when multiple versions of the inputs are received (i.e., from different loop iterations).

4.1.1 Classical Architectures

The classical architectures that implement the dataflow model are divided into two categories: *static* and *dynamic*. The static approach allows that at most one instance of a node is executable. A node becomes executable when all the input data are available and there are no tokens on the output arc. The dynamic approach allows the simultaneous activation of multiple instances of a node: this is possible because an arc is considered as a buffer that can contain multiple data items. To differentiate the different instances of the node, a *tag* is associated with each token. The tag identifies the context in which that particular token was generated. A node is considered executable when all the inputs with the same tag are available. The static model has a simple mechanism to determine which nodes are executable, but limits the performance in case of loops, since the iterations are performed one for each time unit. The dynamic model allows a larger exploitation of parallelism: this advantage is possible thanks to the tag model but also has a significant cost in creating and managing tags (matching mechanism). The following subsections describe static and dynamic architectures.

4.2. Static Dataflow Architectures

The firing rule for a node is that a token has to be present on each input arc, and that there are no tokens present on any of the output arcs. To implement this, acknowledge arcs are implicitly added to the dataflow graph which go in the opposite direction to each existing arc and carry an acknowledgment token. The major advantage of the static model is the great simplicity and speed in the detection of which nodes are executable. Moreover, the memory can be allocated for each arc at compile time since each arc will contain one or zero tokens. This implies that there is no need to use complex hardware: each arc can be assigned to a particular piece of memory. Figure 12 shows the block diagram of the static architecture.

The memory section is a collection of memory cells. Each memory cell contains a data structure that represents an instruction. An instruction template consists of the following fields (Fig. 12B):

- opcode field;
- two fields contain the values inside tokens in the input arcs, each of which has an associated flag that indicates whether the data are available. An instruction is executed when all the flags related to inputs are set to 1 and all the flags on outputs are set to 0;
- a list of destination addresses for the output tokens.

The *processing section* is composed of five pipelined functional units, each of which performs operations, forms output packets, and sends the resulting token to the memory section. The *arbitration network* sends the data structures

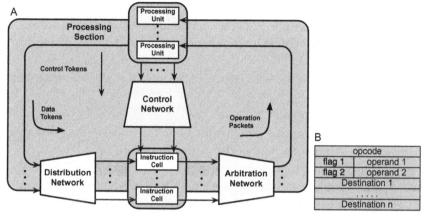

Figure 12 Static architecture (A) [20] and instruction template (B).

representing enabled instructions from the memory section to the processing section. The *distribution network* transfers the output packets from the processing section to the memory section. Finally, the *control network* reduces the load on the distribution network by transferring boolean values in *control tokens* and *acknowledge signals* from the processing section to the memory section. Control tokens convey values that are either *true* or *false*. A control token is generated by a special node, a *decider*, that applies its associated predicate to values in its input arcs. Control tokens direct the flow of data tokens by means of gates and merge actors as described in Section 2.1. In spite of its simplicity, this model has many serious problems. The addition of the acknowledge arcs considerably increases the data traffic in the system (approximately two times). Since a node must wait for the arrival of the acknowledgment signals to be executable, the time between two successive executions increases. This may affect the performance, particularly in situations where there is not a high degree of parallelism. This model only allows an arc to contain a single token which is its most significant limitation. A subsequent iteration of a loop cannot start until the previous iteration has completed its execution even if there are no dependencies between iterations. This constraint limits the amount of concurrency that is possible in the execution within loops.

4.3. Dynamic Dataflow Architectures

The dynamic approach exposes a higher degree of parallelism by allowing multiple invocations of a subgraph as is the case with loops. Only one copy of the graph is kept in memory, and the tags are used to discern the token among different invocations. A tag is composed of the following fields:

- a field that uniquely identifies the context (instance) of a token (*invocation ID*);
- a number that identifies the iteration of the loop associated with a token (*iteration ID*);
- instruction address; and
- an identifier that indicates whether the value contained in the token will be the left or right operand of the instruction (*port*).

This information is commonly known as the *color* of the token. Unlike the static model, the dynamic model represents each arc as a buffer that can contain any number of tokens, each with a different tag. In this scenario, a node is executable when the same tag is found in all its input arcs.

It is important to note that the tokens are not ordered. This may lead to an execution order that is different from the token's entrance order in the buffer. However, the tag ensures that there are no conflicts between tokens.

The tags themselves are generated by the system. The token invocation ID is unique for each subgraph. The iteration ID is initially set to 0. When a token reaches the end of the loop and it is fed back at the top of the loop, a special control operator increments the iteration ID. Whenever a token finally leaves the loop, another control operator sets its iteration ID back to 0. Figure 13 shows the block diagram of the dynamic architecture.

The matching unit is a memory that contains the tokens waiting to be consumed. This unit groups the tokens that have the same tag. If there are tokens with the same tags, they are extracted from the matching unit

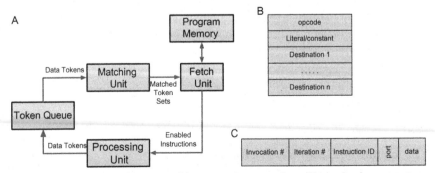

Figure 13 Dynamic architecture (A), instruction template (B), and token structure (C) [22].

and passed to the fetch unit. In the fetch unit, tags uniquely identify an instruction to be fetched from memory that contains the program. The instruction and its tokens (Fig. 13C) form the enabled instruction. The processing unit (PU) executes enabled instructions and produces the results. Then PU sends the results to the *matching unit* through the *token queue*. The main issues with the dynamic dataflow model relative to the static dataflow model are the following:

- overhead due to the process of comparing the tags; and
- need for more memory, since each arc can contain multiple tokens.

The tag-matching mechanism is the key aspect of the dataflow dynamic model. Various tests have shown that the performance directly depends on the speed of the tag-matching process. It should be noted that set-associative cache memories were not available when the dynamic dataflow systems were originally designed. Existence of such technologies could have greatly simplified the matching process of dynamic dataflow architectures and increased their performance dramatically. The typical operations executed in an execution cycle are as follows:

1. recognize the executable nodes;
2. determine the operations that must be performed;
3. compute results; and
4. generate and communicate the resulting token to destination nodes.

Compared to the execution cycle of a control-flow system, these operations incur higher overheads. For example, the comparison of the tag is a more complex operation than incrementing the program counter. *Point 4* imposes an overhead which is comparable to the writing of the result in memory or in a register.

4.4. Explicit Token Store

The problems described above have led to the introduction of the explicit token store (ETS) model. Storage (called *activation frames*) is allocated dynamically for all the tokens that can be generated by a code block (a code block represents a function or a loop iteration). The utilization of memory locations is defined at compile time, while memory allocation takes place directly at runtime. A code block is represented by the pair <FP, IP>, called a *continuation*, where *FP* is the pointer to the activation frame and *IP* is set initially to the first statement in the block. A typical instruction specifies the opcode, an offset within the activation frame where it checks the availability of inputs and one or more offsets, called *displacements*, which define the instructions that will receive the result calculated by the node. Each displacement also has an associated indicator (left/right) that specifies whether the result will be the left or right operand of the destination instruction. Figure 14 shows an example of code block invocation with its instruction memory and frame memory.

When a token arrives at a node, in this case the node ADD, the IP points to the relative instruction in the instruction memory. The system executes the process of comparing the inputs in the slot that is specified by FP + r. If the slot is empty, the system writes the value in the slot and sets the presence bit to indicate that the slot is full. If the presence bit is already set, it means that one of the two operands of the instruction is already available, so the system can now execute the instruction. The steps that the system performs are as follows:

- extract the value, leaving the slot empty and free;
- perform the operation of the instruction;
- communicate the result token to the destination instructions according to the displacement; and
- update the instruction pointer.

For example, once the ADD instruction is completed, two tokens are generated: one is directed to the instruction NEG with token $<$FP, IP + 1, 3.55$>$ and the other is directed to the instruction SUB with token $<$FP, IP + 2, 3.55$>$.

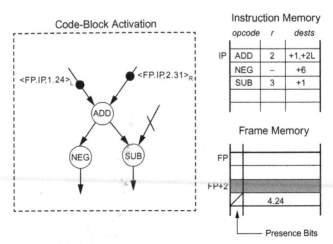

Figure 14 ETS code block [20].

4.5. Dataflow Limitations

After describing some of the initial implementations of dataflow systems, we can now discuss some of the inherent limitations of the dataflow paradigm. While the dataflow model offers advantages in terms of expressing concurrency and synchronization, dataflow is more difficult to implement using conventional hardware technologies. These limitations can be summarized as the following:

- difficulty in exploiting memory hierarchies
- too fine-grained computations—each instruction is an independent activity
- asynchronous triggering of instructions
- implementing imperative memory system and memory ordering

4.5.1 Localities and Memory Hierarchy

Since pure dataflow only operates on values, the values must be communicated to functional units. Implementation of this communication can be very inefficient. Most control processor designs rely on the use of memory hierarchies including multiple levels of cache memories. Arithmetic functional units operate on registers, which are very fast devices for containing data. Control-flow architectures benefit from the concept of localities in using memory hierarchies, and the localities are an artifact of control flow-based sequencing (or ordering) of operations in the processor. Instructions are sequenced by using a program counter. Although branch operations may change the sequence of instructions, in most cases, it is easy to predict the location of the next instruction and data.

On the other hand, a dataflow model defines no such sequencing. Thus, it is difficult to predict which instruction will be executed next. However, reordering of instructions of such a program based on certain criteria [23, 24] can produce synthetic localities. The recurrent use of instructions (in different activation frames) also causes the existence of temporal localities. Another ordering can be created on the basis of their expected order. This can done by grouping instructions into execution levels (or E-levels [25]). Instructions that become ready (i.e., all inputs are available) at the same time unit are said to be in the same level. Instructions at level 0, for example, are ready for execution at time unit 0. Similarly, those at level 1 become ready for execution at time unit 1 and so on. Instruction locality can be achieved using the E-level ordering. Since the execution of an instruction may produce operands that may be destined for the instructions in the subsequent blocks, we need to prefetch more than one block of operand locations from the operand memory. We refer to these blocks as a *working set*. Block size and working set size are optimized for a given cache implementation to achieve a desired performance. While the optimum working set depends on the program, we have found that a block size of two instructions and working sets of four to eight instructions yield significant performance improvements.

The locality for the operand cache is related to the ordering of the instructions in the instruction cache. When the first instruction in a block is referenced, the corresponding block is brought into the instruction cache. Simultaneously, operand locations for all the operands corresponding to the instructions in the *working set* of these instructions are prefetched into the operand cache. As a result of this, the operand cache will satisfy any subsequent references to the operand cache caused by the instructions within this block. Note that the operand cache block consists of a set of waiting operands or empty locations for storing the results. By prefetching, we ensure that future stores and matches caused by the execution of instructions in the block will take place in the operand cache. These principles were used to design cache memories with ETS architecture [26].

4.5.2 Granularity of Computations

Older dataflow architectures treated each dataflow activity as an independent thread of computation. This requires that each instruction or activity be uniquely identified causing excessive overheads for finding and associating data with instructions. In the most control-flow architectures, instructions are grouped into manageable entities such as functions, modules, or threads. A computation is responsible for executing such groups of instructions. In this case, we can first identify the group and then use offsets to identify individual instructions within the group. Dataflow programs can also be grouped to create blocks, frames, or threads, as is the case in some hybrid architectures described in Section 4.6. However, the instructions within the group still use a data-driven model of execution. Other hybrid architectures, as described in Section 4.6, use dataflow synchronization at thread level (a thread is enabled when it receives all its inputs) and use sequential control flow for instructions within a thread.

This model is a compromise to fully benefit from modern technology advances and minimize overhead in managing fine-grained threads of computations.

4.5.3 Synchronous Execution

In control flow, instructions are not triggered when data are available; they are executed using a program control. It is assumed that the data are already available when the instruction is scheduled. The violation of this assumption is the cause for many problems associated with parallel programs based on control-flow languages. However, this assumption allows for more efficient implementations. In the dataflow, the data-driven execution model causes asynchronous triggering of instructions. As can be seen from the previous discussions on some dataflow architectures, an instruction requiring two inputs will require two cycles through the processor pipeline: the first cycle simply stores the first input in some location, while awaiting the second input. The second cycle, initiated when the second input arrives, retrieves the previously saved input along with the instruction (or opcode and destinations) and executes the instruction. To be practical, dataflow architectures must move away from a data-driven paradigm and use instruction-driven paradigms like control flow at the execution unit level. The instruction-driven model requires space for saving inputs to instructions until they are scheduled, but each instruction requires only one cycle to execute. SDF (Section 6) relies on the instruction-driven model of execution.

4.5.4 Memory Ordering

To be viable, dataflow processors must execute concurrent programs written using imperative languages. Assuring correct execution of concurrent programs in these languages requires adherence to the sequential consistency paradigm, which defines an order on memory accesses. WaveScalar (described in Section 5.3) proposes a solution for defining memory orders within the context of tagged token dataflow architecture.

We describe some recent architectures that have modified the pure dataflow model to achieve practical implementations in Section 5.

4.6. Hybrid Dataflow/Controlflow Architectures

The pure dataflow model eliminates WAR and WAW dependencies and exploits the parallelism inherent in a program, but its performance is poor for applications having a low level of parallelism. Because of the problems encountered in the pure dataflow model, researchers investigated various hybrid solutions. Most of these models used an instruction clustering paradigm; various instructions are clustered together in a thread to be executed in a sequential manner through the use of a conventional program counter. The thread is enabled to run when the inputs necessary for its execution are available.

The spectrum of hybrid control-flow/dataflow systems ranges from simple extensions of the von Neumann paradigm to nearly pure dataflow architectures where the level of execution granularity is increased. In the pure dataflow model, each machine-level instruction is seen as a thread. In a hybrid dataflow model, groups of instructions form threads that are executed through control flow. The method of grouping instructions and the average number of instructions in a group differentiate the various hybrid systems. Various projects based on this approach have shown that the dataflow model and the control-flow model are not disjoint, but are the two extremes within a spectrum of computer architectures with hybrid models occupying the middle of the spectrum. The following sections outline some approaches for hybrid architectures.

4.6.1 Coarse-Grain Dataflow

This approach is based on *macro instructions*, activated according to dataflow concepts. The individual instructions within the *macro instruction* are executed in a sequential manner. Systems using this approach usually separate the token control phase from the execution phase through the use of a FIFO buffer. Dedicated microprocessors are usually used to support the execution phase.

4.6.2 Complex Dataflow

This technique is based on the use of machine-level complex instructions, for example, vector instructions. These instructions can be implemented through pipelines as in vector systems. Structured data are accessed in blocks rather than by accessing the individual item. This approach differs from the I-structure where each field of a structure is accessed individually from memory. The advantage of this type of architecture is the ability to exploit the subinstruction-level parallelism, since subinstructions can be performed in parallel (or almost) within their complex instruction. Even in this case, the process of enabling the execution and the execution itself is separated. The major difference compared to the original dataflow model is that the tokens do not carry values. The data are collected and only used inside the PU.

4.6.3 RISC Dataflow

Systems that use this approach support the execution of code written for conventional control-flow systems. The basic aspects of this type of systems are the following:

- conventional RISC-like instructions;
- support for multithreading with the introduction of *fork* and *join* instructions to create and synchronize threads;
- synchronization of memory accesses through the use of the I-structure semantic.

4.6.4 Threaded Dataflow

The idea behind this approach is the grouping of a certain number of instructions that are executed in a sequential manner. In particular, each subgraph that exhibits a low level of parallelism is identified and converted into a sequential thread. In this way, when a thread is executed, it is not necessary to perform the data availability verification process for all its instructions, but only for the first. The instructions within a thread use registers to transmit data to other instructions. These registers may be used by any instruction in the thread. The advantage of the threaded dataflow approach is that those parts of the dataflow graph that do not exhibit good potential parallelism can be executed without the associated overhead, while those that do show potential parallelism can take advantage of it. In this type of architecture, the main issue is the implementation of an efficient mechanism for synchronization between threads. ETS-like methods can be used for this.

5. RECENT DATAFLOW ARCHITECTURES

Recent improvements in computer technology (such as network-on-a-chip and higher density integration) and limitations to instruction and thread-level parallelization within conventional control-flow architectures have led to a new interest in the dataflow computing model. The following sections describe some recent dataflow-based projects.

5.1. Tera-op Reliable Intelligently Adaptive Processing System

The Tera-op Reliable Intelligently adaptive Processing System (TRIPS) [27, 28] system employs a new instruction set architecture (ISA) called *Explicit Data Graph Execution* (EDGE). Two defining features of EDGE ISA are block-atomic execution in which blocks are composed of dataflow instructions and direct instruction communication within a block. An EDGE microarchitecture maps each compiler-generated dataflow graph to a distributed execution substrate. The TRIPS ISA aggregates up to 128 instructions in a block. The block-atomic execution model logically fetches, executes, and commits each block as a single entity. Blocks communicate through registers and memory. Within a block, *direct instruction communication* delivers results from producer to consumer instructions in dataflow fashion. Figure 15 shows the TRIPS architecture.

Each TRIPS chip contains two processors and a secondary memory system, each interconnected by one or more micronetworks. Each processor contains five types of units: 1 global control unit (GU), 16 execution units (EU), 4 register units (RU), 4 data caches (DU), and 5 instruction caches (IU). The units communicate via six micronetworks that implement distributed control and data protocols. The *GU* sends a block address to the *IU* which delivers the block's computation instructions to the reservation stations in the 16 execution units, 4 per unit as specified by the compiler. The *IU* also delivers the register read/write instructions to reservation stations in the *RU*s. The *RU*s read values from the global register file and send them to the *EU*s, initiating the dataflow execution. The commit protocol updates the data caches and register file with the speculative state of the block. The *GU* uses its next block predictor to begin fetching and executing the next block, while previous blocks are still executing. The prototype can simultaneously execute up to eight 128-instruction blocks giving it a maximum window size of 1024 instructions. On simple benchmarks, TRIPS outperforms the Intel Core 2 by 10%, and using hand-optimized TRIPS code, TRIPS outperforms the Core 2 by a factor of 3 [28].

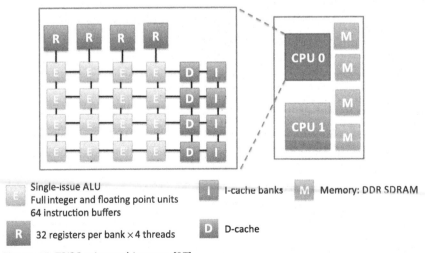

Single-issue ALU
Full integer and floating point units
64 instruction buffers

I   I-cache banks   M   Memory: DDR SDRAM

R   32 registers per bank × 4 threads   D   D-cache

Figure 15 TRIPS microarchitecture [27].

5.2. Data-Driven Workstation Network

D^2NOW [29] is a parallel machine based on the data-driven multithreading (DDM) model of execution. This model decouples the synchronization from the computation portions of a program allowing them to execute asynchronously, similar to the decoupling used in SDF [16, 30]. This aspect provides effective latency tolerance by allowing the computation processor to produce useful work, while a long latency event is in progress. In the DDM model, scheduling of threads is determined at runtime based on data availability; a thread is scheduled for execution only if all of its input data are available in the local memory (dataflow paradigm). Figure 16 shows a DDM processing node.

The processing node consists of a workstation augmented with the thread synchronization unit (TSU). The computation processor communicates with the TSU via two queues: the *ready queue* (RQ) and the *acknowledgment queue* (AQ). These queues are memory-mapped; there is no need for modifying the processor or adding extra instructions. The RQ contains pointers to the threads that are ready for execution. The AQ contains identification information and status of executed threads. The main storage units in the TSU are the *graph memory* (GM) and the *synchronization memory* (SM). The GM contains the information related to the instructions, to the data memory and to the consumer threads. The SM contains the number of input

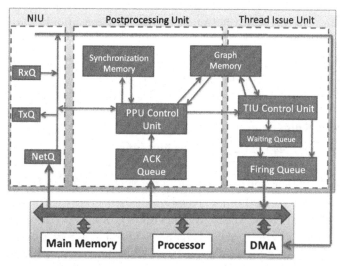

Figure 16 DDM processing node [29].

data items that are necessary for a thread. The processor reads the address of the next thread to be executed from the RQ. After the processor completes the execution of a thread, it stores in the AQ the identification number and status of the completed thread and then reads the address of the next thread to be executed from the RQ. The control unit of the TSU fetches the completed threads from the AQ, reads their consumers from GM and then updates the counter of input data needed of the corresponding consumer threads in the SM. If any of these consumers are ready for execution, they are placed in the RQ and wait for their turn to be executed.

D^2NOW is built using Intel Pentium microprocessors connected through a fine-grained interconnection network. The most interesting aspect of this architecture is the communication mechanism. Like the other dataflow architectures, the main problem is the overhead due to the communication between scheduling quantums (in this case, threads). To tolerate the communication latency, the communication is classified into three types: *fine grain* (one data value per message), *medium grain* (up to a few tens of values per message), and *coarse grain* (hundreds to thousands of values per message). In the fine-grain mechanism, all the information is passed to the NIU (see Fig. 16). In the second mechanism, the computation processor stores data in a buffer within the NIU, the consumer thread's identification as well as the starting address and size of the memory block. In the background, an embedded processor together with a DMA engine process the communication though the fine-grain interconnection network. The coarse-grain mechanism uses an Ethernet network to support large block data transfers. In this way, the latency due to the large amount of data does not affect the transfers on the fine-grain network. For 16- and 32-node machines, the observed speedup, compared to the sequential single node execution, is 14.4 and 26, respectively [29].

5.3. WaveScalar

WaveScalar [31, 32] is a tagged-token, dynamic dataflow architecture. The goal of this architecture is to minimize the communication costs by ridding the processor of long wires and broadcast networks. To this end, it includes a completely decentralized implementation of the *token-store* dataflow architecture (Section 4) and a distributed execution model. WaveScalar supports the execution of code written in general purpose, imperative languages (C, C++, or Java). Conceptually, a WaveScalar binary is a dataflow graph of an executable and resides in memory as a collection of *intelligent* instruction words. Each instruction is intelligent because it has a dedicated functional unit. In practice, since placing a functional unit at each word of instruction memory is impractical, an intelligent instruction cache, the *WaveCache*, holds the current working set of instructions and executes them in place. The WaveScalar compiler breaks the control-flow graph of an application into pieces called *waves*. Figure 17 shows a loop divided into waves.

The *wavenumber* specifies different instances of specific instructions. Waves are very similar to *hyperblocks*, but they are more general, since they can contain control-flow joins and can have more than one entrance. Consider the waves in Fig. 17. Assume the code before the loop has wavenumber 0. When the code executes, the two CONST instructions will produce *0.0* (wavenumber 0, value 0). The *WAVE-ADVANCE(WA)* instructions will take these as inputs and each will output *1.0*, which will propagate through the body of the loop as before. At the end of the loop, the right-side *STEER (S)* instruction will produce 1.1 and pass it back to the *WA* at the top of its side of the loop which will then produce 2.1. A similar process takes place on the left side of the graph. The execution ends when the left-side *S* produces the value 5.10.

One of the most interesting aspects is the method used by WaveScalar to order memory operations, to assure memory consistency. Within a basic block, memory operations receive consecutive sequence numbers. By

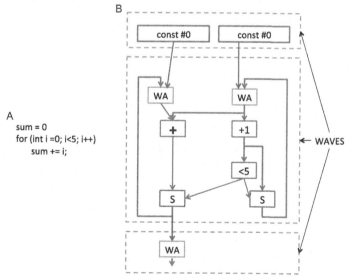

Figure 17 WaveScalar waves [31].

assigning sequence numbers in this way, the compiler ensures that sequence numbers increase along any path through the wave. Next, the compiler labels each memory operation with the sequence numbers of its predecessor and of the successive memory operation, if they can be uniquely determined. The combination of instruction sequence number and predecessor and successor sequence numbers forms a *link*, which is denoted *<pred, this, succ>*. Figure 18 provides an example of annotated memory operations in a wave.

The main element in this architecture is the *WaveCache* (Fig. 19). The WaveCache is a grid of 2048 processing elements *PEs*) arranged into clusters of 16. Each PE contains logic to control instruction placement and execution, input and output queues for instruction operands, communication logic, and a functional unit. Each PE contains buffering and storage for eight different instructions. The input queues for each input require only 1 write and 1 read port and as few as 2 entries per instruction, or 16 entries total. Matching logic accesses and updates the bits as new inputs arrive, obviating the need for content addressable memories. In addition to the instruction operand queues, the WaveCache contains a store buffer and a traditional L1 data cache for each four clusters of PEs. The caches access DRAM through a conventional, unified, nonintelligent L2 cache.

5.4. Teraflux

Teraflux [33] is a 4-year project started in 2010 within the *Future and Emerging Technologies Large-Scale Projects* funded by the European Union with the partnership of companies like HP and Microsoft, and universities in several countries. The dataflow paradigm is used at the thread level. The Teraflux system is not constrained to only follow the dataflow paradigm. The system

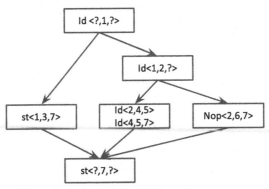

Figure 18 WaveScalar memory operations [32].

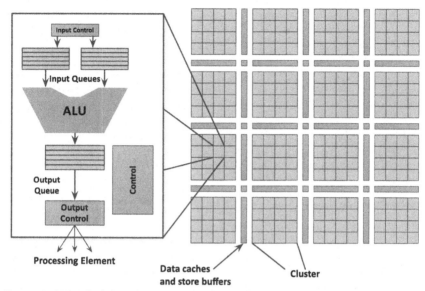

Figure 19 WaveCache [32].

distinguishes among legacy and system threads (L- and S-threads) and dataflow threads (DF-threads). The execution model of Teraflux [34] relies on exchanging dataflow threads in a producer–consumer fashion. To support the data-driven execution of threads each core includes a hardware module that handles the scheduling of threads, the *local thread scheduling unit* (L-TSU). In addition to the cores, the nodes also contain a hardware module to coordinate the scheduling of the data-driven threads across nodes, the *distributed thread scheduling unit* (D-TSU). The set of all L-TSU and D-TSU composes the *Distributed Thread Scheduler* (DTS). Nodes are connected via an internode network, using *Network on Chip* (NoC). Figure 20 shows the general architecture of the Teraflux system and a scheduling example.

In Fig. 20B, the L-TSU is represented in grey inside each C_{ij} core. The two D-TSUs are represented in black inside each node. Moreover, the x86–x64 ISA is extended. The key points of this extension are:

- enables an asynchronous execution of threads based on dataflow rather than program control flow;
- the execution of a DF-thread is decided by the D-TSU;
- the types of memory that are used are distinguished in four types (1-to-1 communication or Thread Local Storage, N-to-1 or Frame Memory,

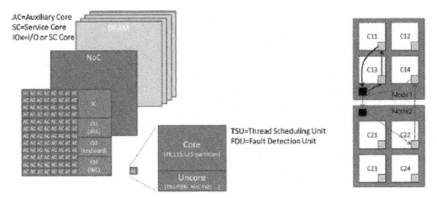

Figure 20 (A) Teraflux basic architecture and (B) scheduling example [34].

1-to-N or Owner Writable Memory, and N-to-N or Transactional Memory).

The DF-thread scheduling policy is very similar to the one used in the SDF architecture discussed in Section 6. Since Teraflux is an ongoing project no performance data is available for the completed system. Performance data is available for DFScala [35], a library for constructing and executing dataflow graphs in the Scala[1] language. DFScala has been constructed as part of the Teraflux project and has been tested on Intel- and AMD-based systems. Figure 21 shows the speedup relative to a single-threaded solution.

5.5. Maxeler

Maxeler Technologies is a company specializing in the development of "*dataflow computing,*" a class of special-purpose computers that are programmable and can be specialized to different applications at different points in time [36]. The Maxeler system contains x86 CPUs attached to dataflow engines (DFEs) via a second-generation PCI Express bus. Data are streamed from memory onto the Maxeler DFEs, where operations are performed and data are forwarded directly from one function unit (a dataflow core) to another as the results are needed, without ever being written to the off-chip memory until the chain of processing is complete. There is no need for instruction-decode logic with this configuration as the flow of data is predetermined by the functionality programmed into the DFEs. The Maxeler dataflow machine does not require techniques such

---

[1] http://www.scala-lang.org/.

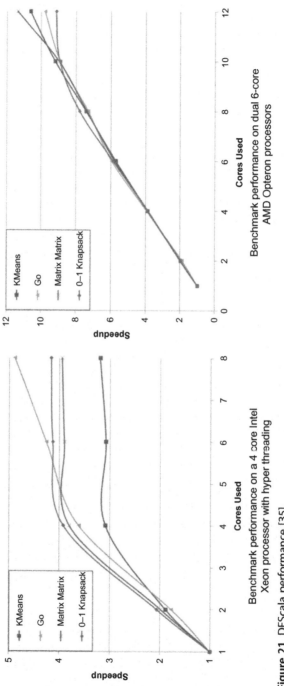

Figure 21 DFScala performance [35].

as branch prediction as these cores execute pure dataflow, or out-of-order scheduling as there are no instructions to schedule. As the data are always available on chip, general-purpose caches are not needed. The minimum amount of buffering memory is utilized automatically as necessary. The Maxeler architecture and use are discussed in chapter, Sorting Networks on Maxeler Dataflow Supercomputing Systems.

5.6. Codelet

The *Codelet* [37] project is based on the exploration of a *fine-grain, event-driven* model in support of the operations executed by high-core-count and extreme parallelism machines. This model breaks applications into *codelets* (small bits of functionality) and *dependencies* (control and data) between these objects. It then uses this decomposition to accomplish advanced scheduling, to accommodate code and data motion within the system, and to permit flexible exploitation of parallelism in support of goals for performance and power. Figure 22 shows the abstract machine used to explain the execution model.

The abstract machine consists of many nodes that are connected via an interconnection network. Each node contains a many-core chip. The chip may consists of up to 1–2 thousand processing cores being organized into groups (clusters) linked together via a chip interconnect. Each group contains a collection of computing units (CU) and at least one scheduling unit (SU), all brought together by their own chip interconnect.

The building blocks of an application are *Thread Procedures* and *Codelets*. A codelet is a collection of machine instructions that can be scheduled as a unit of computation. When a codelet has been allocated and scheduled to a computation unit, it will be kept usefully busy until its completion. Since codelets are more fine grained than a conventional thread, context switching is more frequent resulting in more overhead for the application.

A codelet becomes enabled once tokens are present on each of its input arcs. An enabled codelet actor can be fired if it has acquired all the required resources and is scheduled for execution. A codelet actor behaves as a dataflow node.

A threaded procedure (TP) is an asynchronous function which acts as codelet graph container. A TP serves two purposes, first it provides a naming convention to invoke codelet graphs (similar to a conventional dataflow graph), and second, it acts as a scope for codelets to efficiently operate within. Figure 23 shows three TP invocations.

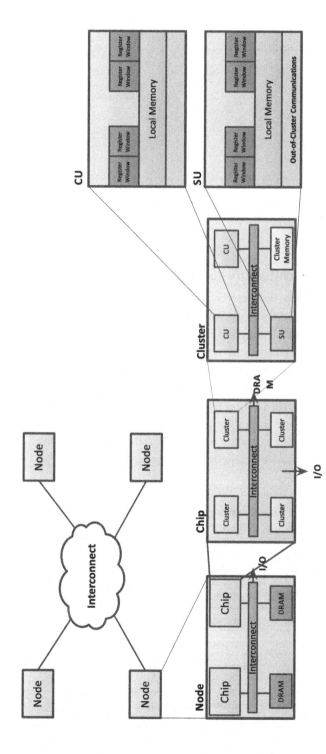

Figure 22 Codelet abstract architecture [37].

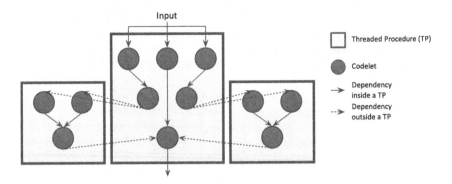

Figure 23 Codelets and threaded procedures [37].

5.7. Recent Architectures Summary

Table 1 provides a summary of the recent architectures discussed in this chapter. The *Granularity* column indicates the general level at which dataflow techniques are applied. The *Maturity* column indicates the maturity level of the research by listing the most complex demonstration of the architecture at the date of this paper. The *Implementation* column indicates if the research requires a full custom processor, uses a custom coprocessor, or can be implemented with existing devices. The *Programming* column indicates if special languages are needed for programming the architecture. The *Current* column indicates the currency of the research by providing the year of the most recent publication at the time this paper was written.

Table 1 Summary of Recent Architectures

Architecture	Granularity	Maturity	Implementation	Programming	Current
TRIPS	Block	Prototype	Custom	General	2006
D^2NOW	Thread	Prototype	Existing	General	2006
WaveScalar	Superblock	Simulation	Custom	General	2010
Teraflux	Thread	Prototype	Existing	General	2013
Maxeler	Task	Commercial	Coprocessor	General	2013
Codelet	Thread	Abstract machine	Existing	General	2013
SDF	Superblock	Simulation	Custom	General	2013

6. CASE STUDY: SCHEDULED DATAFLOW

SDF architecture [16, 30] applies the dataflow execution model at the thread level, where each thread consists of the instructions to execute a compiler basic block rather than at the instruction level of conventional dataflow architectures. SDF is a multithreaded hybrid control-flow/dataflow architecture that improves performance by moving the overhead of dataflow firing semantics to threads of dozens of instructions rather than each instruction. This architecture is examined in more detail as a case study. The hybridization between the control-flow model and the dataflow model is as follows:

- the *dataflow model* is used to enable the threads for executing;
- the *control-flow model* is used to schedule instructions within a thread using a *program counter.*

6.1. Organization

SDF decouples memory accesses from execution. The first example of a decoupled architecture was proposed by Smith [38]. Smith's architecture required a compiler to explicitly slice the program into memory access slices and computational slices. The two slices execute on different PEs and communicate through buffers. A synchronization mechanism is used to guarantee the correct execution. In contrast, SDF divides a thread into three phases: the first phase preloads the input data from memory into registers; the second phase computes the thread results; and the third phase stores the results into memory. Memory access operations (first and third phase) are executed on a different pipeline called *synchronization pipeline* (SP). The functional operations (second phase) are executed on the main pipeline which is called *execution pipeline* (EP). This allows the memory phases of a thread to be overlapped with the execution phases allowing SDF to reduce the impacts of the *memory wall.*

Threads in SDF are nonblocking. A thread completes execution without blocking the processor for synchronization with other threads. Thread context switching is controlled by the compiler, generating new threads rather than blocking a thread for synchronization. This leads to a reduction of synchronization overhead due to thread blocking and avoidance of starvation situations. This approach generates more fine-grained threads, which may increase the overhead if not implemented in an efficient manner.

6.2. Instruction Format

Unlike conventional dataflow architectures, the SDF instructions within a thread are executed in a conventional control-flow manner. Each thread has an associated *program counter* that controls execution. The instruction format of SDF is similar to the MIPS instruction format. Most instructions in SDF have two source operands and one destination operand. SDF uses both the conventional memory paradigm and the I-structure semantics. For this reason, SDF has two sets of memory access instructions for memory accesses. SDF has four instructions for referencing I-structures:

- *IALLOC RS,RD:* an I-structure of the specified size is allocated (the size is contained in the register RS). I-structure flags are initialized to E (empty); a pointer to the allocated memory is returned in RD.
- *IFREE RS:* frees the I-Structure whose address is specified in RS.
- *IFETCH RS—offset, RD:* given the I-structure whose address is specified in RS and the offset, the instruction loads the specified value into RD if the presence flag is set to F (Full or data present). Otherwise, the request is queued and the flag is set to W (Waiting for data to arrive). It should be noted that SDF can also be programmed to skip I-structure semantics and use memory as a conventional memory.
- *ISTORE RS, RD—offset:* this instruction stores the value contained in RS in the I-structure location specified by the couple (RD, offset). The instruction also sets the presence flag to F (data present).

MALLOC, READ, WRITE, MFREE instructions support the management of the data frame memory architecture; this memory contains inputs to SDF threads. SDF has a special instruction for creating threads (FALLOC instruction), to manage the thread's enabling process (LOAD and STORE instructions) and to support the decoupled architecture (FORKSP and FORKEP instructions). These special instructions are described in detail in the following sections.

6.3. Execution Paradigm

As specified before, the SDF architecture is a multithreaded control-flow/dataflow architecture. Threads are the key component of the SDF execution paradigm. A thread is enabled for execution when all its input data are available according to the dataflow execution model. To better understand the SDF execution paradigm, we need to focus first on the dynamic scenario that can be generated at run time. SDF uses ETS-like *continuation* (described in Section 4.4) to maintain useful information for thread execution. Each thread has an associated continuation. A continuation, in its basic form, consists of the following four fields:

- *FP (frame pointer)*, pointer to a memory area allocated for the thread. This memory area is used to store the input data for the thread;
- *SC (synchronization count)*, this field indicates the number of inputs which are necessary, to enable a thread to begin execution;
- *RS (register set identifier)*, this field indicates the identifier of the private register set used by a thread;
- *IP (instruction pointer)*, pointer to the code to be executed by the thread.

A thread, and its related continuation, is created through the *FALLOC* special instruction. This instruction takes three operands:

- a register as input that contains the pointer to the code related to the new thread (IP);
- a register as input that contains the synchronization count (SC);
- a register as output that is used to store the frame pointer of the frame memory allocated to the new thread (FP).

The synchronization count is decreased every time a thread (the parent thread or another thread that knows the frame pointer to the new thread) stores data into the frame memory associated with the new thread. This operation is executed through the *STORE* instruction. This instruction takes three operands:

- a register as input that contains the data a thread wants to "transmit" to the new thread;
- a register as input that contains the frame pointer for the new thread;
- an offset that indicates the location into the frame memory of the new thread.

A continuation can be in one of the four following states:

1. *Waiting continuation* (WTC): Initial state after thread creation until all inputs have been received.
2. *Preload continuation* (PLC): When a thread has received all of its inputs and is ready to be activated.
3. *EXecution continuation* (EXC): All input data have been loaded into the registers and the thread is waiting for execution.
4. *Poststore continuation* (PSC): The thread has completed its computations and is ready to store the results in other threads' frames.

Figure 24 shows how a continuation moves through its sequence of states and which SDF unit possesses the thread for each state.

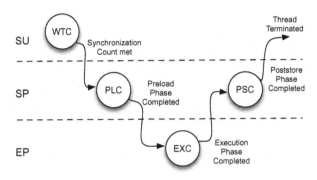

Figure 24 Continuation transitions [30].

When a continuation is created, it is in state *WTC*. In this state, a thread has not yet had a register set assigned to it. Figure 25 shows the SDF assembly code related to the creation and enabling of a new thread.

Since SDF is a decoupled memory access/execution architecture, the compiler divides thread execution in three phases: *preload* phase, *execution* phase, and *poststore* phase. These three phases correspond perfectly to the other three states (PLC, EXC, and PSC) of a continuation. When the synchronization count of a thread reaches zero, indicating that all of the inputs necessary for the thread to execute are available, the continuation moves from state WTC to state PLC. A register set is allocated to the thread before it starts its preload phase. The thread is enqueued into the preload queue and it waits for a free SP where it can execute LOAD memory operations. Figure 26 shows SDF thread phases and related continuation states.

In the preload phase, a thread takes the input data from its frame memory and stores it into its private registers using *LOAD* instructions. A LOAD instruction takes three operands:

- *RFP*, a special register that contains the frame pointer of the current thread. This register is set when an enabled thread is scheduled for execution on the SP;

```
          PUTR1    thread
          PUT      1,R2
          FALLOC   R1,R2,R11      ; create a continuation, go to WTC
          PUTR1    main.2
          FORKSPR1
main.2:
          PUT      5,R5
          STORE    R5,R11|1       ; decrease the SC
```

Figure 25 Thread creation and enabling.

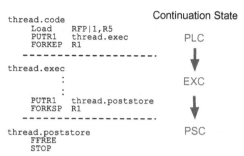

Figure 26 SDF thread phases.

- an offset that indicates the location into the frame memory;
- a register as output where the data from memory are stored.

At the end of the preload phase, the thread is moved to the execution pipeline by executing the *FORKEP* special instruction. This instruction has an input register operand that points to the code to be executed. There is a conditional form for this instruction that uses a boolean register operand to execute or skip the *FORKEP* instruction. The *FORKSP* instruction is used to move the thread from the execution pipeline to the SP (going from the EXC state to the PSC state, Fig. 26). The only difference between the FORKSP instruction and the FORKEP instruction is the destination queue where the continuation is enqueued. In this phase of processing, the thread can store the results of its computation in memory (I-structures or Frame memory) or pass them to other threads to enable them for execution. Figure 27 shows a possible SDF program threads' structure.

6.4. Architecture

An SDF processor is mainly composed of three parts: one (or more) SPs, one (or more) execution pipelines, and the TSU. Figure 28 shows the general organization of the original nonspeculative SDF architecture.

6.4.1 Synchronization Pipeline

Figure 29 shows the general organization of an SP. The main job of an SP is to execute preload and poststore phases of a thread. An SP implementation is similar to a MIPS in-order pipeline and consists of six functional units:

1. *Instruction fetch unit* fetches an instruction belonging to the current thread using the program counter;

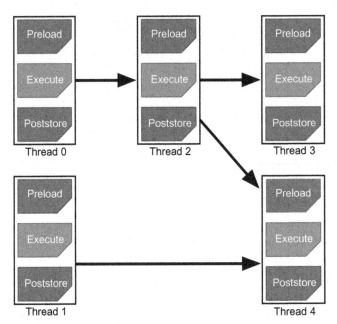

Figure 27 SDF program threads' structure.

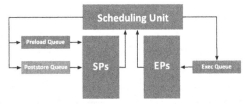

Figure 28 Nonspeculative SDF architecture.

2. *Instruction decode unit* decodes the instruction and fetches register operands using the register set identifier;
3. *Effective address computation unit* uses the frame pointer and offset to compute the effective address for LOAD and STORE instructions (or an
   I-structure memory location) to access frame memories allocated to
   threads;
4. *Memory access unit* completes memory accesses;
5. *Execute unit* contains a simple integer ALU to support effective address
   calculations;
6. *Write-back unit* writes the value extracted from memory into the specified
   destination register.

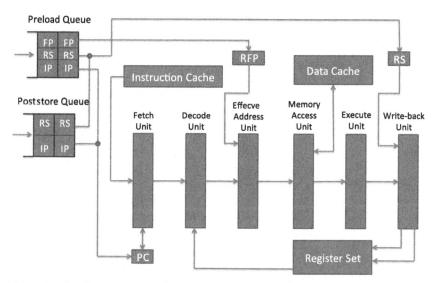

Figure 29 Synchronization pipeline.

6.4.2 Execution Pipeline

Figure 30 shows the general organization of the execution pipeline. The execution pipeline performs the computations of a thread using only register accesses. This pipeline is very similar to a simple in-order MIPS pipeline and is composed of four stages: *instruction fetch, instruction decode, execute*, and *write-back*. As can be seen, the EP behaves like a conventional pipeline. Moreover, the EP does not access data memory and therefore requires no pipeline stalls (or context switches) due to data cache misses.

6.4.3 Scheduling Unit

Figure 31 shows the general organization for the SU. The *SU* is responsible for the management of threads. Special instructions that are executed on SPs and/or execution pipelines communicate with the SU. For example, consider the *FALLOC* instruction that is responsible for the creation of a thread. When this special instruction is executed on the execution pipeline, a request for a frame memory is transmitted to the SU. The Scheduler maintains a *stack of indexes pointing to the available frames*. To simplify the hardware, SDF allocates fixed sized frames. The SU makes an index available to the EP by extracting the first available frame. The SU is also responsible for allocating register sets to the threads, when they have received all of their inputs. When the synchronization count for a thread reaches zero, the scheduler

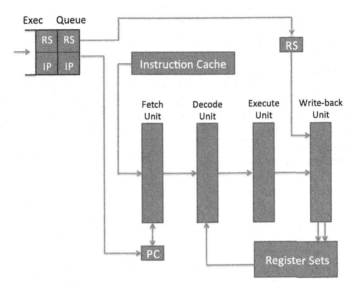

Figure 30 Execution pipeline.

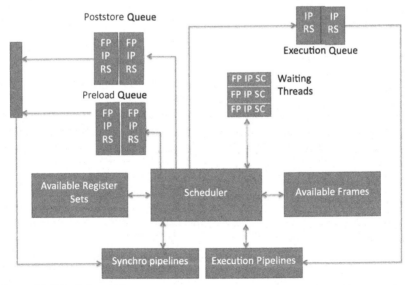

Figure 31 Scheduling unit.

extracts the continuation of the thread from the waiting queue and assigns it a register set. The register sets are viewed as a circular buffer. The SU pushes indexes of a de-allocated frame to the *available register set stack* every time an *FFREE* instruction is executed at the end of the poststore phase of a thread.

This instruction is also responsible for deallocating the frame memory related to the thread. Note that the SU operates at thread-level rather than instruction level and requires much simpler hardware to perform its tasks.

6.5. Support for Thread-Level Speculation

Thread-level speculation (TLS) [39] allows the compiler to automatically parallelize portions of code in the presence of statically ambiguous data dependencies. Figure 32 shows an example of code where TLS can be applied. This loop cannot be statically parallelized due to possible data dependencies through the array *hash*. While it is possible that a given iteration will depend on data produced by an immediately preceding iteration, these dependencies may in fact be infrequent if the hashing function is effective. Threads can therefore be executed in parallel by speculating that no data dependencies exist. Figure 32B shows a *read-after-write* data dependency between the thread with epoch 1 and the thread with epoch 4. A violation occurs if the epoch 4 thread reads the value before the epoch 1 thread writes. In this case, the thread is squashed and restarted to read the correct value and to calculate the correct result.

6.5.1 TLS Schema for SDF

The TLS schema [40, 41] implemented in SDF not only supports speculative execution within a single node of an SDF cluster consisting of multiple EPs and SPs but also supports speculation in SDF clusters using a distributed shared memory (DSM) protocol. The design is derived from a variation of the invalidation-based MESI protocol. The MESI protocol consists of the following cache line states:

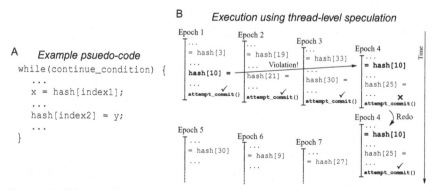

Figure 32 TLS example [39].

- *exclusive or modified* (E/M), which indicates when the cache line is present in the current cache. If the value matches with the value in main memory the state is exclusive. If the value has been modified from the value in main memory, the value is *dirty* and the state is *modified.* The write-back to main memory changes the line to the *exclusive* state;
- *shared* (S), which indicates that this cache line may be stored in more than one cache of the machine and the value matches with the value in main memory. The line may be discarded at any time;
- *invalid* (I), which indicates that this cache line is invalid.

The SDF schema extended the MESI protocol with two more states:

- *SpR.Ex*, speculative read of an exclusive data;
- *SpR.Sh*, speculative read of a shared data.

6.5.2 Speculation Extensions to SDF

The SDF TLS mechanism is supported by a new continuation consisting of a seven-tuple <FP, IP, RS, SC, *EPN, RIP, ABI* >. The added elements are epoch number (EPN), retry instruction pointer (RIP), and address-buffer ID (ABI). The epoch number is used to establish the execution order of the thread based on the program execution order. Speculative threads must commit in the order of their epoch numbers. RIP defines the instruction at which a failed speculative thread must start its retry. ABI defines the buffer ID that is used to store the addresses of the speculatively read data. For the nonspeculative threads, the new fields are set to 0. Figure 33 shows how the architecture is extended to control the order of thread commits.

The SU tests the epoch field of the continuation to check if it is zero (normal thread) or nonzero (speculative thread). Speculative threads commit strictly in the order of epoch numbers. The commit protocol maintains the epoch number of the next thread that can commit based on the program order and will test the epoch number of a continuation that is ready for

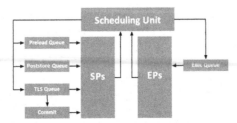

Figure 33 TLS architecture extension.

commit. If these numbers are the same and no data access violations are found in the ABI buffer associated with the thread, the commit controller will schedule the thread for commit. If there is a violation, the commit controller sets the IP of that continuation to the RIP value and places the thread back in the preload queue for reexecution. At this time, the thread becomes nonspeculative. To check if there are violations on accessing data, each thread has an associated buffer whose identifier is the ABI field of its continuation. When a speculative read request is issued by a thread, the address of the data being read is stored in the associated address buffer assigned to the thread and the entry is set to valid. When the speculative read data are subsequently written by a nonspeculative thread, the corresponding entries in the address buffer are invalidated, and this will prevent a speculative thread from committing.

The SDF instruction set is extended with three instructions. The first instruction (*SFALLOC Rip, Rsc, Rfp*) is for speculatively spawning a thread. The second instruction (*SREAD Raddr/IMM,Rd*) is for speculatively reading data. The third instruction (*SCFORKSP Rip*) is for committing a speculative thread. This instruction places the speculative thread continuation into the speculative thread commit queue rather than the standard poststore queue.

7. CONCLUSIONS

In this chapter, we have described how dataflow properties can be used to support concurrency, synchronization, and speculation, which are essential for achieving high performance. We have provided an overview of dataflow-based programming languages and historical dataflow architectural implementations. We have introduced some hybrid control-flow/dataflow designs. The SDF architecture is used to illustrate how a dataflow architecture can be designed to exploit concurrency and speculative execution.

The dataflow model of computation is neither based on memory structures that require inherent state transitions, nor does it depend on history sensitivity. This "purity" permits the use of the model to represent maximum concurrency to the finest granularity and facilitates dependency analysis among computations. Despite the advantages of the dataflow model, there are no commercially successful implementations of the data-driven model. Critics of dataflow argue that functional semantics and freedom from side effects may be nice, but well-known compiler techniques applied to imperative languages can allow exploitation of parallelism equal to that of dataflow. They claim that the dataflow model is weak in handling recursion and arrays, and all proposed dataflow solutions to these problems are complicated. The implementation of fine-grain parallelism leads to performance penalties in detecting and managing the high-level of parallel activities. The lack of memory (and memory hierarchy) makes the dataflow model inefficient to implement on register-based processing units.

Hybrid dataflow/control-flow architectures are proposed to address some of these criticisms. These attempts also failed in part due to the dominance of imperative programming languages. The implementation of imperative memory systems within the context of a dataflow model is not satisfactorily addressed. In addition to the management of structures, techniques for the management of pointers, dealing with aliasing and dynamic memory management, are needed. Ordering of memory updates (a critical concept in shared memory concurrency) is a foreign concept to pure dataflow. However, to be commercially viable, it is essential to provide shared memory-based synchronization among concurrent activities. Some ideas such as those presented in WaveScalar and SDF hold some promise in this area.

Nevertheless, several features of the dataflow paradigm have found their place in modern processor architectures and compiler technology. Most modern processors use complex hardware techniques to detect data dependencies, control hazards, and support dynamic parallelism to bring the execution engine closer to an idealized dataflow engine. Compilers rely on static single-assignment analysis to eliminate anti and output dependencies among computations. Some multithreaded systems use dataflow like triggering to enable threads.

There appears to be some renewed interest in hybrid systems that use dataflow-like synchronization at the thread level, but use sequential control-flow execution within a thread. Extensions to the pure dataflow model to permit "producer–consumer" and "barrier" synchronization are being proposed. Speculative execution and support for transactional memory models is yet another sign of interest in dataflow systems. But most importantly, there is a growing interest and some evidence of commercial success in using dataflow as a coprocessor to a conventional control-flow processing unit. The dataflow-based coprocessor is responsible for executing computations rich with concurrency, while the main processor will handle scheduling and memory management. A dataflow-based coprocessor offers the potential for a simplified alternative to conventional GPUs. We are optimistic that such systems will play an increasing role in the next generation of high-performance computer systems.

REFERENCES

[1] A. Benveniste, G. Berry, The synchronous approach to reactive and realtime systems, Proc. IEEE 79 (9) (1991) 535–546.

[2] P. Le Guernic, T. Gauthier, M. Le Borgne, C. Le Maire, Programming real-time applications with signal, Proc. IEEE 79 (9) (1991) 1321–1336.

[3] N. Halbwachs, P. Caspi, P. Raymond, D. Pilaud, The synchronous dataflow programming language lustre, Proc. IEEE 79 (9) (1991) 1305–1319.

[4] J. Buck, S. Ha, E. Lee, D. Messerschmitt, Ptolemy: a framework for simulating and prototyping heterogeneous systems, Int. J. Comput. Simulat. 4 (1994) 155–182.

[5] E.A. Lee, T.M. Parks, Dataflow process networks, Proc. IEEE 83 (5) (1995) 773–799.

[6] G. Kahn, The semantics of a simple language for parallel programming, Proceedings of IFIP Congress Information Processing Conference, 1974, pp. 471–475.

[7] K. Kavi, B. Buckles, U.N. Bhat, A formal definition of dataflow graph models, IEEE Trans. Comput. C-35 (11) (1986) 940–948.

[8] J.B. Dennis, First version of dataflow procedural language, in: B. Robinet (Eds.), Proceedings, Colloque sur la Programmation Paris, April 9–11, 1974, vol. 19, Springer–Verlag, pp. 362–376.

[9] K. Kavi, B. Buckles, U.N. Bhat, Isomorphisms between petri nets and dataflow graphs, IEEE Trans. Softw. Eng. SE-13 (10) (1987) 1127–1134.

[10] A.K. Deshpande, K.M. Kavi, A review of specification and verification methods for parallel programs, including the dataflow approach, IEEE Proc. 77 (12) (1989) 1816–1828.

[11] K. Kavi, A.K. Deshpande, Specification of concurrent processes using a dataflow model of computation and partially ordered events, J. Syst. Softw. 16 (2) (1991) 107–120.

[12] J. Backus, Can programs be liberated from von Neumann style? A functional style and its algebra of programs, Commun. ACM 21 (8) (1978) 613–641.

[13] R. Cytron, J. Ferrante, B.K. Rosen, M.N. Wegman, F.K. Zadeck, Efficiently computing static single assignment form and the control dependence graph, ACM Trans. Program. Lang. Syst. 13 (1991) 451–490.

[14] W.M. Johnston, J.R.P. Hanna, R.J. Millar, Advances in dataflow programming languages, ACM Comput. Surv 36 (1) (2004) 1–34, doi: 10.1145/1013208.1013209.

[15] Arvind, R.S. Nikhil, K.K. Pingali, I-structures: data structures for parallel computing, ACM Trans. Program. Lang. Syst 11 (4) (1989) 598–632, doi: 10.1145/69558.69562.

[16] K. Kavi, J. Arul, R. Giorgi, Execution and cache performance of the scheduled dataflow architecture, J. Univ. Comput. Sci. Special Issue Multithreaded Processors Chip Multiprocessors 6 (2000) 948–967.

[17] B. Lee, A. Hurson, B. Shirazi, A hybrid scheme for processing data structures in a dataflow environment, IEEE Trans, Parallel Distrib. Syst. 3 (1) (1992) 83–96, doi: 10.1109/71.113084.

[18] Arvind, K.P. Gostelow, W. Plouffe, An asynchronous programming language and computing machine, Technical report, University of California, Irvine, December 1978.

[19] W.B. Ackerman, J.B. Dennis, Val—a value-oriented algorithmic language, Technical report, Massachusetts Institute of Technology, February, 1979.

[20] A.R. Hurson, K.M. Kavi, Dataflow computers: their history and future, in: B. Wah (Eds.), Wiley Encyclopedia of Computer Science and Engineering, John Wiley & Sons, December 14, 2007.

[21] D. Cann, J. Feo, W. Bohm, R. Oldehoeft, The SISAL 2.0 reference manual, Technical report, Computing Research Group, LLNL and Computer Science Department, Colorado State University, December 1991.

[22] B. Lee, A.R. Hurson, Dataflow architectures and multithreading, Computer 27 (8) (1994) 27–39, doi: 10.1109/2.303620.

[23] M. Tokoro, J.R. Jagannathan, H. Sunahara, On the working set concept for data-flow machines, Proceedings of the 10th Annual International Symposium on Computer Architecture, 1983, pp. 90–97.

[24] M. Takesue, Cache memories for data flow architectures, IEEE Trans. Comput. 41 (1992) 667–687.

[25] S.A. Thoreson, A.N. Long, A feasibility study of a memory hierarchy in data flow environment, Proceedings of the International Conference on Parallel Computing, 1987, pp. 356–360.

[26] K.M. Kavi, A.R. Hurson, P. Patadia, E. Abraham, P. Shanmugam, Design of cache memories for multi-threaded dataflow architecture, Proceedings of the 22nd International Symposium on Computer Architecture (ISCA-22), ISCA-22, ACM, New York, NY, USA, 1995, pp. 253–264.

[27] D. Burger, S.W. Keckler, K.S. McKinley, M. Dahlin, L.K. John, C. Lin, C.R. Moore, J. Burrill, R.G. McDonald, W. Yoder, The TRIPS Team, Scaling to the end of silicon with EDGE architectures, IEEE Computer 37 (7) (2004) 44–55, doi: 10.1109/MC.2004.65.

[28] M. Gebhart, B.A. Maher, K.E. Coons, J. Diamond, P. Gratz, M. Marino, N. Ranganathan, B. Robatmili, A. Smith, J. Burrill, D. Keckler, S.W. Burger, K.S. McKinley, An evaluation of the TRIPS computer system, SIGPLAN Not 44 (3) (2009) 1–12, doi: 10.1145/1508284.1508246.

[29] C. Kyriacou, P. Evripidou, P. Trancoso, Data-driven multithreading using conventional microprocessors. IEEE Trans. Parallel Distrib. Syst 17 (10) (2006) 1176–1188, http://dx.doi.org/10.1109/TPDS.2006.136.

[30] K.M. Kavi, R. Giorgi, J. Arul, Scheduled dataflow: execution paradigm, architecture, and performance evaluation, IEEE Trans. Comput 50 (8) (2001) 834–846, doi: 10.1109/12.947003.

[31] S. Swanson, A. Schwerin, M. Mercaldi, A. Petersen, A. Putnam, K. Michelson, M. Oskin, S.J. Eggers, The wavescalar architecture, ACM Trans. Comput. Syst 25 (2) (2007) 4:1–4:54, doi: 10.1145/1233307.1233308.

[32] S. Swanson, A. Schwerin, K. Michelson, M. Oskin, Wavescalar, Proceedings of the 36th Annual IEEE/ACM International Symposium on Microarchitecture, MICRO 36, IEEE Computer Society, Washington, DC, USA, 2003. pp. 291–302, http://dl.acm.org/citation.cfm?id=956417.956546.

[33] R. Giorgi, Teraflux: exploiting dataflow parallelism in teradevices, Proceedings of the 36th Annual IEEE/ACM International Symposium on Microarchitecture, CF '12, ACM, 2012. New York, NY, USA, 2012, pp. 303–304, http://doi.acm.org/10.1145/2212908.2212959.

[34] A. Portero, Z. Yu, R. Giorgi, Teraflux: exploiting tera-device computing challenges, Procedia CS 7 (2011) 146–147.

[35] D. Goodman, S. Khan, C. Seaton, Y. Guskov, B. Khan, M. Luján, I. Watson, Dfscala: high level dataflow support for scala, in: Second International Workshop on Data-Flow Models for Extreme Scale Computing (DFM), 2012.

[36] O. Pell, V. Averbukh, Maximum performance computing with dataflow engines, Comput. Sci. Eng. 14 (4) (2012) 98–103, doi:10.1109/MCSE.2012. 78.

[37] S. Zuckerman, J. Suetterlein, R. Knauerhase, G.R. Gao, Using a "codelet" program execution model for exascale machines: position paper, Proceedings of the 1st International Workshop on Adaptive Self-Tuning Computing Systems for the Exaflop

Era, EXADAPT '11, ACM, 2011. New York, NY, USA, 2011, pp. 64–69, http://doi. acm.org/10.1145/2000417.2000424.

[38] J.E. Smith, Decoupled access/execute computer architectures, SIGARCH Comput. Archit. News 10 (3) (1982) 112–119. http://dl.acm.org/citation.cfm?id=1067649. 801719.

[39] J.G. Steffan, C.B. Colohan, A. Zhai, T.C. Mowry, A scalable approach to thread-level speculation, SIGARCH Comput. Archit. News 28 (2) (2000) 1–12, doi: 10.1145/ 342001.339650.

[40] W. Li, K. Kavi, A. Naz, P. Sweany, Speculative thread execution in a multithreaded dataflow architecture, Proceedings of the 19th ISCA Parallel and Distributed Computing Systems, 2006.

[41] A.H. Krishna, M. Kavi, Wentong Li, A non-blocking multithreaded architecture with support for speculative threads, Algorithms Archit. Parallel Process. 5022 (2008) 173–184.

ABOUT THE AUTHORS

Dr. Krishna Kavi is currently a Professor of Computer Science and Engineering and the Director of the NSF Industry/University Cooperative Research Center for Net-Centric Software and Systems at the University of North Texas. During 2001–2009, he served as the Chair of the department. He also held an Endowed Chair Professorship in Computer Engineering at the University of Alabama in Huntsville and served on the faculty of the University of Texas at Arlington. He was a Scientific Program Manger at US National Science Foundation during 1993–1995. He served on several editorial boards and program committees.

Kavi's research is primarily on Computer Systems Architecture including multithreaded and multicore processors, cache memories, and hardware-assisted memory managers. He also conducted research in the area of formal methods, parallel processing, and real-time systems. He published nearly 200 technical papers in these areas. He received more than US$6 million in research grants. He graduated 145 PhDs and more than 35 MS students. He received his PhD from the Southern Methodist University in Dallas Texas and a BS in EE from the Indian Institute of Science in Bangalore, India.

Domenico Pace spent 4 months at the University of North Texas to develop his master degree thesis. During this period, he worked on Scheduled Dataflow architecture. Domenico graduated on June 2013 at Università di Pisa with an MS degree. He also received his BS in Computer Engineering from the same university. Domenico also coauthored another paper, titled "MT-SDF: Scheduled Dataflow Architecture with Mini-threads" presented on Workshop on Dataflow Models (DFM 2013), with the same coauthors as this book chapter. Currently, he is working as an automotive software developer in Italy.

Charles Shelor is currently a PhD student in Computer Engineering at the University of North Texas with research interests in computer architecture, dataflow processing, and embedded systems. He received an MS in Electrical Engineering and a BS in Electrical Engineering, Magna Cum Laude from Louisiana Technical University. He has been a professional engineering since 1982. He has been granted 13 patents and has more than 25 years of industrial experience including at Lockheed-Martin, Efficient Networks, Alcatel-Lucent, Cyrix, and Via Technologies. He also was an ASIC and FPGA design methodology consultant teaching structured, reusable design techniques for 4 years as Shelor Engineering. He was the author of the "VHDL Designer" feature for the "VHDL International Times" newsletter for 2 years. He won the VHDL International programming contest in the industry category in 1994.

CHAPTER THREE

Dataflow Computing in Extreme Performance Conditions

Diego Oriato, Stephen Girdlestone, Oskar Mencer
Maxeler Technologies, London, United Kingdom

Contents

Advances in Computers, Volume 96
ISSN 0065-2458
http://dx.doi.org/10.1016/bs.adcom.2014.11.002

Abstract

Reconfigurable computers, generally based on field programmable gate array technology, have been used successfully as a platform for performance critical applications in a variety of industries. Applications targeted at reconfigurable computers can exploit their fine-grained parallelism, predictable low latency performance and very high data throughput per watt. Traditional techniques for designing configurations are, however, generally considered time consuming and cumbersome and this has limited commercial reconfigurable computer usage. To solve this problem, Maxeler Technologies Ltd, working closely with Imperial College London, have developed powerful new tools and hardware based on the dataflow computing paradigm. In this chapter, we explore these tools and technologies and present a case study on how they have enabled a weather forecast application to be accelerated almost two orders of magnitude compared to conventional widespread technologies.

ABBREVIATIONS

BOLAM Bologna limited-area model
CFL Courant–Friedrichs–Lewy
CLBs configurable logic blocks
CPU central processing unit
DFC dataflow core
DFE dataflow engine
DMA direct memory access
DRAM dynamic random-access memory
ECC error-correcting code
FLOPs floating-point operations
FPGA field programmable gate array
GALS globally asynchronous locally synchronous
GPGPU general-purpose computing on graphics processing units
HPC high-performance computing
LAM limited-area model
MPC-C maximum performance computer C-series
MPI message passing interface
MTBF mean-time-between-failures
SAN storage area networks
SLiC simple live CPU interface SLIC
TCO total cost of ownership
TOR top-of-rack

1. INTRODUCTION

The continuously increasing speed and memory capacity of supercomputers has, over the past few decades, allowed for the creation of ever more complex and accurate mathematical simulations. There are challenges facing high-performance computing (HPC), however. As microprocessors reach the limits of attainable clock frequencies and acceptable power consumption, hardware vendors are scaling up the number of cores per node, thereby enabling higher degrees of parallelism. To take advantage of potential and often only modest, speed improvements [1], existing software must be heavily reorganized by using parallelization libraries (MPI, OpenMP, etc.).

The obvious form of parallel processor is simply a replication of multiple processors starting with a single silicon die (multicore) and extended to racks and racks of interconnected processor–memory server units. Even when the application can be expressed in a completely parallel form, this approach has its own limitations especially when accessing a common memory. The more processors used to access the same common data, the more likely contention develops to limit the overall speed.

The architectures used by these chips are still based on control flow paradigm and suitable for a wide range of tasks. This means that their low-level architectures are not necessarily optimal for the applications the supercomputer is designed to run. Figure 1 shows how little of a modern central processing unit (CPU) is dedicated to actual computation. The rest of the chip is dedicated to subsystems such as caches, branch predictors, and schedulers designed to speed up the instruction decoding and execution.

Currently the top 500 supercomputers [2] are built from relatively general-purpose servers which rely on multicore CPUs and more recently on general-purpose many-cores GPUs for computation. The emphasis on speed as the ultimate metric has forced scientist and business to face huge monetary and environmental costs involved in purchasing and running HPC systems (total cost of ownership, TCO); the electricity costs alone for an exascale supercomputer are estimated to be more than $80 million [3] a year. Since 2006, awareness of other performance metrics such as floating-point operations (FLOPs) per watt has been raised within the HPC community, and the Green500 list

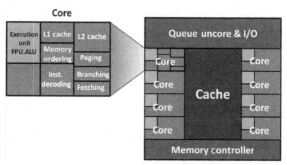

Figure 1 Architecture diagram of Intel Sandy Bridge CPU.

was created to rank the most energy efficient supercomputers in the world. Heterogeneous systems (CPU + general-purpose computing on graphics processing units, GPGPU) claim the top positions also in the Green500 list but the gain in efficiency is often linked to advancement in cooling systems rather than in the computational technology [2].

Alternative computing technologies are emerging as a powerful solution to overcome the slowdown of scaling with traditional processors and the spiraling running costs. To create a supercomputer that achieves the maximum possible performance for a given power/space budget, the architecture of the system needs to be tailored to the applications of interest. This involves optimally balancing resources such as memory, data storage, and networking infrastructure based on detailed analysis of the applications. As well as these high-level optimizations, the architecture of the chips in the system needs to provide both speed and low power consumption.

Maxeler Technologies developed an alternative paradigm to parallel computing: Multiscale dataflow computing. Dataflow computing was popularized by a number of researchers in the 1980s, especially by Dennis [4]. In the dataflow approach, an application is considered as a dataflow graph of the executable actions; as soon as the operands for an action are valid, the action is executed and the result is forwarded to the next action in the graph. There are no load or store instructions as the operational node contains the relevant data. Creating a generalized interconnection among the action nodes proved to be a significant limitation to dataflow realizations in the 1980s. Over recent years, the extraordinary improvement in transistor array density allowed emulations of the application dataflow graph. The Maxeler dataflow implementations are a generalization of the earlier work employing static, synchronous dataflow with an emphasis on data streaming. Indeed "multiscale" dataflow incorporates vector and array processing to offer a multifaceted parallel computing platform.

In this chapter, we will talk through both the basics of dataflow computing and how to use Maxeler dataflow engines (DFEs), as well as cluster design and management for clusters containing dataflow nodes. Finally, we will finish with a case study showing how this has been put into practice for a complex atmospheric simulation.

2. DATAFLOW COMPUTING

In a software application, a program's source code is transformed into a list of instructions for a particular processor (control flow core), which is then loaded into the memory, as shown in Fig. 2.

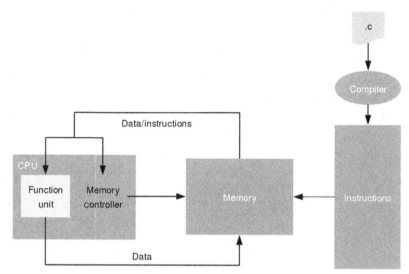

Figure 2 Data movement in a control flow core.

Instructions move through the processor and occasionally read or write data to and from memory. Modern processors contain many levels of caching, forwarding and prediction logic to improve the efficiency of this paradigm; however, the programming model is inherently sequential and performance depends on the latency of memory accesses and the time for a CPU clock cycle.

Dataflow programming focuses on modeling a program as a directed graph. DFEs exploit the intrinsic parallelism of a directed graph of operations to achieve high performance, by arranging the calculation in a parallel pipeline where thousands of operations are computed every cycle at relatively low clock frequencies.

In a dataflow program, we describe the operations and data choreography for a particular algorithm (see Fig. 3). In a DFE, data streams from memory into the processing chip where data is forwarded directly from one arithmetic unit (dataflow core, DFC) to another until the chain of processing is complete. Once a dataflow program has processed its streams of data, the DFE can be reconfigured for a new application in a very short time, e.g., less than a second in the current Maxeler technology. Each DFC computes only a single type of arithmetic operation (for example, an addition or multiplication) and is thus simple so thousands can fit on one DFE. In a DFE processing pipeline, every DFC computes simultaneously on neighboring data items in a stream. Unlike control flow cores where operations are computed at different points in time on the same functional units (computing in time), a dataflow computation is

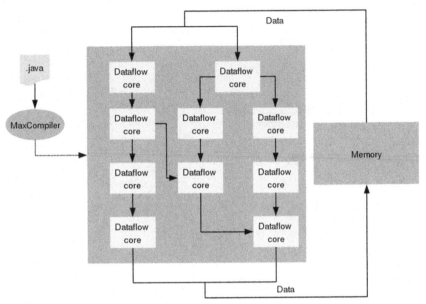

Figure 3 Data movement in a data flow core.

laid out spatially on the chip (computing in space). Dependencies in a dataflow program are resolved statically at compile time.

One analogy for moving from control flow to dataflow is replacing artisans with a manufacturing model. In a factory, each worker gets a simple task and all workers operate in parallel on streams of products and parts. Just as in manufacturing, dataflow is a method to scale up a computation to a large scale. The DFE structure itself represents the computation thus there is no need for instructions per se; instructions are replaced by arithmetic units laid out in space and connected for a particular data processing task. Because there are no instructions, there is no need for instruction decode logic, instruction caches, branch prediction, or dynamic out-of-order scheduling. By eliminating the dynamic control flow overhead, all available resources of the chip are dedicated mainly to performing computation. At a system level, the DFE handles large-scale data processing while CPUs manage irregular and infrequent operations, IO and internode communication.

3. MAXELER MULTISCALE DFEs

Maxeler has developed DFEs to provide a high-performance reconfigurable dataflow computing platform. A DFE has at its heart a modern high-speed, large area, reconfigurable chip. Wired to this chip, also named dataflow core (DFC), is a significant quantity of memory for storing application data and various high bandwidth interconnects that allow the DFE to communicate quickly with other DFEs, networks, and general-purpose computers.

Figure 4 illustrates the architecture of a Maxeler maximum performance computer C-series (MPC-C) dataflow processing system, which comprises six DFEs with their on-board memories of 48 GB attached by a Peripheral Component Interconnect Express (PCIe) Gen2 channel to a CPU. Multiple DFEs are connected together via a high-bandwidth MaxRing interconnect, as shown in Fig. 4. The MaxRing interconnect allows applications to scale linearly with multiple DFEs in the system while supporting full overlap of communication and computation. This system allows a stand-alone deployment of dataflow technology with a fixed combination of CPUs and dataflow compute engines. Within a heterogeneous system with a dynamically changing balance of resources, a more flexible solution is represented by the Maxeler MPC-X as show in Fig. 5. Here, the DFEs connect directly

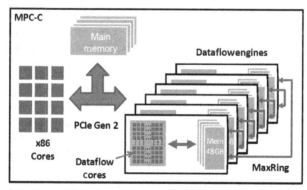

Figure 4 Architecture of Maxeler MPC-C dataflow node.

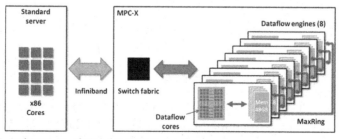

Figure 5 Architecture of Maxeler MPC-X dataflow node.

to a switch fabric and through an infiniband cloud to clusters of CPU cores. The ratio of CPU cores and DFEs can be changed dynamically at runtime based on application requirements.

The common part in these two configurations is the individual Maxeler DFE hardware. Each DFE can implement multiple kernels, which perform computation as data flows between the CPU, DFE, and its associated memories. The DFE has two types of memory: Fast Memory (*FMem*) which can store several megabytes of data on-chip (DFC) with terabytes/second of access bandwidth and Large Memory (*LMem*) which can store many gigabytes (48 GB in Fig. 5) of data off-chip. The bandwidth and flexibility of FMem is a key reason why DFEs are able to achieve such high performance on complex applications—for example, a Maxeler Vectis DFE can provide up to 10.5 TB/s of FMem bandwidth within a chip. Applications are able to effectively exploit the full FMem capacity because both memory and computation are laid out in space so data can always be held in memory close to computation. This is in contrast to traditional CPU architectures with multilevel caches where only the smallest/fastest cache memory level is close to the computational units and data is duplicated through the several cache levels.

The reconfigurable chips used so far in DFEs have been field programmable gate arrays (FPGAs). FPGAs have a very flexible fabric in which dataflow graphs can be emulated. The development of reconfigurable integrated circuits developed specifically for DFEs could bring significant performance improvements to applications and improve programmability. There are also modifications that could be incorporated into FPGAs to make them more suitable for dataflow applications. The buffers used to enforce schedules in dataflow graphs, for example, are currently implemented using dedicated FPGA memory resources such as block RAMs with separate addressing logic implemented in configurable logic blocks (CLBs). This creates routing congestion around the memory block and reduces the frequency at which they can be clocked. Autonomous memory blocks [5] could solve this problem by creating a dedicated configurable addressing circuit within the memory block itself; as well as reducing congestion autonomous memory blocks would reduce the amount of work required from compilation tools to place the CLBs.

4. DEVELOPMENT PROCESS

It is well known that measuring and modeling application characteristics is essential for the optimization of the design of a cluster, in particular in terms of interconnections, memory, and distribution of computational resources. The same idea can be extended to every level in a computer system, developing dedicated, problem-specific computer architectures to address different domains of scientific problems in the most efficient way to achieve the maximum performance.

A team of mathematicians, physicists, computer scientists, and engineers working together to plan a system all the way from the formulation of the computational problem down to design of the best possible computer architecture is a proven method to achieve maximum application performance. The key factor of this approach is to adapt the application algorithm to match the capabilities of the computer at the same time as change the computer to match the requirements of the algorithm. Dataflow computing provides a fundamental part of the solution by providing flexibility, maximum performance, and high efficiency.

Figure 6 shows the process for maximizing application performance with dataflow computing. We identify four distinct steps: Analysis, Transformation, Partitioning, and Implementation.

4.1. Analysis

To understand the application, its algorithm and the potential performance bottlenecks, it is important to carry out an in-depth analysis of the application. This analysis should cover all the aspects involved in a computational problem, from the mathematics in the algorithms to the low-level electrical engineering aspects. This includes considerations such as:

1. Nature of computation
2. Proportion of computation versus memory access
3. Balance between local computation and network communication
4. Balance between computation and disk I/O
5. Trade-offs between (re)computation and storage

All of these can have a great impact on the final system performance and an improvement in one factor could be defeated by limitations in others, hence the need for approaching the whole system.

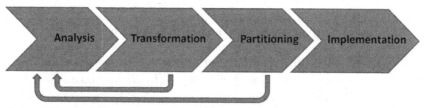

Figure 6 The Maxeler application acceleration process.

4.2. Transformation

After the analysis and the design of the best architecture, the next step is to transform the application to create a structure that is suitable for acceleration. This might include the transformation of the algorithm (or the use of an equivalent one) as well as computation reordering and data layout or data representation transformations. The analysis and transformation steps are those that involve the largest amount of multidisciplinary cooperation. Scientists with expertise in the problem domain collaborate with computer experts and engineers to make sure that the full range of options are explored.

4.3. Partitioning

After transformation, one should consider how to partition the code and the data of the application between CPU resources and DFEs. For program code, the choice is only whether to run it on the conventional CPUs or in DFEs. For data, we define data access plans as the locations of each significant data array used during the computation. In the DFE, data can be present in the large off-chip memory or in the smaller and faster on-chip memory (few megabytes, typically). For the CPU, data can obviously be on disk, main memory, or on-chip cache and registers.

4.4. Implementation

Each transformation and partitioning will provide a certain level of performance in exchange for a certain amount of development effort. This process of analyze, transform and partition, can go through several iterations as new possibilities are explored. High-level performance modeling is used to quickly narrow down to a small set of promising options most likely to deliver best performance. Then more detailed analysis can be used to select one particular option. Once the best architecture has been identified, the implementation stage starts. The following section describes implementation tools and basic dataflow programming concepts used.

5. PROGRAMMING WITH MAXCOMPILER

Maxeler's dataflow computers are programmed using several high-level and scripting languages such as MatLab, Python, standard C/C++/FORTRAN, and Java combined with Maxeler's language extensions to drive generation of dataflow graphs.

Figure 7 shows the logical organization of a dataflow computing system. The programmer creates a dataflow application with three parts:

1. an application typically written in Matlab, python, C/C++, Excel VB, FORTRAN which runs on conventional CPUs;

2. one or more dataflow kernels, written in Java; and

3. a manager written in Java.

Kernels are at the heart of the Maxeler Dataflow concept. Kernels describe computation and data manipulation in the form of dataflow graphs. MaxCompiler transforms kernels into fully pipelined synchronous circuits. The circuits are scheduled automatically to allow them to operate at high frequencies and make optimal use of the resources on the DFE.

MaxCompiler designs use an architecture that is conceptually similar to the globally asynchronous locally synchronous (GALS) architecture previously used in FPGA design [6]. As well as enabling the maximum exploitation of low-level parallelization, the fully pipelined nature of kernels allows them to be easily modeled at a high level, which helps avoiding wasted programming effort sometimes seen with other, less predictable, programmable systems.

The Manager describes the connections between kernels and streams connecting kernel to off-chips I/O channels such as CPU interconnect (e.g., PCI express, Infiniband), inter-DFE Maxeler propriety connections named MaxRing and DRAM memory (LMem). These connections are the asynchronous parts of a DFE configuration which are connected together using a simple point-to-point interconnection scheme [7]. The

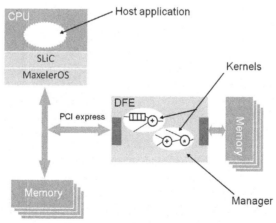

Figure 7 Architecture of a Maxeler dataflow computing system.

manager allows developers to connect resources such as memory and PCI-express streams to kernels to keep them fed with data. The streaming model used for these off-chip communications naturally adapts to the hardware data paths exploiting the maximum bandwidth available.

The separation of computation and communication into kernels and a manager is the key idea that solves the problem of synchronization, which plagues parallel programming on control flow cores; the computation in the kernels can be deeply pipelined and no synchronization code is required. This and the ability of extending the pipeline over many DFEs are responsible for the degree of high performance that can be achieved. The maximum number of pipelines within a kernel and the maximum number of kernels in a DFE is bound only by the intrinsic parallelism of the application and the hardware resources available on the DFE.

Figure 8 depicts the compilation process of a typical MaxCompiler application. Both kernels and manager are described using the MaxJ programming language, an extension of the conventional Java language with Maxeler features (operator overloading). MaxJ is a meta-program that describes the structure of the dataflow graph of instructions that should be created in the DFE. When the MaxJ program is executed inside MaxCompiler a data flow chip configuration file is generated. This chip configuration file also known as "max" file contains the hardware configuration binary data (bitstream), the readable meta information about the user configuration and also CPU function calls enabling it to be easily integrated

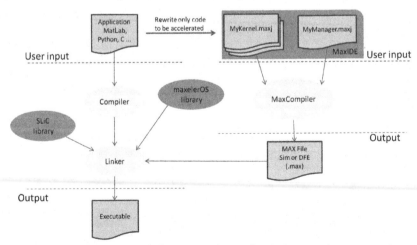

Figure 8 Compilation process of MaxCompiler application.

into the CPU application. During the compilation of the CPU code, the max file is compiled and linked with the MaxCompiler Simple Live CPU interface (SLiC) library to the application executable. The single executable file thus generated contains all the binary code to run on both the conventional CPUs and the DFEs in a system. When the application calls a function which uses a DFE the hardware will automatically be configured with the correct dataflow graph of instructions to perform that function.

The compilation of the kernel and manager MaxJ files can be slow (typically several hours) due to the complex nature of mapping a dataflow graph into a hardware design. However, during development and debugging it is more appropriate to use simulation. In this case, the MaxCompiler program is compiled into native CPU code and executed as a standard process, which emulates the DFE. The resulting simulated DFE is much slower than real hardware but can be compiled in few minutes and allows a better debugging experience. MaxCompiler simulation is few order of magnitudes faster than commercial low-level HDL simulators.

A simple example of a MaxJ kernel is the following:

```
DFEVar x = io.input("x", dfeFloat(8,24));
DFEVar y = io.input("y", dfeFloat(8,24));
DFEVar z = x*x+y*y;
io.output("z", z, dfeFloat(8,24));
```

This snippet of code creates a kernel that computes the $z = x^2 + y^2$ where x and y are two input arrays and z the output array. The three arrays are streamed in/out of the kernel one value at the time. It is evident how the math is very similar to what it would be in a conventional software language. The loop over the arrays is implicit in the streaming process. The DFE will have to run for a number of cycles equal to the size of each array. Inputs and outputs are single precision floating-point numbers and the operations involved respect the IEEE single precision floating-point rules. Conditional instructions can easily be dealt with as in the following code:

```
DFEVar x = io.input("x", dfeFloat(8,24));
DFEVar y = io.input("y", dfeFloat(8,24));
DFEVar x2 = x*x;
DFEVar y2 = y*y;
DFEVar z = x2>y2?x2:y2;
io.output("z", z, dfeFloat(8,24));
```

Now this new kernel outputs the array z that contains the largest square of the two inputs on each iteration. The ternary operator $(--?-:-;)$ inside the Kernel represents effectively the conditional if-statement of many programming languages. The design created will have the two branches of the conditional statement physically present and executed each iteration. The result will be the product of the selection of the output from one of those branches. Of course ternary operators can be chained together to create multiple possibilities.

In the previous kernels, the output was depending only on the current (i.e., same index of the array) values of the inputs. When this is not the case as, for example, in the following three point moving average computation:

$$z[i] = \frac{(x[i-1] + x[i] + x[i+1])}{3}$$

then a new operator has to be introduced, capable to capture data at a different point in the stream.

```
DFEVar prev=stream.offset(x,-1);
DFEVar next=stream.offset(x,1)
DFEVar z=(prev+x+next)/3;
```

Because the input x is a stream, rather than indexing into the array (as we do in software) the kernel code uses the "stream.offset" operator with offset value relative to the current position in the stream to access the previous and next element of the input.

The center section of Fig. 9 shows the small MaxJ program where we use to create a manager that includes a simple $y = x^2 + 30$ kernel and connects its input and outputs to the CPU. The left section shows the CPU code and the invocation to the function MyKernel() with the allocated array x and y. This represents a stub code whose implementation is auto generated inside the max file during the compilation of the MaxJ KERNEL. Once the MyKernel() function is executed by the CPU, data in the array x is transferred through direct memory access (DMA) to the DFE. In the DFE, computation happens while data is streaming through the chip. As the output is available out of the DFE, it is transferred back to the CPU as one single pipeline process. Because of the streaming paradigm, I/O in and out of the DFE is overlapped with computation. Configuration of the hardware is done automatically as first step in the MyKernel() function.

The MaxelerOS and the SLiC libraries constitute the software layer that controls the streaming process. DFEs are controlled from a CPU using the SLiC API. This API comes in a variety of flavors ranging from the basic and advanced automatically generated static APIs to the more flexible dynamic API. As well as a C API MaxCompiler can generate bindings in a variety of

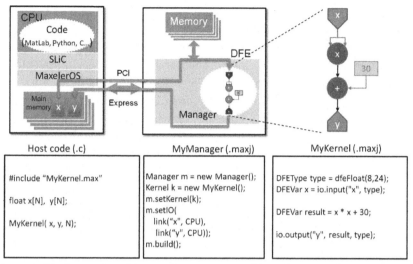

Host code (.c)	MyManager (.maxj)	MyKernel (.maxj)

#include "MyKernel.max"
 	
float x[N], y[N];
 	
MyKernel(x, y, N);
	Manager m = new Manager();
	Kernel k = new MyKernel();
	m.setKernel(k);
	m.setIO(
	    link("x", CPU),
	    link("y", CPU));
	m.build();
		DFEType type = dfeFloat(8,24);
		DFEVar x = io.input("x", type);
		
		DFEVar result = x * x + 30;
		
		io.output("y", result, type);

Figure 9 The interaction of host code, manager, and kernel in a dataflow application.

other languages so that DFEs can be used to accelerate portions of Matlab, R and Python code without the need for users to write their own wrappers.

6. DATAFLOW CLUSTERS

Only recently, the dataflow computing paradigm and its incarnation in the DFE have been considered for real production systems. The stigma of "exotic academic research subject" is slowly fading as the single node dataflow system is replaced by large clusters in the data centers. As ever with technology, hardware scalability is not a guaranteed result, even in the case of dataflow applications where the datagraph is inherently parallel.

A dataflow cluster would have a mix of DFEs and CPUs, the number of each usually constrained by limitations of power or space budgets. However, by using the MPC-X dataflow nodes, the ratio between CPU and DFEs in use can be changed dynamically.

6.1. Power Efficient Computing

Physical space, the power supply, cooling capacity, network capacity, and the access to storage are key factors to take into account when designing a cluster. Medium size data centers have space for 40–50 racks (the physical containers of nodes and switches). Each rack can contain up to 50 computing servers each occupying a rack unit (1U). As 1U server typically requires between 400 and 600 W, racks need to be supplied with tens of kilowatts when at full load. A matching amount of cooling is required since almost all power consumption is converted into heat. Typically maximum weight of the floor per square feet and maximum heat dissipation per cubic feet limit the number of computing servers to <50.

Since the power consumed by a single DFE is typically in the range of 50–100 W, adding DFEs to a compute rack has a small impact on power consumption. Assuming a typical speedup of 30× that is commonly achieved by a dataflow node compared to a CPU node, and assuming an additional 25% in reduced power consumption the overall improvement in power per Watt is considerable, 24× to be precise. The dataflow cluster is therefore 30× smaller for a fixed performance and consumes 24× less electricity. For a fixed power budget, the dataflow cluster could be 80% the size of the conventional CPU cluster but still delivering 24× in speedup.

6.2. Data Storage

Since each DFE contains a very large amount of memory, there are many applications that would not be able to run on a single CPU node for lack of memory, which could be easily run on a DFE. This means that the use of mechanisms such as message passing interface (MPI) is less common for dataflow accelerated application, as they are not required.

The large quantity of dynamic random-access memory (DRAM) available in a dataflow node, possibly combined with the ability to compress/decompress data without performance penalties, is also useful in applications where disk storage might otherwise be required for storing temporary data. When disk storage is required, the ratio of disks to DFEs can also be dynamically changed when using MPC-X dataflow nodes.

Sometimes data needs to be shared over multiple nodes. In this case, centralized storage is usually the optimal solution, provided the centralized resources can deliver sufficient bandwidth to all the nodes. Generally, a data partitioning strategy is used whereby each node spends most of the time computing with local data set, and the global storage deals with requests for missing data.

Systems based on storage area networks (SAN) and parallel file systems (e.g., Lustre) are the preferred choices. The key factors in the performance of a storage system are:

1. cost;
2. capacity;

3. linear access throughput (MB/s); and

4. I/O operations per second (random access).

Ultimately, the success of the storage system is how it answers the requirements of the applications that need to run on it.

6.3. Interconnections

High-performance network traffic in current clusters uses networks such as Gigabit Ethernet, 10 Gigabit Ethernet or Infiniband. Usually the nodes within a rack communicate through top-of-rack (TOR) switches. TOR switches then provide up-links to the wider network, thus creating a tree network structure. Separate management networks are usually present to provide remote access to each node, but do not require high bandwidth. Local networks for other subsystem (SAN) are also present but they use dedicated interconnect such as Fibrechannel. A further network is installed in dataflow clusters where CPU nodes communicate with local dataflow nodes over faster links than is provided globally. Global networks might not be tree based as different network topologies can provide substantially superior performance if they are a better fit to the application. DFEs usually have their own dedicated networks; Maxeler nodes contain internal DFE torus networks (MaxRing) which connect each DFE to its neighbors.

6.4. Cluster-Level Management

Support for cluster-level management is essential for large-scale dataflow computing deployment. Tasks of a cluster management, such as monitoring status of the cluster nodes, scheduling the compute jobs, and providing a control interface between users and the cluster, are essential.

Conventional widely adopted CPU-centric cluster management software is not designed for clusters with dataflow computing elements. The two main issues are allocation and scheduling of DFE resources and coping with nodes that compute substantially faster. The difference between CPU and DFE, as far as the scheduler is concerned, is in the ability of time sharing for multiple applications. The performance benefit of a DFE comes, in part, from the locality of the data to the chip. By time sharing DFEs, the overhead of swapping data in and out for different applications would be highly detrimental to performance.

Since the locality of data is critical, dataflow programming models force the user application to decide the number of resources and their topology in order to maximize efficiency. At the same time, Maxeler's MaxelerOS management software allows users to access and submit individual processing operations. MaxelerOS abstracts the specific hardware in use and allocate pools or groups of DFE to serve specific applications. DFE groups can also grow or shrink automatically depending on demand, something particularly useful when there is more than one application using the DFE resources.

MaxelerOS also monitors various characteristics of the DFEs, including health, ownership, temperature, and utilization. Users can query the status of DFEs through tools such as maxtop and maxstatuscheck; the output of these utilities can be integrated into cluster-level systems, as long as the management system can be extended with this extra functionalities and translate it into useful information for the management process.

Cluster schedulers often deal with relatively long-running processes, where any scheduling overhead is minimal compared to the process runtime. However, this overhead can become critical when dealing with dataflow nodes running $100\times$ faster. One solution to this is to modify the application level to increase the amount of work performed per scheduling unit; another is to modify the cluster scheduler to improve performance for scheduling small jobs.

6.5. Reliability

Conventional CPU nodes may fail for reasons such as disk failure, power failure, memory error, or failures within the processor. Dataflow nodes may fail for similar reasons; in addition DFEs based on FPGA technologies can be affected by memory errors both in the FMem and LMem.

The mean-time-between-failures (MTBF) of a cluster is directly proportional to the number of nodes in the cluster. Thus, an intrinsic advantage of a dataflow accelerated cluster is that by utilizing a smaller number of nodes to perform the same amount of computation, the rate of failure can be reduced if DFE nodes have a similar individual MTBF to CPU nodes.

In addition, DFE nodes may not have direct disk storage as the engines make use of large amount of on-board DRAM for temporary local storage. As a large proportion of all failures are due to the hard disk drives, a diskless DFE node can be more reliable than a disk-based CPU server. The higher rate of failures caused by the larger amount of memory in a DFE node is balanced by the fact that error-correcting code (ECC) memory is largely used as a standard. Using ECC memory, 1-bit errors can be corrected and 2-bit errors can be detected in each 64-bit memory word. Moreover, a DFE can be customized to use more sophisticated ECC schemes, offering greater protection, depending on the requirements of the application.

7. CASE STUDY: METEOROLOGICAL LIMITED-AREA MODEL

Climate and weather modeling is a significant user of HPC due to the hard deadlines inherent in predicting weather. Given the large data volumes and runtimes involved, climate and weather modeling is ideally suited for dataflow computation. The aim of this case study is to describe the steps involved in the acceleration of a real-world application using dataflow computing. We will show that by using dataflow nodes it is possible to achieve performances in excess of $70 \times$ when comparing to a conventional x86-based CPU node.

7.1. The Application

The application accelerated is a research-oriented complex atmospheric model developed by ISAC-CNR (Bologna, Italy) [8]. The application falls in the category of a hydrostatic limited-area model (LAM) parallelized using domain decomposition and message passing libraries [9].

Historically hydrostatic models present a considerable computational advantage over their nonhydrostatic counterpart. By avoiding dependence on the solution of the full vertical momentum equation, hydrostatic models significantly lengthen the time step used within the model's run and therefore increase computational speed. This is very important both for global area models, where spatial resolution is limited by the dimension of the domain that can be computed, and for climate models, where long time integration is required. Furthermore, in the field of ensemble forecasting, many instances of the same model or different models are conducted using different, but equiprobable, initial conditions. This is a form of Monte Carlo analysis used to characterize forecast uncertainty. In this scenario, the ability to run multiple simulations in a short time becomes essential.

Typical spatial resolutions of state-of-the-art hydrostatic LAMs are in the order of 10 km. The increase of spatial resolution required by accurate local weather forecasts is hampered by the limit of validity of the hydrostatic approximation underpinning these hydrostatic models. This limit stands conventionally at about 10 km. At this resolution, the necessary Courant–Friedrichs–Lewy (CFL) condition for convergence imposes small time steps that significantly reduce the speed benefit of the hydrostatic approximation [10]. With the loss in computational advantage hydrostatic LAMs are in need of hardware acceleration.

7.2. The Model

The Limited-Area meteorological model we study integrates the primitive equations (PE) in time over a regional horizontal domain covering only part of the Earth. The PE are a set of nonlinear three-dimensional partial differential equations that are used to approximate global atmospheric flow. They consist of three main sets of equations:

- the two equations for the horizontal conservation of momentum for the zonal velocity u and the meridional velocity v

$$\frac{\partial u}{\partial t} = -\frac{u}{ah_x}\frac{\partial u}{\partial \lambda} - \frac{v}{a}\frac{\partial u}{\partial \phi} - \dot{\sigma}\frac{\partial u}{\partial \sigma} - \frac{R_d T_v}{ah_x}\frac{\partial \ln p_s}{\partial \lambda} - \frac{1}{ah_x}\frac{\partial \Phi}{\partial \lambda} + F_u \quad (1)$$

$$\frac{\partial v}{\partial t} = -\frac{u}{ah_x}\frac{\partial v}{\partial \lambda} - \frac{v}{a}\frac{\partial v}{\partial \varphi} - \dot{\sigma}\frac{\partial v}{\partial \sigma} - \frac{R_d T_v}{a}\frac{\partial \ln p_s}{\partial \varphi} - \frac{1}{a}\frac{\partial \Phi}{\partial \varphi} + F_v, \quad (2)$$

- the continuity equation for the atmospheric pressure p and surface pressure p_s

$$\frac{\partial p_s}{\partial t} = -\int_0^1 \nabla \cdot \left(\vec{V}_h \frac{\partial p}{\partial \sigma} \right) d\sigma \quad (3)$$

- the continuity equation expressing conservation of specific humidity q and temperature θ

$$\frac{\partial q}{\partial t} = -\frac{u}{ah_x}\frac{\partial q}{\partial \lambda} - \frac{v}{a}\frac{\partial q}{\partial \phi} - \dot{\sigma}\frac{\partial q}{\partial \sigma} + F_q. \quad (4)$$

$$\frac{\partial \theta}{\partial t} = -\frac{u}{ah_x}\frac{\partial \theta}{\partial \lambda} - \frac{v}{a}\frac{\partial \theta}{\partial \phi} - \dot{\sigma}\frac{\partial \theta}{\partial \sigma} + F_\theta. \quad (5)$$

The PE (1)–(5) describe the time evolution for the five prognostic variables u, v, p_s, q, and θ.

The hydrostatic approximation assumed in the PE can be described explicitly by

$$\frac{\partial \Phi}{\partial \sigma} = -\frac{R_d T_v}{p}\frac{\partial p}{\partial \sigma} \quad (6)$$

relating the geopotential field to the vertical variation of the pressure and the virtual temperature T_v.

Terms F_u, F_v, F_q, and F_θ in Eqs. (1), (2), (4), and (5) represent contributions to the tendencies from the parameterization of several physical processes such as radiation [11], convection [12], dry adiabatic adjustments, surface friction, soil water and energy balance, large-scale precipitation, and evaporation.

7.3. The Algorithm

The system of differential equations is solved through integration in time, achieved by using a leapfrog scheme based on the staggered Arakawa C-grid [13]. First, time derivatives (tendencies) are calculated, at time t, and the prognostic variables are advanced to time $t + \Delta t$, where Δt is the time step of integration. Asselin time filtering [14] is then applied to variables at time t to suppress the computational noise arising from the three time level integration scheme. To suppress nonlinear instability and to limit energy concentration on grid scales, all prognostic variables except p_s are subjected to the horizontal fourth-order diffusion operator. Both zonal and meridional velocity are further processed using a divergence damping operator of the second order solved using an Euler time scheme.

Two types of boundary conditions are applied at the edges of the horizontal plane. Fixed values for the prognostic variables imposed by the initial condition at the very edge of the horizontal plane. In the next internal edge, a weighted average between the fixed boundary value and the value computed by the model is applied (Karlberg relaxation scheme [15]). In the vertical dimension, pressure is set to zero at the highest altitude.

7.4. Analysis

The Bologna limited-area model (BOLAM) algorithm uses an explicit finite difference time domain scheme. The time step computation can be decomposed into five logical blocks as shown in Fig. 10A.

1. *Pressure Tendency*: Calculation of the continuity equation (3) for the surface pressure integrated over the vertical dimension.
2. *Diaged*: Calculation of the logarithm of the surface pressure, calculation of the vertical profile of the pressure, virtual temperature, geopotential, and vertical velocity as in Eq. (6).
3. *Tendency*: Computation of the dynamic contributions to the prognostic equations as in Eqs. (1), (2), (4), and (5).
4. *Diffusion*: Computation of the artificial horizontal diffusion for the prognostic variables.

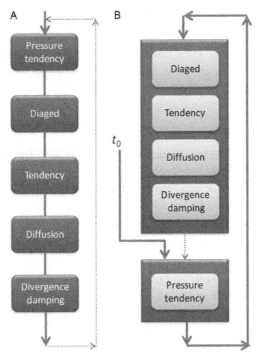

Figure 10 The reordering of the logical blocks required for efficient DFE acceleration.

5. *Divergence & Damping*: Calculation of the horizontal divergence and damping with a diffusion coefficient function of time.

Each block is structured as a three-dimensional loop where longitude, latitude, and altitude are respectively fast, medium, and slow dimensions. Incrementing counters are employed for longitude and latitude corresponding to west-to-east and south-to-north movements. The vertical dimension is described by the sigma coordinate σ, which represents the ratio of pressure over surface pressure; its value is highest at the surface level. Consequently, a decreasing counter is employed for altitude, even if it is incremented during the loop iterations.

Due to the tight coupling nature of the PE, each block either modifies the prognostic variables or computes intermediate variables required by the next block making the computation of the blocks a strictly orderly serial process. Parallelization of the original algorithm was done using 2D domain decomposition in the horizontal plane. MPI was used for the exchange of the ghost regions. The size of the ghost region is determined by the 2D cross-shaped five-point stencil used by the diffusion operator in the *Diffusion* block.

7.5. Partitioning

We used the Maxeler Parton toolset to analyze the CPU time spent on each logical block of the application.

Figure 11 reports the profile of the application run on an Intel Xeon core. The *Tendency* block is responsible for over 40% of the compute time, followed by the *Divergence Damping* and the *Diffusion*. A relatively large overhead is caused by some memory management (*Array Swap* in Fig. 11) and by the treatment of boundaries conditions (*Boundary Fix*) and by the advancing time integration scheme (*Advance* and *Filter*). This cost is evenly spread over all the five blocks described previously.

We base the decision of which blocks require acceleration on the CPU profiling report. The *Tendency* block is the first candidate for acceleration; with 160 FLOPs (96 additions/subtractions, 60 multiplications/divisions, and 4 exponentials). Since we aim for acceleration of $100 \times$ or more, all the blocks would have to be migrated to the DFE. By moving all the computation to the DFE, we also minimize data transfer between CPU and DFE. We kept the time step control loop in the CPU and invoked the DFE computation per time step.

7.6. Transformation

Whereas a traditional program consists of a series of statements, a dataflow program is an assembly line where its "workers," the operations B1 and B2,

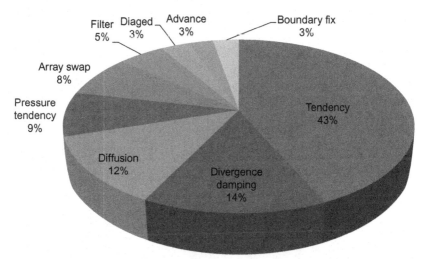

Figure 11 Breakdown of CPU time inside the case study application.

do their assigned tasks as soon as data arrive. The aim is therefore to group all the computational logic inside a single loop as on the transformation depicted in Fig. 12 and to replace the loop with a deterministic data access pattern. For this reason, it is important to understand the data dependency among the different parts of the algorithm. In our application, for example, the *Pressure Tendency* block consists of a 3D loop whereas the surface pressure is reduced over the altitude in 2D. Before the surface pressure variable can be used in the successive *Diaged* block, the reduction process has to be concluded. This fact prevents the merging of the 3D loops in the *Pressure Tendency* and the *Diaged* blocks.

To overcome this, there are usually two common approaches: temporarily buffering the full three-dimensional data between the two blocks or computing those blocks in two separate dataflow steps. The first would require a very large buffer to temporary store the full problem size. The second solution forces us to carry out the time step computation in two streaming phases, which would double the time it takes to stream the data. Neither of these options is ideal so we exploited a feature of the order in which the functional blocks are executed in the algorithm. We observed that the "Pressure Tendency" block is actually the first computation done in the time step. Therefore in order to compute the *Pressure Tendency* block at time step t, only data at time step $t-1$ are required. As a consequence, it is

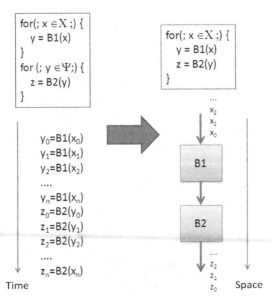

Figure 12 Combining loops for more efficient dataflow.

possible to execute the *Pressure Tendency* block in advance as the last part of time step $t-1$. Figure 10B shows the reordering of the logic that was required for the dataflow transformation.

7.7. Parallelization

Intrinsic parallelism of the dataflow transformation derives from the fact that each spatial logic block is executed in parallel to all the others on each clock cycle for different data items. In this regard, the meteorological model is a good candidate for this type of acceleration thanks to its large number of arithmetic operations, which results in a long pipeline and therefore a high degree of parallelism is inherently achieved.

At the same time, data need to be fed into the pipeline at a rate determined by the hardware implementation. A DFE comprises memory coupled to a chip implementing many DFCs. The DFCs are arranged in a pipeline which processes one item of data per clock cycle. Typical clock speeds are around 100–200 MHz. Given that to compute one grid point we need the five prognostic variables, their previous and next time step values and a few other constants describing the geometry and the Physics of the problem, we estimated that a single pipeline would use only 50% of the memory bandwidth.

Besides the length of the pipeline, another degree of parallelization can be achieved by increasing the capacity of the pipeline. In our model, this translates to computing more than one grid point per clock cycle by physically replicating each block of the pipeline. Two main obstacles usually limit the size of the pipeline: the memory bandwidth required to sustain the increased dataflow and the number of DFCs that fit on the chip. Given that a single capacity pipeline requires 50% of the memory bandwidth available in the DFE, there should be sufficient for a pipeline of double capacity.

To be able to duplicate the meteorological model pipeline, we converted part of the computation to use fixed-point arithmetic. In general, fixed-point arithmetic is more efficient in term of silicon area per operation than the equivalent floating-point arithmetic. A detailed study was performed on each block of the algorithm to establish the optimal fixed-point representations to be used. We determined that due to the very high dynamic range of the prognostic variables a single representation was impossible. Therefore we first scaled all variables by applying a scaling coefficient, different for each prognostic variable. We then adjusted the fixed-point representation along the computational pipeline to maximize precision and avoid overflow.

Some parts of the pipeline were implemented using floating-point representation to allow for high dynamic variability. For simplicity, we kept the
number of bits for these different representations constant to 32, but further
optimizations could be achieved by varying the bit width. With these modifications, we were able to replicate the logic in the pipeline to compute two
items of data in parallel.

The last axis of parallelism is derived from the fact we had six DFEs available in a single MPC-C compute node. One option was to decompose the
problem among the DFEs and reduce further the computation time. Since
the grid of real-world datasets have a contained number of points (<1 mil-
lion) we opted for a one-to-one mapping of serial simulation to DFE thus
giving the capability of running six independent simulations in parallel. In
future, if tackling larger problem sizes we could utilize a decomposition
approach as shown possible by a past study [16].

7.8. Experimental Setup

We ran the dataflow application on a Maxeler MPC-C dataflow node with
eight Intel Xeon E5506 @ 2.13 GHz CPU cores and six Vectis DFEs
connected to the CPUs via PCI Express. Each Vectis DFE utilizes a Xilinx
Virtex 6 SX475T FPGA to implement the DFCs and 48 GB of memory.

Maxeler's MaxCompiler development environment was used to implement the dataflow pipeline and integrate it into the original application. The
tested dataflow design with two replicated pipelines occupies 80% of the
chip's internal memory and 58% of the DSPs (multipliers), and was set to
run at 150 MHz.

The DFE memory was used to store all the variables needed during the
computation. The prognostic variables were initialized from CPU and transferred out at the last time step of the simulation. The CPU controlled the
time step loop by triggering the dataflow process and waiting for it to finish
before repeating the trigger. No computation was executed on the CPU
other than for initialization and post processing.

7.9. Results

The dataset used is, for a LAM, a medium size domain of 13,600 km (160
points) in longitude, 3333 km (120 points) in latitude and 30 km (32 points)
in altitude. We used a baroclinic atmosphere for the initial condition [17].
The time step $\Delta t = 15$ s was chosen to satisfy the CFL criteria which guar-
antees the stability of the solutions. The hardware was run on a larger

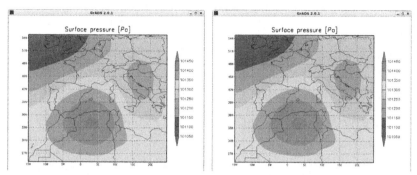

Figure 13 Surface pressure results after 500 time steps.

problem size ($160 \times 128 \times 32$) giving 93% efficiency compared to software. The larger problem size is due to constraints of memory alignment in the DFE imposed by the "bursty" nature of DDR memory: alignment of the problem size to an integer number of memory bursts (each 192 bytes) required the latitude size to be 128 rather than 120.

Figure 13 depicts the surface pressure result, after 500 time steps, obtained using the original software application (left) and the dataflow hardware accelerated solution (right). The isobars are similarly placed with small differences only visible for low values of pressure. These small differences arise from the changes we have made to the number representations for some parts of the dataflow, and were judged at an acceptable level.

The baroclinic condition generates vorticity, i.e., the curl of the velocity field. A contribution to the vorticity is given by advection (vortex tube moving with the flow), which has been implemented using single precision floating-point in the dataflow application. The advection is a critical contribution to the zonal and meridional velocities, which, unlike the surface pressure, have a high dynamic range.

Figure 14 shows the zonal wind component u after 500 time steps, both for software and hardware. It exhibits a high degree of agreement between software and hardware results, even for variables which are highly unstable and described by complex nonlinear differential equations.

7.10. Speedup

To accurately determine the speedup of the dataflow implementation, it is important to analyze the dynamic behavior of the parallel version of the software to understand how efficiently the software exploits a multicore node.

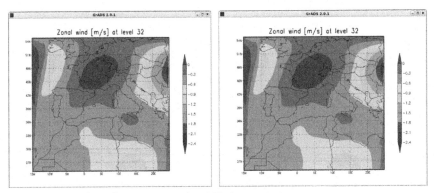

Figure 14 Zonal wind component after 500 time steps.

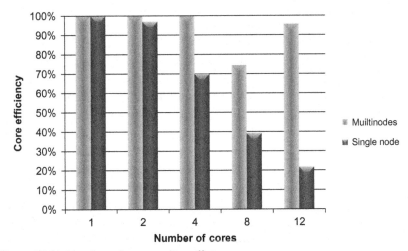

Figure 15 Multinode and -core scaling efficiency.

In this study, we define the "task" as an independent simulation of 5000 time steps.

The parallel software was run in two configurations: single node and multinode. For the single node measurements, we used two Intel Xeon X5650 @ 2.7 GHz six-core CPUs coupled to 192 GB DDR3 memory. For the multinode configuration, we used 12 nodes, each a dual Intel Xeon E5440 @ 2.8 GHz quad-core CPU with 24 GB DDR3 memory. All 12 nodes were connected through Infiniband.

As shown in Fig. 15 (purple (gray in the print version) bars), the software does not scale very well when using more than two cores. It struggles to extract more than 70% of the single-core capacity if four cores are in use.

This means that running with four cores gives only a speedup of 2.8 × compared to a single core. Using all 12 cores becomes less efficient than running with four cores as the efficiency drops to 22% and the speedup is only 2.6 ×. The highest speedup of 3.1 × is reached with 8 cores.

This lack of scalability is usually either due to memory bus contention or a consequence of the overhead of the interprocesses communication. To understand this problem, we eliminated the possible memory bottleneck by running a single task across multiple nodes, with only one core utilized on each. The multinode measurements are represented by the red (dark gray in the print version) bars in Fig. 15. We can see an efficiency of more of 95% when running on 12 nodes, equivalent to an 11.5 × speedup compared to a single node. This indicates that the MPI ghost region exchange (over infiniband) is not the bottleneck, costing very little in the efficiency of a single core. Investigation of the drop in core efficiency for the 8-node configuration shows that this behavior is caused by inefficient domain decomposition automatically produced by the software for the problem size we tested.

Previous results showed that the software is limited by the speed of the memory bus. To understand whether it is the memory bandwidth or the contention in accessing the same data that constitutes the bottleneck, we tested the performance of an Intel Xeon X5650 @ 2.7 GHz 12-core CPU node varying the number of independent tasks concurrently run. Figure 16 again shows the core efficiency for three cases: running tasks using a single core (blue (dark gray in the print version) bars); running tasks using

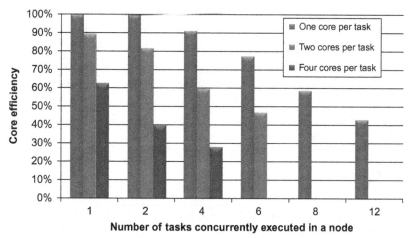

Figure 16 Multicore scaling with multiple concurrent tasks.

two cores each (green (light gray in the print version) bars); running tasks using four cores each (red (gray in the print version) bars).

As can be seen running 12 independent tasks reduces the efficiency of the single core to 43%. However, the speedup equivalent is 5.2 × that is the highest achieved by a single node. This is preferable to using all the cores of the node for fewer tasks. In the worst case, four tasks, each using four cores, return an efficiency of only 28% also in light to the fact that only 12 cores are available and sixteen processes present.

So far, we have compared relative efficiency of the parallel software version of the code as function of the number of cores, tasks, and nodes. In absolute terms, the task of 5000 time steps for a problem size of $160 \times 120 \times 32$ executes in an average of 960 s on a single Intel Xeon X5650 @ 2.7 GHz CPU core. To compare CPU-only node performance with dataflow node performance, we use the parallelization configuration for that node (i.e., number of independent tasks and processors per task) that provides the maximum overall throughput, and compare the throughputs achieved. The configuration that gives highest throughput for the software is the one reported by Fig. 16 with 12 tasks each using one core. The average execution time of each task was 2235 s. We ran the problem size $160 \times 128 \times 32$ on the DFE for 5000 time step iterations in 15.1 s. Exactly the same time was achieved with six tasks running concurrently. Since the computation is performed entirely within the DFE, there is no contention for the CPU resources of the MPC-C node. Table 1 shows the speedup measurements relative to the Intel Xeon X5650 @ 2.7 GHz architecture. We compare one DFE against one core, measuring 64 × performance speedup. We also compared the MPC-C node, containing six DFEs, against the 12-core Intel node. We obtained a speedup of 74 × compared to the fastest CPU solution.

Table 2 reports the speedup number in the optimal case of software running on many conventional nodes. In each node, only one core is used. One MPC-C node with six DFEs is 35 × faster than 12 conventional nodes.

Table 1 Performance speedup of a single DFE and an MPC-C node compared to Intel Westmere technology

	Intel Xeon X5650 @ 2.7 GHz	
Speedup	Core	Node (12 cores)
1 DFE	64 ×	12 ×
MPC-C node	381 ×	74 ×

Table 2 Performance speedup of a single DFE and an MPC-C node compared to the software running over several Intel Harpertown nodes

	Intel Xeon E5440 @ 2.8 GHz		
Speedup	1 Node	4 Nodes	12 Nodes
1 DFE	65 ×	16 ×	6 ×
MPC-C node	398 ×	99 ×	35 ×

As far as the operation cost is concerned, the advantage is clearly with the dataflow solution. Peak power usage of a MPC-C node was measured to be around 900 W. Considering a peak value of 400 W per Intel node, we need 74 12-core nodes and therefore around 30 kW to match the performance of the dataflow solution. The power necessary for a solution using many one-core nodes as for Table 2 would be even higher; although the power usage per node will be significantly lower than 400 W (less cores, idle cores, less memory per node), almost 400 single-core nodes are required to match the MPC-C speed, bringing the power requirement to values in excess of 40 kW.

8. CONCLUSION

Achieving challenging science goals in the coming years will require development of powerful computational technology at new levels of performance. However, building exascale computers by 2020 will be impossible within reasonable power budgets by simply scaling current CPU technology with silicon process.

Maxeler has pioneered a multidisciplinary approach to scientific computing that takes a team of natural and computer scientists and engineers all the way from the formulation of the computational problem down to design of the best possible computer architecture for its solution. Morphing the computer architecture, based on the problem it solves, is the fundamental concept of multiscale dataflow computing. The added complexity of choreographing the data movement and resolving data dependencies is well repaid by a great increase in computational speed and a considerable reduction in power consumption. The case study on a weather forecasting application described in this work shows how powerful a dataflow approach can be in comparison to conventional CPU technology.

REFERENCES

[1] H. Esmaeilzadeh, E. Blem, R.S. Amanat, K. Sankaralingam, D. Burger, Dark silicon and the end of multicore scaling, in: Proc. 37th International Symposium on Computer Architecture, ISCA 2011, 2011.

[2] Top 500 supercomputer types (http://www.top500.org) and the Green500 list (http://www.green500.org) accessed on 19 September 2013.

[3] O. Pell, O. Mencer, Surviving the end of frequency scaling with reconfigurable dataflow computing, HEART workshop, 2011.

[4] J.B. Dennis, Data flow supercomputers, Comput. Series 13 (1980) 48–56.

[5] W.J.C. Melis, P.Y.K. Cheung, W. Luk, Autonomous memory blocks for reconfigurable computing, in: IEEE International Symposium on Circuits and Systems, ISCAS'04, Vol. 2, 2004, pp. 581–584.

[6] A. Royal, P.Y.K. Cheung, Globally asynchronous locally synchronous FPGA architectures, in: 13th International Conference on Field-Programmable Logic and Applications, Berlin, Springer, Berlin, 2003, Lecture Notes in Computer Science,.

[7] T.S. Mak, P. Sedcole, P.Y.K. Cheung, W. Luk, On-FPGA communication architectures and design factors, in: 16th International Conference on Field Programmable Logic and Applications (August 2006), IEEE, 2006, pp. 1–8.

[8] A. Buzzi, M. Fantini, P. Malguzzi, F. Nerozzi, Validation of a limited area model in cases of Mediterranean cyclogenisis: surface fields and precipitation scores, Meteorol. Atmos. Phys. 53 (1994) 137–153.

[9] M. Marrocu, R. Scardovelli, P. Malguzzi, Parallelization and performance of a meteorological limited area model, Parallel Comput. 24 (1998) 911–922.

[10] P. Malguzzi, G. Grossi, A. Buzzi, R. Ranzi, R. Buizza, The 1966 "century" flood in Italy: a meteorological and hydrological revisitation, J. Geophys. Res. 111 (2006) D24106.

[11] B. Ritter, J.-F. Geleyn, A comprehensive radiation scheme for numerical weather prediction models with potential applications in climate solutions, Mon. Weather Rev. 120 (1992) 303–325.

[12] K.A. Emanuel, A scheme for representing cumulus convection in large scale models, J. Atoms. Sci. 48 (1991) 2313–2335.

[13] F. Mesinger, A. Arakawa, Numerical Methods Used in Atmospheric Models, Volume 1, WMO and ICSU, Geneva, 1976, GARP Publications Series No. 17.

[14] A. Asselin, Frequency filter for time integration, Mon. Weather Rev. 100 (1972) 487–490.

[15] P. Karlberg, Test of later boundary relaxation scheme in a barotropic model: Internal report No. 3, Res. Dept., ECMWF, 1977.

[16] D. Oriato, O. Pell, C. Andreoletti, N. Bienati, FD modeling beyond 70 hz with FPGA, SEG 2010 HPC Workshop.

[17] J.G. Charney, The dynamics of long waves in a baroclinic westerly current, J. Meteor. 4 (1947) 135–162.

ABOUT THE AUTHORS

Diego Oriato is a distinguished acceleration architect at Maxeler Technologies and a high-performance computing expert. Prior to joining Maxeler, he was a Java developer and performance developer at the IBM Hursley Labs in UK. He holds a bachelor degree in Electronics and a PhD in Physics.

Stephen Girdlestone is a distinguished acceleration architect at Maxeler Technologies and algorithm expert. He has a PhD in Maths from Imperial College London.

Prior to founding Maxeler, Oskar was Member of Technical Staff at the Computing Sciences Center at Bell Labs in Murray Hill, leading the effort in "Stream Computing". He joined Bell Labs after receiving a PhD from Stanford University. Oskar was Consulting Professor in Geophysics at Stanford University and he is also affiliated with the Computing Department at Imperial College London.

CHAPTER FOUR

Sorting Networks on Maxeler Dataflow Supercomputing Systems

Anton Kos*, Vukašin Ranković†, Sašo Tomažič*
*Faculty of Electrical Engineering, University of Ljubljana, Ljubljana, Slovenia
†School of Electrical Engineering, University of Belgrade, Belgrade, Serbia

Contents

Abstract

The primary contribution of this study is the implementation and evaluation of network sorting algorithms on a Maxeler dataflow computer. Sorting is extensively used in

Advances in Computers, Volume 96
ISSN 0065-2458
http://dx.doi.org/10.1016/bs.adcom.2014.10.001

139

numerous applications. We discuss sequential, parallel, and network sorting algorithms. The major part of this study is dedicated to the properties, construction, and testing of sorting networks. We introduce and compare principal network sorting algorithms with predominant sequential and parallel sorting algorithms. We implement network sorting algorithms in an entry model of the Maxeler dataflow supercomputing system. The goal of our study is to compare the sorting times of network sorting algorithms using a Maxeler dataflow computer with the sorting times of optimal sequential and parallel sorting algorithms using a control flow computer. In different testing scenarios, we demonstrate that high sorting speedups can be achieved with network sorting using a Maxeler dataflow computer. We sorted arrays of 128 values. Using different testing parameters, we achieved speedups that ranged from approximately 10 to more than 200. Sorting networks that execute parallel sorting using the dataflow computational paradigm offer a possible solution for expanding volumes of data. By converting to more advanced Maxeler systems and researching new ideas and solutions, we aim to sort large arrays and achieve large speedups.

ABBREVIATIONS
BRAM block random access memory
CPU central processing unit
FF flip flop
FPGA field programmable gate array
LUT lookup table
PC personal computer

1. INTRODUCTION

Sorting is a critical operation in the realm of computer systems. According to Ref. [1], sorting accounts for approximately one-quarter of the total running time on computer systems and approximately one-half of the running time in some cases. These estimated figures suggest that (a) sorting is employed in numerous applications, (b) sorting is not always necessary, or (c) inefficient sorting algorithms are prevalent. Therefore, a constant quest for improved sorting algorithms and their proper use and practical implementation is necessary.

In numerous application domains, sorting is an indispensable part of applications with or without the knowledge of users. A common example is searching for information on the Internet, in which search algorithms work with sorted data; a natural method to present search results is an ordered list of items that matches the search criteria [2].

The majority of applications and computer systems employ well-studied comparison-based sequential sorting algorithms [3]. Parallel processing and the use of parallel sorting algorithms enable speedups. Parallelization is commonly achieved with the use of *multi-core* or *many-core* systems, which can produce speedups that are approximately proportional to the number of cores. A new paradigm termed *dataflow computing* has re-emerged and is being successfully employed in numerous computationally intensive application domains. Dataflow computing offers immense parallelism by utilizing thousands of tiny simple computational elements to improve the performance by orders of magnitude.

The exponential increase in data volumes demands faster communication networks and high-speed computing [4]; thus, it is a driving force for the search for efficient, faster, and parallelized computer algorithms [5]. Due to rapidly increasing data volumes, sorting algorithms face similar challenges. Although the field of sorting algorithms has been well studied during the entire era of computer science, new technologies, new paradigms, and new applications are constantly reshaping the demands and conditions for sorting algorithms. Algorithms that previously were impractical or inadequate have re-emerged with the development of new technologies.

This chapter is organized in the following manner. In Section 2, we present the motivation for this study, which defines the framework for our ideas, experiments, and results. In Section 3, we provide a short tutorial on sorting algorithms and include several tables and graphs for their classification and comparison, with a special emphasis on network sorting algorithms. Section 4 addresses sorting networks, which is the theoretical core of this study. We present the basic properties, construction, algorithms, operating examples, and comparisons of sorting networks. In Section 5, we explain the implementation of the sorting networks on the dataflow computer. In Section 6, we define our experimental setup. Section 7, which is extensive, is dedicated to the presentation of our experimental results. Finally, we present the conclusions of this study in Section 8.

2. MOTIVATION

The primary motivation of this study is to investigate the potential use of a dataflow computing paradigm for sorting algorithms and their implementation on a dataflow computer. This study requires that several tasks to be performed in different fields of computing.

We had the opportunity to use the Maxeler MAX2 card, which is an entry model of the Maxeler dataflow supercomputing systems. The MAX2 card is considered to be an field programmable gate array (FPGA) hardware accelerator. Although the performance of our dataflow computer is positioned at the low end of the Maxeler product portfolio, its application development environment (MaxCompiler) is equivalent to the application development environment of advanced models of Maxeler systems. The applications developed and the skills mastered on any of the Maxeler systems are employable and reusable throughout its product portfolio. The attractiveness of Maxeler systems is also demonstrated by its MaxCompiler, which eases application development. The application for a Maxeler system is written in (a) C code that runs on the host system (control flow computer) and (b) kernel Java code that is compiled and executed on a MAX2 card (dataflow computer) but launched from the C code on the host. MaxCompiler is responsible for the integration of both types of codes. A detailed explanation of the implementation and the development of the application, which is sorting in our case, are provided in Section 5.

In this study, we have identified sorting networks as a suitable sorting method for dataflow computers. Our objective is to explore the adaptability of the FPGA-based dataflow computer and its development environment for the implementation of sorting network algorithms. We focus on exploitation of the dataflow computer parallelism. We do not intend to implement parallel sorting algorithms on control flow computers to directly compare the results with network sorting algorithms on a dataflow computer; this lies beyond the scope of this work. However, we will compare both sets of algorithms using a theoretical analysis (refer to Section 4.7).

An additional objective of our study is to compare the performance of the automated and generalized FPGA programming performed by MaxCompiler with the more conventional methods of custom programming in standard hardware description languages.

An interesting fact that has significantly contributed to our motivation is that dataflow computing and sorting networks are both more than half a century old. At the time of their discovery, their implementation was impossible or impractical. With the emergence of new technologies, they may soon re-appear and outperform contemporary prevailing computing paradigms and sorting algorithms.

Therefore, our study focuses on the advantages and benefits of network sorting algorithms and dataflow computing. Network sorting and dataflow computing are a natural match; by combining them, we expect large sorting speedups.

3. SORTING ALGORITHMS

Sorting algorithms have been extensively investigated during the entire era of computer science. Numerous different approaches have been utilized and an immense number of sorting algorithms have been developed and analyzed.

Sorting algorithms can be classified based on different criteria, such as computational complexity (best, average, and worst), memory usage, stability, general sorting method (insertion, selection, merging, exchange, and partitioning), and whether they involve comparison sorting [6]. Because the detailed study of all sorting algorithms is not the focus of this chapter, we will concentrate only on comparison-based sorting algorithms. The most popular sorting algorithms and network sorting algorithms are members of this group.

Comparison-based sorting algorithms examine data by repeatedly comparing two elements from an unsorted list with a comparison operator, which defines their order in the final sorted list. In this chapter, we classify comparison-based sorting algorithms into three groups based on the time order of the execution of comparison operations, as follows:

- *sequential sorting algorithms* consecutively execute the comparison operations;

- *parallel sorting algorithms* simultaneously execute several comparison operations; and

- *network sorting algorithms* are parallel algorithms; they exhibit the property in which the sequence of comparison operations is identical for all possible input data.

In a particular comparison-based sorting algorithm, one or more versions belong to one or more of these groups. For example, *merge sort* can be sequentially executed; it has its parallel version and can be implemented as a network sorting algorithm. Each of the previously mentioned implementations requires some modifications of the algorithm. Typically, the sequential versions of the algorithm require the least comparison operations; the parallel version may use additional comparisons but is faster due to parallel execution; and the network version is inferior to both versions in the number of comparisons but is faster than the parallel version when implemented using specialized hardware.

3.1. Sequential Sorting

A plethora of comparison-based sequential sorting algorithms and their versions have been developed. Comparison-based sequential sorting algorithms

Table 1 Properties of the Most Popular Comparison-Based Sorting Algorithms Sorting Time—$O(x)$ Notation

Algorithm	Average	Best	Worst
Insertion sort	N^2	N	N^2
Selection sort	N^2	N^2	N^2
Bubble sort	N^2	N	N^2
Shell sort	$N \cdot (\log_2 N)^2$	N	$N \cdot (\log_2 N)^2$
Quicksort	$N \cdot \log_2 N$	$N \cdot \log_2 N$	N^2
Merge sort	$N \cdot \log_2 N$	$N \cdot \log_2 N$	$N \cdot \log_2 N$
Heap sort	$N \cdot \log_2 N$	$N \cdot \log_2 N$	$N \cdot \log_2 N$
Binary tree sort	$N \cdot \log_2 N$	N	$N \cdot \log_2 N$

Columns show the average, the best, and the worst sorting times in $O(x)$ notation of each algorithm, where N represents the number of items to be sorted. For some algorithms, the sorting time is also dependent on the configuration of input data, which may be random, partially sorted, and sorted in reverse order.

require a minimum of the time proportional to $O(N \cdot \log_2 N)$ on average [1], where N is the number of items to be sorted.

The properties of prevalent comparison-based sorting algorithms are summarized in Table 1. The average, the best, and the worst sorting times vary considerably among algorithms. The best sorting time is highly dependent on the configuration of the input data. For example, an insertion sort has the average and the worst sorting time of $O(N^2)$; however, with nearly sorted input data, it requires only $O(N + d)$ operations, where d is the number of required inversions. Quicksort has the average and the best sorting time of $O(N \cdot \log_2 N)$; however, in some special cases, it encounters problems with the nearly sorted input data with the worst sorting time of $O(N^2)$ [2].

The best choices are quicksort, merge sort, heap sort, and binary tree sort. Quicksort should be avoided because its worst sorting time in some rare cases is $O(N^2)$. If a favorable configuration of data is expected (nearly sorted, for example), the best choice may be one of the algorithms with a sorting time that is linearly proportional to N (insertion, bubble, binary tree, and shell sort). The selection of the best sorting algorithm is a challenging task that is dependent on the expected input data.

3.1.1 Optimal Algorithm for Small Input Data Sizes

Table 1 summarizes the sorting times of algorithms in big-O notation, which presents the order of change (growth rate) for sorting time in terms of the

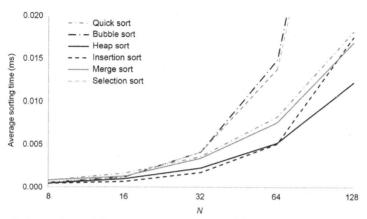

Figure 1 Comparison of the average sorting times for the most popular sequential sorting algorithms. Sorting times are expressed in terms of the input data size N. The results are obtained by running the algorithms written in C code on a PC. We observe that for small values of N, the $O(N^2)$ insertion sort algorithm is the fastest; however, with the growing value of N, all $O(N \cdot \log_2 N)$ algorithms become faster.

change of input array size. Several algorithms contain an identical expression. This finding does not signify that the actual sorting times are also equivalent. The big-O notation does not include a constant of an algorithm; for example, the expression $O(C \cdot N)$ is written as $O(N)$.

In real implementations of sorting algorithms, the constant C will vary across different algorithms. When comparing sorting algorithms of identical order, the sorting algorithms with a lower constant C will exhibit shorter sorting times for all possible input data. How do the sorting times compare for algorithms of different orders? Can an algorithm of the order $O(N^2)$ with a small constant C_1 be faster than an algorithm of the order $O(N \cdot \log_2 N)$ with a large constant C_2? If the ratio C_2/C_1 is not large, this statement is true for small values of N. We have measured the average sorting times for some of the most popular sequential sorting algorithms from Table 1 for small values of N. The results presented in Fig. 1 indicate that the insertion sort, which is an $O(N^2)$ algorithm, has a lower constant C than all measured $O(N \cdot \log_2 N)$ algorithms, which makes it faster for small values of N. This result is important for subsequent comparisons with network sorting algorithms, which are currently implemented for only small input data sizes.

3.2. Parallel Sorting

Several of the aforementioned sequential sorting algorithms also have parallel versions. Ideally, parallelization that uses N processors would decrease the sorting times summarized in Table 1 by the factor N.

The parallelization of sorting algorithms can be implemented using *multi-core* and *many-core* processors [7]. These terms commonly refer to microprocessors with more than one core that are produced on the same integrated circuit (die). Generally, the term *multi-core* refers to processors with a maximum of 20 cores, whereas the term *many-core* refers to processors with a few tens or even hundreds of cores [8]. In most practical cases, this approach is not optimal. For a true parallel sorting, this type of system requires the number of cores in the order of the number of items to be sorted (N). For the majority of applications, N grows into thousands and millions of items to be sorted.

Comparison-based sorting algorithms are computationally undemanding because the computational operations comprise simple comparisons between two items. To sort a set of N items, we require a set of N basic computational cores, which are primarily designed to perform the mathematical operation of comparison. Additionally, these computational cores require some control logic to execute a specific sort algorithm.

If we expand this consideration, we can simplify the computational cores by removing the control logic and implementing the sorting algorithm control and logic into the core interconnections. In this scenario, computational cores perform only the comparisons. In this step, we leave the world of control flow computing and enter the world of dataflow computing. Let us briefly illustrate the major differences between control flow and dataflow:

- *Control flow* focuses on the processes and operations that are required to complete them. Data enter and exit the process on an as-needed basis. For example, when the process requires some data, it is read from the memory. The process uses the data in the defined manner, possibly transforms it, and the results are written back to the memory when needed. The process flow can be significantly influenced by the intermediate results and used data.
- *Dataflow* focuses on data streams. Streams originate from the data source(s) and are passed to the destination(s) through the dataflow computer using (predefined) data paths between the components that transform the passing data. The process can be modeled as a directed graph of the data that flows between operations.

In comparison-based sorting algorithms, the computational cores in the control flow computer determine where to obtain the data, read the data, compare the data, and write the results (back) to memory. In the final step of the algorithm, the sorted data resides in a certain memory location. In dataflow computers, the stream of unsorted data is passed to the computer, where it is sorted by transpositions on their path to the destination. The source and the destination can include any type of memory or data streams, which comprise inputs/outputs to internal or external processes.

The following two questions arise. Do dataflow computers exist? Do suitable sorting algorithms for dataflow computers exist? Positive answers will be comprehensively discussed in the following sections. First, let us briefly discuss the appropriate comparison-based sorting algorithms.

Dataflow computing is a suitable match for parallel sorting algorithms due to the potential for executing thousands of operations in parallel. Each operation is executed inside a simple dedicated computational core. The only limitation is the absence of control over the sorting process in terms of intermediate results, which indicates that the sequence of operations in the sorting process must be defined in advance. This fact prevents the direct use of algorithms from Table 1 because they are designed for control flow computers. Thus, these algorithms determine the order of item comparisons based on the results of previous comparisons. A possible solution is the adaptation of these sorting algorithms in a manner that ensures their conformance to dataflow principles. For example, if we can assure that the parallel sorting algorithm can be modeled as a directed graph, the sorting process conforms to the dataflow paradigm. In the following section, we demonstrate that these parallel sorting algorithms exist.

3.3. Network Sorting

In the middle of the twentieth century, several researchers extensively examined *sorting networks* that employ an *oblivious* comparison-based algorithm, in which the sequence of performed comparisons is identical for all possible inputs of any given size. Sorting networks are interesting because their structure is fixed. However, until recently, sorting networks had no practical implementation due to technological limitations. A detailed explanation of sorting networks is provided in the following section.

Network sorting algorithms are parallel sorting algorithms with a fixed structure. Several network sorting algorithms have evolved from the parallel versions of comparison-based sorting algorithms and use identical sorting methods (insertion, selection, and merging). The structure of sorting networks must form a directed graph, which ensures that the output is always sorted regardless of the configuration of the input data. Due to this constraint, network sorting algorithms that are derived from parallel sorting algorithms generally perform some redundant operations. This finding makes these algorithms inferior to their originating parallel sorting algorithms in the number of operations (comparisons) that they must perform.

Theoretically, the number of sequential operations or comparisons for the quicksort sorting algorithm is on the order of $O(N \cdot \log_2 N)$ and on the order of $O(N \cdot (\log_2 N)^2)$ for the network version of bitonic merge sorting [1–3,9]; that is, theoretically, the quicksort algorithm is superior to the bitonic merge algorithm by a factor of $\log_2 N$.

Because network sorting algorithms conform to the dataflow paradigm, they do not impose a computational overhead, which indicates that process control is not required; i.e., deciding what items must be compared next is dependent on the previous operation results. Thus, the network version of bitonic merge sorting has the small algorithm constant C_B. Quicksort decisions are highly dependent on the results of previous operations; thus, quicksort has a large algorithm constant C_Q. Therefore, considering only the algorithm constants, bitonic merge is superior to quicksort by the factor $\alpha = C_B / C_Q$.

Considering the algorithm constants, the number of operations for the quicksort algorithm is on the order of $O(C_Q \cdot N \cdot \log_2 N)$ and on the order of $O(C_B \cdot N \cdot (\log_2 N)^2)$ for the bitonic merge algorithm, which yields the ratio $C_B \cdot \log_2 N / C_Q$ or $\log_2 N / \alpha$. For small N values, $\log_2 N < \alpha$, the quicksort algorithm becomes slower than the bitonic algorithm. For large N values, $\log_2 N > \alpha$, the quicksort algorithm becomes faster than the bitonic algorithm. This consideration is presented in Fig. 2, which shows the sorting times of the quicksort algorithm and the network version of the bitonic merge sorting algorithm. Both results are obtained by sequential computation (no parallelism is employed) on a personal computer (PC) using the algorithm written in C code.

We have performed a similar comparison for the most popular sequential sorting algorithms and the most popular network sorting algorithms, and these results are shown in Fig. 3. Let us emphasize that all results for all algorithms are obtained by sequential computation. For smaller values of N, network sorting algorithms outperform all sequential sorting algorithms. When N increases, the higher order computational complexity of network algorithms prevails over algorithm constants, and sequential algorithms become faster.

The practical network sorting algorithms contain a number of comparisons on the order of $O(N \cdot (\log_2 N)^2)$ and the best comparison-based sorting algorithms on the order of $O(N \cdot \log_2 N)$. The following question arises: how can we expect that network sorting will outperform sequential

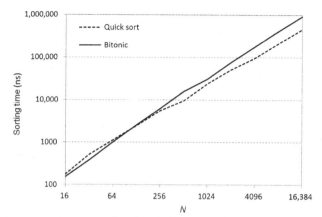

Figure 2 Comparison of the sorting times for the sequential computation of the quicksort sorting algorithm and the network version of the bitonic merge sorting algorithm in terms of the number of items being sorted (N). The results are obtained by the sequential computation of both algorithms on a PC using C code. We observe that for $N < 256$, the bitonic algorithm performs faster due to the smaller algorithm constant C (refer to a detailed explanation in the text).

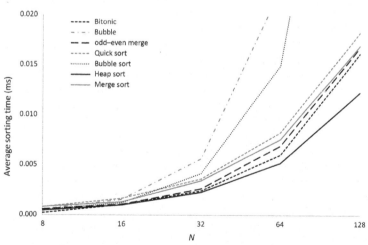

Figure 3 Comparison of the average sorting times between the popular sequential sorting algorithms (solid lines) and the network sorting algorithms (dashed lines). The sorting times are provided in terms of the input data size N. The results are obtained by sequential computation of all algorithms on a PC using C code. As observed in Fig. 2, network sorting algorithms perform better for small values of N and worse for large values of N when compared with sequential algorithms.

comparison-based sorting for larger values of N? If we exploit parallelism, would it reduce the computational time by an identical factor (the number of computational cores) and would the performance ratio remain unchanged? The answer is dependent on the change of computational paradigm and moves to the domain of dataflow computing. Let us illustrate this situation using an example.

For a true parallel execution of a sorting algorithm, we require N computational cores. The sorting times for this parallel algorithm are on the order of $O(N \cdot \log_2 N)$ for classical algorithms (e.g., quicksort) and $O((\log_2 N)^2)$ for network algorithms. Let us assume that the best parallel control flow system has a maximum of P computational cores. With an increasing N, we will reach the point where $N > P$, and the sorting times of classical parallel algorithms will be on the order of $O(N \cdot \log_2 N)/P$; the sorting times increase faster than linearly and the algorithm is no longer truly parallel. Because this situation is not desirable, the sorting should move to the dataflow computers that can ensure a sufficient number of cores for a true parallel execution.

Because the best classical sorting algorithms are not suitable for dataflow computers, we must employ network sorting algorithms. In the following sections, we provide a short tutorial on network sorting algorithms and subsequently compare the fastest sequential sort algorithms on the control flow computer with the implementation of the best practical network sorting algorithms on the dataflow computer.

4. SORTING NETWORKS

Sorting networks, which are a subset of comparison networks, are abstract machines that are solely constructed of wires and comparators. In comparison networks, the wires that interconnect comparators must form a directed acyclic graph [3].

A sorting network is a comparison network with wires and comparators that are connected in a manner to perform the function of sorting their input data. The input to a sorting network is an array of items in an arbitrary order, whereas the output of a sorting network always consists of a sorted array of items.

4.1. Basic Properties

The basic building blocks of a sorting network are shown in Fig. 4. The values to be sorted are present on the input ports that enter the comparator and are sorted on its output ports; the higher value exists on the bottom port, and the lower value exists on the top port. We assume that each comparator works in $O(1)$ time.

By connecting additional comparators, we can construct a sorting network. Generally, we construct a sorting network for N items as a set of N parallel horizontal lines that are connected by vertical lines, which represent comparators. The items to be sorted enter the network on the left and are passed to the right through the network. A pair of items is exchanged, if necessary, each time a comparator is encountered. The sorted items exit the network on the right. A simple example of a network that sorts four values is depicted in Fig. 5. The first comparator does not exchange values, whereas the other comparators do exchange values.

A sorting network can be characterized by its size and depth. The *size* of a sorting network is defined by the total number of comparators in the network. The *depth* of the sorting network is defined as the maximum number

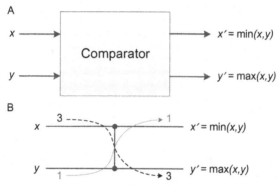

Figure 4 A comparator with two input ports (x, y) and two output ports (x', y') that performs the functions $x' = \min(x, y)$ and $y' = \min(x, y)$. Representation (A) is not practical for larger networks; therefore, we use representation (B), in which the comparator box is replaced by a vertical line connecting the ports.

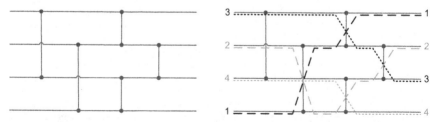

Figure 5 An example of a simple sorting network with four wires and five comparators. Each comparator connects two wires. Two comparators on the left-hand side and two comparators in the middle can work in parallel. The parallel operation of this sorting network sorts the input numbers in three steps.

of comparators along any valid path from any input to output. For example, the sorting network in Fig. 5 has a size of 5 and a depth of 3, whereas the sorting networks in Fig. 7 have a size of 15 and a depth of 9.

4.2. Constructing Sorting Networks

Although construction of an efficient sorting network is not a simple task, the construction of a simple, nonoptimal sorting network is straightforward. A general principle is provided in Fig. 6 [1]. Assuming that we already have a working N-port sorting network, we can readily construct an $(N+1)$-port sorting network.

For example, when we begin with $N=2$, only one comparator is necessary to represent our 2-port sorting network. Next, we construct a 3-port network using our 2-port sorting network (comparator) and add two additional comparators using one of the principles in Fig. 6. By repeating this process, we can construct sorting networks of any size.

Both versions of a 6-port sorting network are shown in Fig. 7. As we will demonstrate in a subsequent section, a network that is constructed using the principles in Figs. 6 and 7 is not optimal; however, it has a straightforward structure and correctly sorts all possible inputs.

An efficient sorting network can be constructed using a divide-and-conquer principle. We briefly explain it here; details are provided in Ref. [3]. Our goal is to construct a block named *Sorter [N]*, which represents our sorting network and sorts an arbitrary sequence of N values; refer to structure (A) in Fig. 8.

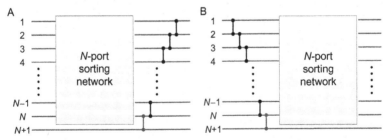

Figure 6 Construction of an $(N+1)$-port sorting network from an N-port sorting network using the principle of insertion (A) and selection (B). In (A), inputs from 1 to N are sorted by the existing N-port sorting network. Input $N+1$ is subsequently inserted into the sorted output of the N-port sorting network by additional N comparators that work in series and propagate the inserted value to its proper position. Similarly, the N comparators on the input side in (B) work in series and ensure that the highest value of all $N+1$ inputs is selected and propagated to the bottom port. The remainder of the values on the ports from 1 to N are sorted by the N-port sorting network.

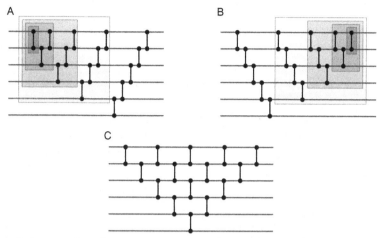

Figure 7 Construction of a 6-port sorting network using the insertion (A) and selection (B) principles. We begin with the comparator (2-port sorting network) boxed in dark gray. We subsequently work down to a 6-port sorting network, in which each construction step is depicted in a lighter shade of gray. When we allow the nonoverlapping comparators to work in parallel, networks (A) and (B) become identical and are represented in (C), which is the network version of the bubble sort and is described in Section 4.4.1.

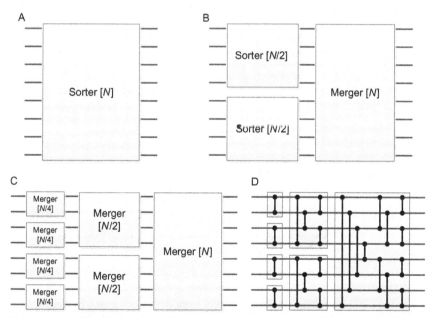

Figure 8 An efficient 8-port sorting network that is constructed using a divide-and-conquer principle. The Sorter [N] block in (A) is replaced by two Sorter [N/2] blocks that produce two sequences of N/2 values, which are merged by a Merger [N] block (B). By unrolling the recursion, we obtain a structure of mergers (C). Replacing each of the merger blocks with the corresponding merging networks yields a final sorting network (D). The constructed sorting network has a size of 24 and a depth of 6.

Let us assume that we can construct a block with N inputs and N outputs with the following property: if we bring two previously sorted sequences of $N/2$ values to its inputs, the block will merge the two sequences into a sorted sequence of N values on its outputs. We denote this block as *Merger [N]*. To produce the two sorted sequences of $N/2$ values for the Merger [N] inputs, we can use two $(N/2)$-port sorting networks that are presented by two Sorter [N/2] blocks; refer to structure (B) in Fig. 8. We first replace the Sorter [N] block by two Sorter [N/2] blocks and one Merger [N] block. Subsequently, we replace each of the Sorter [N/2] blocks by two Sorter [N/4] blocks and one Merger [N/2] block. We repeat this recursive division process until the point at which we would use the Sorter [1] block, which comprises a single value (wire) that does not require sorting. The result of this recursive process is a structure of mergers; refer to structure (C) in Fig. 8. The final step of the sorting network construction is the replacement of the merger boxes by actual merging networks. An example is shown in structure (D) in Fig. 8.

4.3. Testing Sorting Networks

Although it is straightforward to show that a sorting network constructed by the previously described process correctly sorts all possible inputs, this task is challenging for sorting networks with more complicated layouts. The *zero-one principle*, which is proven in Ref. [1], states that if a network with N inputs sorts all 2^N possible sequences of zeroes and ones $\{0,1\}$ in nondecreasing order, it will sort any arbitrary sequence of N numbers into a nondecreasing order.

4.4. Network Sorting Algorithms

For a given array of N values, several different sorting networks can be constructed. In addition to the two conventional construction methods presented in Section 4.2, other methods yield different network layouts with different properties. In the construction process, the primary goal can be a minimum-comparison network (minimum size) or a minimum-time network (minimum depth). The first network is a sorting network with the least number of comparators, and the second network is a sorting network that sorts an array of N values in the least amount of time. For the minimum-time sorting network, we assume that all nonoverlapping comparisons are conducted in parallel.

In Ref. [1], several comparators or time-efficient networks for different N are presented. Although it is possible to obtain these networks, proving their validity is challenging. Moreover, each sorting network possesses a different layout that does not follow any pattern or rule [1]. The construction process for these sorting networks can be time consuming.

Our objective is to automatically construct an (efficient) sorting network for any given N. We use a well-known sequential sorting algorithm that can be parallelized and attempt to map it into a sorting network layout. In the following sections, we present common network sorting algorithms. Each algorithm has its origin in sequential sorting algorithms, can be automatically constructed for any given N, and can be compared with their sequential counterpart.

Algorithms that are constructed through a recursive process, such as the algorithm presented in Section 4.2, are the most efficient (size and timewise) and can be automatically constructed when N is a power of 2. Therefore, in all examples, including the sorting networks without this constraint, we will use $N = 2^n$, where $n \in \{1, 2, 3, \ldots\}$.

4.4.1 Bubble Sorting

The network version of bubble sorting is shown in Fig. 9. Although this network exhibits poor efficiency, its construction is simple and straightforward, and its validity is readily proven [1]. A bubble sorting network has a depth $D(N)$ on the order of $O(N)$ and a size $C(N)$ on the order of $O(N^2)$. The exact values are as follows:

$$D_{\text{bubble}}(N) = 2N - 3 \tag{1}$$

$$D_{\text{bubble}}(N) = \frac{N(N-1)}{2} \tag{2}$$

4.4.2 Odd–Even Sorting

Comparators in an odd–even sorting network are organized in a brick-like structure, as shown in Fig. 10. The efficiency of an odd–even sorting network is better than a bubble sorting network. It has a depth $D(N)$ on the order of $O(N)$ and a size $C(N)$ on the order of $O(N^2)$, with the following exact values:

$$D_{\text{odd-even}}(N) = N \tag{3}$$

$$C_{\text{odd-even}}(N) = \frac{N(N-1)}{2} \tag{4}$$

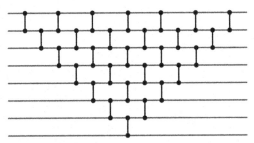

Figure 9 An example of a bubble sorting network with eight inputs ($N=8$), a depth of 13, and a size of 28; refer to Eqs. (1) and (2).

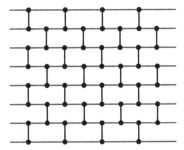

Figure 10 An example of an odd–even sorting network with eight inputs ($N=8$), a depth of 8, and a size of 28; refer to Eqs. (3) and (4).

By comparing the operation of bubble and odd–even sorting networks, we observe that the bubble sorting network will propagate the highest value to the bottom wire and the lowest value to the top wire, whereas the odd–even sorting network simultaneously performs both operations. We also observe that both networks are identical in size; however, the depth of the bubble sorting network is nearly two times the depth of the odd–even sorting network.

4.4.3 Bitonic Merge Sorting

The bitonic merge sorting network was proposed by K.E. Batcher in 1983 [9] and is one of the fastest sorting networks. The depth $D(N)$ of this sorting network is on the order of $O((\log_2 N)^2)$, and the size $C(N)$ is on the order of $O(N \cdot (\log_2 N)^2)$ [9], with the following exact values:

$$D_{\text{biotonic}}(N) = \frac{\log_2 N \cdot (\log_2 N + 1)}{2} \tag{5}$$

$$C_{\text{biotonic}}(N) = \frac{N \cdot \log_2 N \cdot (\log_2 N + 1)}{4} \tag{6}$$

A bitonic sorting network is constructed based on a divide-and-conquer principle; it divides all inputs into pairs and sorts each pair into a bitonic sequence. A bitonic sequence has the following property: $x_1 \leq \cdots \leq x_k \geq \cdots \geq x_N$ for some $k(1 \leq k < N)$. Next, this sorting network performs a merge sort of the adjacent bitonic sequences and repeats the process through all stages until the entire sequence is sorted. Figure 11 depicts an implementation of a simple bitonic merge sorting network for $N = 8$. This process and the algorithm are detailed in Refs. [1–3,6,7,9–12,18].

4.4.4 Odd–Even Merge Sorting

As for the bitonic sorting network, the odd–even merge sorting network was also proposed by K. E. Batcher [9]. The depth $D(N)$ of this sorting network is on the order of $O((\log_2 N)^2)$, and the size $C(N)$ is on the order of $O(N(\log_2 N)^2)$ [9], with the following exact values:

$$D_{\text{merge}}(N) = \frac{\log_2 N \cdot (\log_2 N + 1)}{2} \tag{7}$$

$$C_{\text{merge}}(N) = \frac{N \cdot \log_2 N \cdot (\log_2 N - 1)}{4} + N - 1 \tag{8}$$

An implementation of a simple odd–even merge sorting network for $N = 8$ is shown in Fig. 12. This process and the algorithm are detailed in Refs. [1–3,6,7,9–12].

The operation of an odd–even merge sorting network is similar to the operation of the bitonic sorting network. The major difference is that an

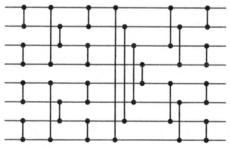

Figure 11 An example of a bitonic merge sorting network with eight inputs ($N = 8$), a depth of 6, and a size of 24; refer to Eqs. (5) and (6).

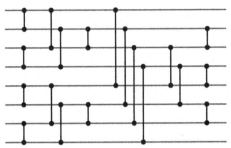

Figure 12 An example of an odd–even merge sorting network with eight inputs ($N=8$), a depth of 6, and a size of 19; refer to Eqs. (7) and (8).

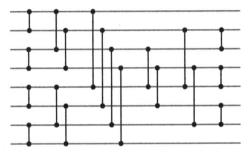

Figure 13 An example of a pairwise sorting network with $N=8$, a depth of 6, and a size of 19.

odd–even merge sorting network uses monotonic subsequences rather than bitonic subsequences in bitonic network sorting.

The properties of the bitonic and odd–even merge sorting networks are similar, with a slight advantage of the latter in the network size. However, the bitonic sorting network is more popular for implementation primarily due to the constant number of comparators in each stage.

4.4.5 Pairwise Sorting

The pairwise sorting network is similar to the odd–even merging network with an equivalent depth $D(N)$ and size $C(N)$ on the order of $O(N(\log_2 N)^2)$. This sorting network was devised by Parberry [13]. The implementation of a pairwise sorting network for $N=8$ is shown in Fig. 13.

4.5. Comparison of Network Sorting Algorithms

Because all sorting networks consist of only comparators and wires, the measures or properties by which we can describe and compare their efficiency can be defined. These two properties consist of the *depth* and the *size*. Both measures have been defined in Section 4.1. Assuming that all comparisons

Table 2 Properties of Network Sorting Algorithms

Sorting Network	Depth	Size
Bubble	$2N-3$	$\dfrac{N(N-1)}{2}$
Odd–even	N	$\dfrac{N(N-1)}{2}$
Bitonic	$\dfrac{\log_2 N \cdot (\log_2 N + 1)}{2}$	$\dfrac{N \cdot \log_2 N \cdot (\log_2 N + 1)}{4}$
Odd–even merge	$\dfrac{\log_2 N \cdot (\log_2 N + 1)}{2}$	$\dfrac{N \cdot \log_2 N \cdot (\log_2 N - 1)}{4} + N - 1$
Pairwise	$\dfrac{\log_2 N \cdot (\log_2 N + 1)}{2}$	$\dfrac{N \cdot \log_2 N \cdot (\log_2 N - 1)}{4} + N - 1$

The depth and the number of comparators for each algorithm, where N is the number of items to be sorted, are summarized.

on each level of the sorting network are performed in parallel, the depth of the network defines the number of steps required to sort N numbers as inputs and the time required to sort the input. The size of the sorting network indicates how many comparisons (and, thus, the number of comparators) are required to construct a sorting network. For example, the size defines the required chip area in hardware implementations.

In the previous section, the most efficient sorting networks have a size on the order of $O(N(\log_2 N)^2)$ and a depth on the order of $O((\log_2 N)^2)$ [2]. Faster variants of sorting networks have been described; however, they have proven to be impractical [14]. Table 2 summarizes the presented network sorting algorithms and their properties.

Based on the properties of the network sorting algorithms in Table 2, we conclude that although the bubble and odd–even algorithms are the simplest algorithms to construct, these algorithms are inferior in all other properties. The remaining algorithms possess identical depths but vary in their size. Although the size of a bitonic network is larger than the size of the odd–even merge and pairwise network, its constant number of comparators at each stage can represent an advantage in certain applications. If the latter is not important, then the best choice would be an odd–even or a pairwise sorting network.

4.6. Network Sorting Algorithm Operation Example

Let us present an example of the sorting process for the odd–even merge sorting network from Section 4.4.4. The sorting network and the sorting process are shown in Fig. 14. The sorting process encompasses three stages,

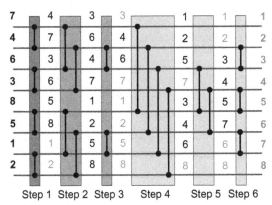

Step 1 Step 2 Step 3   Step 4   Step 5 Step 6

Figure 14 An example of a sorting process in an odd–even merge sorting network. The network has eight inputs $N = 8$, a depth of 6, and a size of 19. If we place an array of numbers in random order on the inputs of the sorting network (red (dark gray in the print version) numbers on the left-hand side of the network), they are sorted on its outputs after the sorting process is completed (green (light gray in the print version) numbers on the right-hand side of the network). The sorting process undergoes three stages (shown in different colors (shades of gray in the print version)) and includes six steps (shown as rectangles). One or more comparators sort the pairs of numbers in parallel in each step, whereas the intermediate results are shown between each step. Numbers that were swapped by the comparator are shown in black; numbers that were not swapped are shown in gray.

which are defined by the construction of the sorting algorithm (refer to Section 4.2). The stages are shown in different colors. The depth of the network is six; thus, the process sorts the numbers in six steps with parallel operation for all comparators of each step. The odd–even merge sorting network contains a different number of comparators in each step. The unsorted array of eight numbers (shown in red (dark gray in the print version)) enters the sorting network on the left-hand side. Following the sorting process, we have only one step in the first stage with three pairs of numbers swapped (shown in black) and one pair (1,2) remaining on the same wires (shown in gray). In the second stage, step 2 makes four swaps and step 3 makes one swap. The third stage is executed in three steps. Step 4 makes three swaps, step 5 makes two swaps, and step 6 makes one swap. The sorted array exits the network on the right-hand side (shown in green (light gray in the print version)).

4.7. Network Sorting Versus Sequential and Parallel Sorting

When we compare the properties of sequential comparison-based algorithms (Table 1) to the properties of the sorting network algorithms

(Table 2), we discover that the sorting times of the most efficient sorting networks are better than the most efficient comparison-based sequential sort algorithms by the factor of $N/\log_2 N$. The sorting time of a sorting network is dependent on its depth. We assume that the comparisons on each level are performed in parallel. Let us also emphasize that we disregard the sorting algorithm constant C, for which we know that it is larger for sequential and parallel sorting algorithms than for network sorting algorithms (refer to Section 3.1.1).

The number of comparisons and sorting times for different implementations of sorting algorithms are summarized in Table 3. For the sequential algorithms, the sorting time is proportional to the number of comparisons. With parallel algorithms, we simultaneously execute N (true parallel sorting) or P (near-parallel sorting) comparisons, and the sorting times are smaller for the corresponding factor. Network algorithms execute all comparisons of each step in parallel.

In Fig. 15, we plot the sorting times for the algorithms from Table 3. The curves indicate that as N increases, the true parallel sorting algorithm is superior, followed by the network sorting algorithm and the near-parallel sorting algorithm. The sequential sorting algorithm is the slowest.

Let us compare the two fastest algorithms from Table 3. The advantages of the true parallel sorting algorithm are the lowest number of comparisons and the shortest sorting time. In a control flow computer, a true parallel sorting algorithm is the first choice. If we use a dataflow computer, the situation changes considerably. In a dataflow computer, data flows between operations are organized as a directed graph. In the case of network sorting algorithms, the sorting network structure is a directed acyclic graph with comparators organized to sort the input array of values (refer to the sorting network figures in this section). When we sort one array, the sorting time is directly proportional to the depth of the sorting network and only one layer

Table 3 Number of Comparisons and the Expected Sorting Times for Different Implementations of Sorting Algorithms

Measure	Values for the Best Algorithm of Type (in $O(x)$ Notation)			
	Sequential	Parallel (N)	Parallel (P)	Network
Comparisons	$N \cdot \log_2 N$	$N \cdot \log_2 N$	$N \cdot \log_2 N$	$N \cdot (\log_2 N)^2$
Sorting time	$N \cdot \log_2 N$	$\log_2 N$	$(N/P) \cdot \log_2 N$	$(\log_2 N)^2$

All values are expressed in $O(x)$ notation, the sorting algorithm constants C are disregarded, and N is the number of items to be sorted.

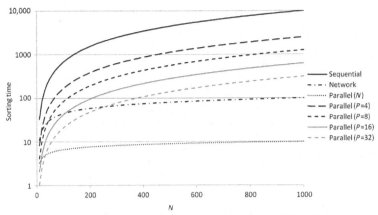

Figure 15 Expected sorting times for the algorithms from Table 3. Sorting times are presented in required cycles to sort an array of N items. One cycle is defined as the time required to perform one comparison. For the sequential algorithms, the number of cycles is identical to the number of comparisons. For the network algorithm, the number of cycles is identical to the depth of the sorting network. For the parallel algorithms, the number of cycles is identical to the number of comparisons divided by the number of parallel computational cores.

of comparators is active in each cycle; a cycle is defined as the time required to perform one comparison step. One layer of comparators represents all comparators of one step of the sorting algorithm (refer to Fig. 14). This sorting scenario is more suitable for control flow computers. Dataflow computers are designed for data flows or data streams, which would consist of a stream of arrays of values to sort, in the case of sorting. For example, if we have M arrays of N values to be sorted, we can consecutively send them to the sorting network. Arrays enter the sorting network in intervals of one cycle. After the first array is sorted, consecutive arrays exit the sorting network in a single cycle interval. Each step of the algorithm operates on a different array. When M reaches the depth of the sorting network, all comparators of the network are active. In this scenario, the sorting time for the first array is on the order of $O((\log_2 N)^2)$; the remaining arrays follow in one-cycle time intervals.

A comparison of the sorting of M arrays of N values on a dataflow computer (sorting network) and the sorting of M arrays of N values on a control flow computer (true parallel sorting) yields interesting results. The sorting time for the control flow computer with the true parallel operation is on the order of $O(M \cdot \log_2 N)$ and on the order of $O((\log_2 N)^2 + M)$ for the dataflow computer with the sorting network. When $M \cong \log_2 N$, both sorting times are comparable; however, when $M \gg \log_2 N$, network sorting on a dataflow computer becomes much faster.

The conclusion of this consideration is that for small M and small N, the best choice is the parallel sorting algorithm on a control flow computer. The dataflow computer will always achieve better performance for large M and small N and a control flow computer will always achieve better performance for large N and small M. When both M and N are large, the results are inconclusive because they are dependent on the $M/\log_2 N$ ratio.

5. IMPLEMENTATION

We have implemented different sorting network algorithms on the MAX2 card, which is the low-end version of the Maxeler dataflow supercomputing system and is an FPGA hardware accelerator. Consequently, the execution of algorithms that run on Maxeler systems must be highly independent of input data or intermediate computational results and only dependent on the number of input data [2].

Maxeler systems are dataflow computers that are capable of employing a large number of tiny interconnected computational cores, which makes them more suitable for the implementation of sorting networks because each computational core or unit can represent one comparator. The major difference between the dataflow and the control flow computer [19] is depicted in Fig. 16.

Sorting networks are implemented on a simple MAX2 PCI Express card version of a Maxeler dataflow supercomputing system. The MAX2 card is inserted into an Intel-based workstation with an Intel® Core™2 Quad processor that runs at a clock rate of 2.66 GHz. The card is connected to the PCI Express x16 slot on the workstation's motherboard. The MAX2 card is equipped with a XILINX Virtex-5 FPGA device, which runs at a clock rate of 200 MHz.

5.1. Dataflow Computer Code (MAX2 Card)

The application development process for the MAX2 card and other Maxeler dataflow supercomputing systems are detailed in Refs. [15,16,20]. Here, we only provide an explanation of the kernel code in Java and the host code in C, which runs on a PC. The execution of the kernel is *embedded* into the execution of the C code on a host PC. The kernel is part of the application code that is compiled and burned onto an FPGA; it executes the sorting on a MAX2 card. The kernel code was generated separately using a dedicated C+

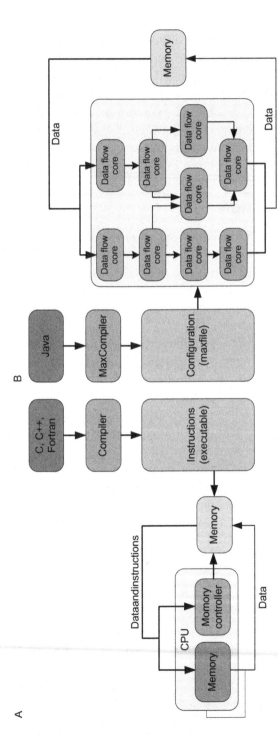

Figure 16 The major difference between a classical control flow computer (A) and a Maxeler dataflow system (B). In (A), a program is compiled and loaded into memory from which the processor reads the instructions and data, executes the program and creates results. At any time of the program execution, the processor has full control over data by deciding which data enters the program, how is it processed and what to do with the results. Program flow and execution can be highly dependent on the intermediate results. In (B), a program is compiled into a configuration file that configures the dataflow engine. Data are streamed through the engine, and the results exit at the output port. Dataflow cores on the data paths transform the data but exhibit little or no control over the data. The data processing is independent of the intermediate results.

+ script. The script takes N as an input parameter and automatically generates the code that represents the appropriate network structure. This code is copied into the MaxCompiler and compiled to a Maxeler system (FPGA). The Java kernel source code that defines the implementation of the bitonic merge sorting network with four inputs ($N=4$) is shown in Fig. 17A, and the corresponding sorting network layout is depicted in Fig. 17B. We provide an example of a sorting network with only four inputs to maintain the size of Figs. 17 and 18 within the space limitations.

A bitonic merge sorting network can be divided into $D(N)$ steps (1); in our case, the number of steps is three. In the kernel code in Fig. 17A, each

```
A
    for (int j = 0; j < 2; j++){
        for (int i = 1; i <= 1; i++){
            y[i+2*j-1] = x[i+2*j-1] > x[2*(j+1) + 1 - i-1] ? x[i+2*j-1] : x[2*(j+1) + 1 - i-
            1];
            y[2*(j+1) + 1 - i-1] = x[i+2*j-1] >
            x[2*(j+1) + 1 - i-1] ? x[2*(j+1) + 1 - i-1]:
            x[i+2*j-1];
        }
    }

    for (int j = 0; j < 1; j++){
        for (int i = 1; i <= 2; i++){
            x[i+4*j-1] = y[i+4*j-1] > y[4*(j+1) + 1 - i-1] ? y[i+4*j-1] : y[4*(j+1) + 1 - i-
            1];
            x[4*(j+1) + 1 - i-1] = y[i+4*j-1] >
            y[4*(j+1) + 1 - i-1] ? y[4*(j+1) + 1 - i-1 :
            y[i+4*j-1];
        }
    }

    for (int j = 0; j < 2; j++){
        for (int i = 1; i <= 1; i++){
            y[i+2*j-1] = x[i+2*j-1] > x[1+i + j*2-1] ? x[i+2*j-1] : x[1+i + j*2-1];
            y[1+i + j*2-1] = x[i+2*j-1] > x[1+i + j*2-1] ? x[1+i + j*2-1] :x[i+2*j-1];
        }
    }
```

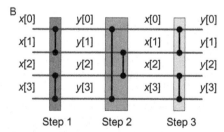

Step 1   Step 2   Step 3

Figure 17 Bitonic merge sorting network with four inputs. (A) Java kernel code that is compiled to the MAX2 card and (B) the corresponding sorting network structure. The kernel code in (A) consists of three double loops. Each loop represents a step of the bitonic merge sorting network algorithm in (B). Comparisons in each step of the algorithm are executed in parallel. Input to the network comprises an array of numbers $x[]$. The results of each step of the algorithm execution are alternately written in array $x[]$ or array $y[]$. The output array for an odd number of algorithm steps is $y[]$, whereas the output array for an even number of algorithm steps is $x[]$.

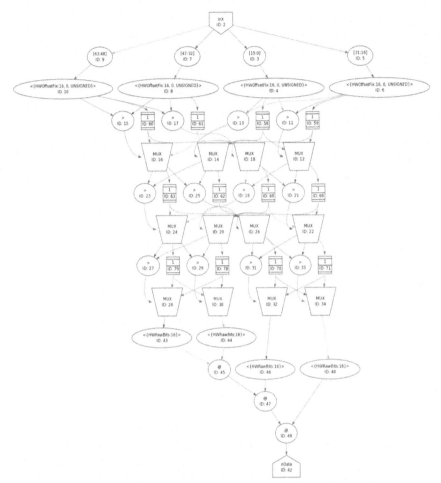

Figure 18 Maxeler graph of the bitonic merge sorting network from Fig. 17 ($N = 4$). An array of numbers from the host to be sorted (in X) is an input stream of bits. The stream is divided into four groups of bits, which are held by entities with the following IDs: 3, 5, 7, and 9. These groups of bits are represented as 16-bit unsigned numbers inside entities with the following IDs: 4, 6, 8, and 10. The array of four 16-bit numbers is sorted by three pairs of comparators. One comparator consists of two comparison elements and two multiplexers. For example, one of the comparators in the first step of the sorting network is represented by entities with the IDs 14–17 inclusive. All elements on an identical horizontal level are executed in parallel. For the correct synchronization of the multiplexer inputs, buffer entities are added. An example of a buffer is an entity with the ID 60. After sorting is completed, the 16-bit values represented by entities with IDs 43, 44, 46, and 48 are assembled into a stream of bits. The operation is performed by entities with the IDs 45, 47, and 49. Finally, the sorted array is transmitted to the host as an output stream of bits (oData).

step is defined by two nested *for* loops; each loop is defined by two comparators. Comparisons are performed with *ternary-if* operators (?:).

The input is defined as an array of four numbers: $x[0]$ to $x[3]$. The first nested loop in Fig. 17A defines the first step, which is depicted as a blue rectangle (gray in the print version) in Fig. 17B. In the first step of the algorithm, pairs of values $(x[0],x[1])$ and $(x[2],x[3])$ are compared; the results are stored in the array $y[\,]$. The second nested loop defines the second step that compares pairs of values $(y[0],y[3])$ and $(y[1],y[2])$; the results are stored in the array $x[\,]$. The third nested loop defines the third step that compares pairs of values $(x[0],x[1])$ and $(x[2],x[3])$; the results are stored in the array $y[\,]$, that is, the output of the sorting algorithm in this case.

MaxCompiler is able to convert the code from Fig. 17A into a dataflow graph by understanding that each step of the algorithm is executed in parallel in one FPGA clock cycle. The generated graph of our sorting network is depicted and explained in Fig. 18. The sorting network performs $N/2$ independent comparisons per layer in parallel. A theoretical speedup factor of $O(N/\log_2 N)$ is expected, given that the complexity of the best sequential sorting algorithm is $O(N \cdot \log_2 N)$ and knowing that the complexity of the parallel bitonic sorting network is identical to its depth $D(N)$, which is defined by Eq. (5).

To send data to the Maxeler card, we used MaxJava's built-in type, which is named KArray. KArray is a structure that holds information about every element of the array. This structure is the most optimized structure for our problem because we can physically connect the array to be sorted to the sorting network inputs.

5.2. Control Flow Computer Code (Host PC)

The kernel code from the previous section, which is executed on a Maxeler card, is accompanied by the code in C executed on a host PC. The pseudo code that reflects the operation of the host code is shown in Fig. 19. The host code controls the calls to the kernel code, the communication between the host and the MAX2 card, and the data transfer. In addition to these tasks, the host code (application) typically performs other bookkeeping tasks that cannot be executed on a Maxeler card. Bookkeeping tasks include preparing the input data, measuring execution times, presenting results, saving results into a file, and using sorted data.

Some constraints should be addressed. The first constraint of implementation of the sorting network is the number of comparators required to build

```
Set number of cycles to K
Set number of arrays in the stream to M
Set array size to N
Set sorting tests [sequentialCPU,networkCPU,networkMaxeler] to 0 or 1

Initialize MAX2 card

If sequentialCPU algorithm test is set
  For number of cycles
    For number of arrays in the stream
      Initialize random array to be sorted
      Get start timing information
      Sort random array using sequentialCPU algorithm
      Get stop timing information
      Write sorting time to results file
    EndFor
  EndFor
EndIf

If networkCPU algorithm test is set
  For number of cycles
    For number of arrays in the stream
      Initialize random array to be sorted
      Get start timing information
      Sort random array using networkCPU algorithm
      Get stop timing information
      Write sorting time to results file
    EndFor
  EndFor
EndIf

If networkMaxeler algorithm test is set
  For number of cycles
    Generate an input stream of M random arrays to be sorted
    Generate an output stream for M sorted arrays
    Get start timing information
    Run MAX2 card
    Send input stream to MAX2 card
    Receive output stream from MAX2 card
    Stop MAX2 card
    Get stop timing information
    Write sorting time to results file
  EndFor
EndIf

Close MAX2 card
```

Figure 19 Pseudo code that represents the operation of the host application that was originally written in C. We set the size of the array to be sorted to N, the number of arrays to be sent in one stream to M, and the number of cycles to K. The number of cycles defines the number of consecutive streams of M arrays of N values being sorted. After initialization of the MAX2 card, the host may perform the sorting of one of the sequential sorting algorithms (sequentialCPU) and/or one of the network sorting algorithms (networkCPU). Both algorithms use the host's CPU for sorting and consecutively sort M arrays of N values. The last part of the pseudo code generates the entire stream of M arrays, runs the MAX2 card, and sends the stream to the card. The arrays inside the stream are sorted by the kernel that runs on the FPGA of the MAX2 card. The sorted arrays are then streamed back to the host. After the host receives the entire stream from the MAX2 card, the card is stopped, the results are written to the file and the MAX2 card is closed. The operations that are directly connected to the Maxeler card are marked in red (gray in the print version).

it, for which the size of the FPGA chip can become a limitation. An additional constraint is the amount of time required to send the entire number array to the MAX card. In the majority of cases, sorting participates in a larger application. We may assume that numbers are already on the MAX card; this assumption lessens this problem. To save space on the FPGA and construct larger sorting networks for longer arrays, we can limit the size of the numbers to 8 or 16 bits. These and other constraints will be addressed in the discussion of the experimental results in the following sections.

6. SETTING UP THE EXPERIMENT

Applications typically use sorting as a part of a more extensive process. Within these processes, sorting can be used occasionally, regularly, or continuously. To cover different frequencies of sorting usage in applications, we have devised two scenarios.

In the first scenario, we consecutively sort several arrays of numbers. Each array is independently sent to the Maxeler card. Consequently, the card must be separately started for each array; this policy increases the total sorting time.

In the second scenario, we sort a stream of arrays that are continuously sent to the Maxeler card. Consequently, the card is initialized and started only once.

The goal of the experiment is to establish the possible acceleration for sorting on a Maxeler system compared with the sorting on a central processing unit (CPU). We define the following variables and functions:

- N is the size of the array to be sorted,
- M is the number of arrays to be consecutively sorted,
- $T_H(N)$ is the time required to sort one array of size N on the host,
- T_0 is the time required to start a Maxeler card,
- $T_C(N)$ is the sum of times required to send one array of size N to the Maxeler card and receive the sorted result,
- $T_S(N)$ is the time required by the sorting network structure on a Maxeler card to sort one array,
- $T_M(N)$ is the total time required to sort one array on a Maxeler system. This time includes the time required to start the card and the time of communication (send and receive data) with the Maxeler card.

The acceleration or speedup S is defined by the ratio between the time required for sorting on a CPU and the time required for sorting on a Maxeler system, as follows:

$$S = \frac{T_H(N)}{T_M(N)} \tag{9}$$

In the first scenario, we must start the Maxeler card, send one array, sort it, and then return the results to the host. The total sorting time is defined as $T_M(N) = T_0 + T_C(N) + T_S(N)$, and the speedup is given as follows:

$$S_1 = \frac{T_H(N)}{T_0 + T_C(N) + T_S(N)} \tag{10}$$

In the second scenario, we sort several arrays in a row. We start the Maxeler card, continuously send M arrays, sort these arrays, and return the results to the host. The total sorting time is defined as $T_M(N) = T_0 + M \cdot T_C(N) + M \cdot T_S(N)$, and the speedup is defined as follows:

$$S_2 = \frac{M \cdot T_H(N)}{T_0 + M \cdot \max(T_C, T_S) + \min(T_C, T_S)} \tag{11}$$

In the first scenario, the speedup (Eq. 10) is highly dependent on each of the denominator factors. For small to medium values of N, the starting time T_0 for the Maxeler card may be relatively high compared with the $T_C(N)$ and $T_S(N)$; thus, we cannot expect significant speedups.

In the second scenario, the speedup (Eq. 11) is primarily dependent on M and the ratios between $T_H(N)$, $T_C(N)$, and $T_S(N)$. With increasing M, the time T_0 becomes negligible. Given that the theoretical ratio between $T_H(N)$ and $T_S(N)$ is on the order of $N/\log_2 N$, the second scenario is expected to yield significant speedups.

After the first set of experiments, we noticed that the time required to start the Maxeler card T_0 and the communication time $T_C(N)$ are significant factors; when added, they are greater than the sorting time $T_S(N)$ in the majority of cases. Consequently, speedups S_1 and S_2 are significantly lower than they would be if we only consider the sorting time $T_S(N)$. Although we do not have a method to measure the $T_S(N)$, we can calculate it if we measure the loopback time $T_{L1}(N) = T_0 + T_C(N)$ in the first scenario or the loopback time in the second scenario, which is defined as follows:

$$T_{L2}(N) = T_0 + M \cdot T_C(N) \tag{12}$$

We have performed a set of experimental *Loopback* tests, in which we send an identical stream of arrays from the host to the Maxeler card. However, the card does not perform any sorting; it only returns the unchanged arrays to the host. We then calculate the net sorting time for the first scenario

$T_{SL1}(N) = T_M(N) - T_{L1}(N)$ and the net sorting time for the second scenario $T_{SL2}(N) = T_M(N) - T_{L2}(N)$. By considering the loopback times, we define the speedups for both scenarios as follows:

$$S_{1L} = \frac{T_H(N)}{T_{SL1}(N)} \tag{13}$$

$$S_{2L} = \frac{M \cdot T_H(N)}{T_{SL2}(N)} \tag{14}$$

7. EXPERIMENTAL RESULTS

We present the experimental results in three categories. First, we discuss some limitations and constraints of the implementation of network sorting algorithms on the MAX2 card. Second, we compare the sorting times of different network sorting algorithms. Finally, we compare the best network sorting algorithm executed on a MAX2 card with the best sequential (and parallel) algorithms executed on a host CPU; the final results comprise the speedup results achieved through the utilization of the network sorting algorithms.

7.1. FPGA Usage

The FPGA chip resources are limited. The implemented sorting networks use three types of FPGA resources: flip flops (FF), lookup tables (LUT), and block R AM (BR_AM). The discussion of the operation and the functionality of each of these FPGA resources is beyond the scope of this chapter. With increasing N, one type of FPGA resource will become exhausted. From Fig. 20, we can conclude that FFs represent the most critical FPGA resource, which becomes exhausted first. In the 16-bit version of the odd–even merge network sorting algorithm, the usage of FFs is 63% for $N = 128$ and exceeds 100% at $N = 256$. These data are not included in the graph because compiling to FPGA failed due to the lack of FFs.

Figure 21 compares the usage of FFs for different network sorting algorithms. Note that the FF usage conforms to the theoretical results for the number of comparators summarized in Table 2. We can conclude that the number of comparators linked to the FF usage on a chip is the primary limiting factor for sorting networks with a larger array size N. Less efficient algorithms, such as the bubble and odd–even algorithms, can sort array sizes

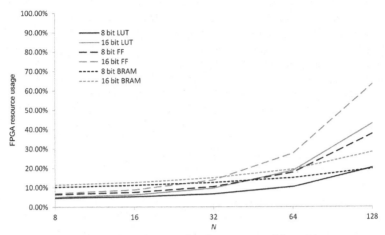

Figure 20 FPGA resource usage for 8- and 16-bit versions of the odd–even merge network sorting algorithm. Flip flops (FF) represent the resource that is rapidly exhausted. When compiling the 16-bit version of the sorting network to FPGA, we can achieve $N = 128$.

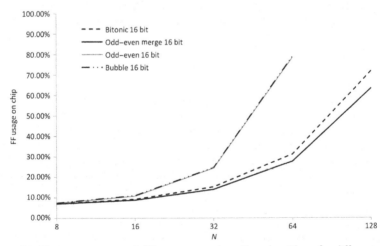

Figure 21 FF resource usage of different network sorting algorithms for different array sizes N. For bubble and odd–even network sorting algorithms, the highest array size is at $N = 64$. Bitonic and odd–even merge network sorting algorithms use fewer FFs; their highest array size is $N = 128$. The results conform to the properties of the algorithms summarized in Table 2.

up to $N = 64$, whereas more efficient algorithms, such as bitonic and odd–even merges, can sort array sizes up to $N = 128$.

The most efficient algorithm in terms of chip usage in Fig. 21 is the odd–even merge network sorting algorithm. We have evaluated this algorithm using different number formats. The results shown in Fig. 22 are as

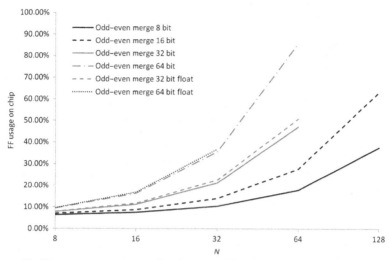

Figure 22 FF resource usage on a chip for the odd–even merge network sorting algorithm for different array sizes *N* with different number formats: 8–64-bit fixed point number format and 32–64-bit floating point number format.

anticipated. The 8- and 16-bit fixed point number formats enable array sizes up to $N=128$; the 32- and 64-bit fixed point number format and the 32-bit floating point format enable array sizes up to $N=64$. The 64-bit floating point format enables array sizes up to $N=32$; the constraint for a 64-bit floating point format is not the number of FFs but the number of LUTs.

Based on these results, we were able to implement a sorting network on a MAX2 card to the size of $N=128$. This result is comparable to other studies on sorting networks using similar FPGA chips [17]. We find this result favorable because MaxCompiler is a general purpose compiler that is primarily oriented toward dataflow computing. The maximum array size is equivalent to the maximum array size achieved with a more customized implementation of sorting networks on FPGAs; this finding indicates the efficiency of the MaxCompiler.

7.2. Performance of Network Sorting Algorithms on the MAX2 Card

We have performed a series of sorting tests for the following four network sorting algorithms: bubble, odd–even, bitonic, and odd–even merge. We have omitted the pairwise algorithm because its properties are identical to the properties of the odd–even merge algorithm with regard to the size and the depth of the sorting network (refer to Table 2).

In our tests, we measured the sorting time by varying the following parameters:

- the size of the array to sort: 8, 16, 32, 64, and 128;
- the number format: 8-, 16-, 32-, 64-bit fixed point, and 32- and 64-bit floating point;
- the number of consecutive arrays to sort M: 1–1,000,000; and
- the scenarios: two different (refer to Section 6).

The results in Figs. 23 and 24 indicate that the sorting times for different network sorting algorithms are dependent on the array size N and the stream

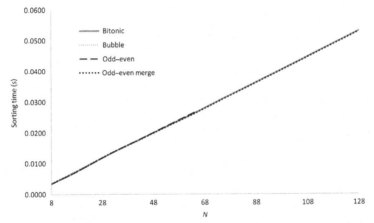

Figure 23 Stream sorting times for different network sorting algorithms are dependent on the array size N. We sorted a stream of $M = 50,000$ arrays of 16-bit fixed point numbers. The sorting times for all algorithms are equivalent.

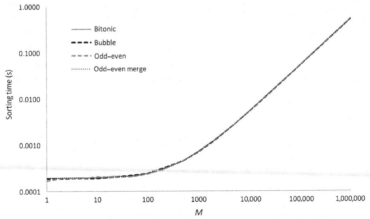

Figure 24 Stream sorting times for different network sorting algorithms are dependent on the stream size M. We sorted a stream of arrays of 16-bit fixed point numbers with $N = 64$. The stream sorting times for all algorithms are equivalent.

size M and are independent of the sorting topology. An additional observation is that the sorting times in Fig. 23 linearly increase with N, which was not expected because the sorting times of sorting networks are proportional to the depth and is on the order of $O((\log_2 N)^2)$.

Similar results are shown in Figs. 25 and 26. These figures show the sorting times of an odd–even merge network sorting algorithm based on various parameters. The sorting time in Fig. 25 increases linearly as the length of the data and array size increases. We observe that 32-bit fixed and floating point numbers have equivalent sorting times. This finding is valid for both 64-bit formats. This result is expected because the depth of the sorting network is not dependent on the number of bits. Similarly, the results in Fig. 26 also exhibit a linear relationship between the sorting time and the length of the numbers.

The results in Figs. 23–26 suggest that the total sorting time $T_M(N)$ exhibits a significant and prevailing linear factor. This factor is proportional to the array size N (Fig. 23), the number of bits, the format (Fig. 25), and the stream size M (Figs. 24 and 26). The prevailing linear factor can be attributed to the loopback time (Eq. 12). Therefore, the loopback time represents the major factor in the total stream sorting time.

We have performed a series of tests to measure the time $T_{L2}(N)$ for different array sizes N and operand formats. These tests enable the possibility to

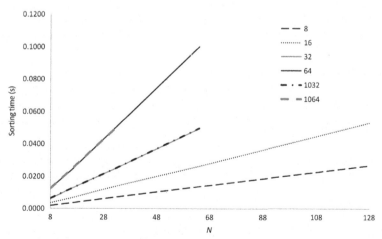

Figure 25 Stream sorting time of the odd–even merge network sorting algorithm for different number formats and array size N. The number formats are as follows: 8-, 16-, 32-, and 64-bit fixed point numbers and 32- and 64-bit floating point numbers (shown as entries 1032 and 1064, respectively, in the legend). We used streams of $M = 50,000$ arrays.

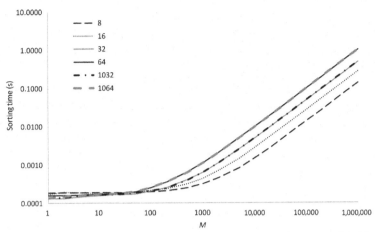

Figure 26 Stream sorting time of the odd–even merge network sorting algorithm for varying number length at stream size M. The number formats are as follows: 8-, 16-, 32-, and 64-bit fixed point numbers and 32- and 64-bit floating point numbers (shown as entries 1032 and 1064 in the legend). We used array sizes of $N = 32$.

subtract the loopback time $T_{L2}(N)$ from the total sorting time $T_M(N)$ to obtain the net sorting time on the MAX2 card.

A comparison of the sorting times for the odd–even network sorting algorithm and the loopback times for sending a stream of M arrays of 16-bit numbers is shown in Fig. 27. This figure indicates that the loopback operations account for the majority of the total sorting time.

The FPGA sorting times for an odd–even merge network sorting algorithm are shown in Fig. 28. We subtracted the loopback times $T_{L2}(N)$ from the total sorting time of the streams for different number formats. The results indicate that the sorting time for the FPGA is not dependent on the number of bits, which conforms to the expectations and theoretical operation of network sorting in an FPGA. Variations of the curves in Fig. 28 are due to the variations in the measurement conditions in which we had limited influence (for example, the resource usage on the host PC).

The differences in total stream sorting time for different number formats observed in Figs. 25 and 26 can be explained by the time required to transfer the data between the host and the Maxeler card; longer number formats required longer communication times. This notion is elaborated in Section 7.3.

Finally, we compared the FPGA sorting time for different network sorting algorithms. The results in Fig. 29 indicate that bitonic and odd–even merge algorithms are faster than bubble sort (according to Table 2) and

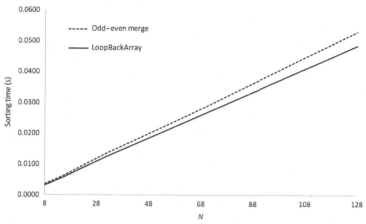

Figure 27 Stream sorting times for the odd–even merge network sorting algorithm and array loopback operation (LoopBackArray) time for different array sizes. We used streams of $M = 50,000$ arrays of 16-bit fixed point numbers. The loopback time linearly increases with the array size. The sorting time increases with increasing N as the depth of the sorting network increases on the order of $O((\log_2 N)^2)$.

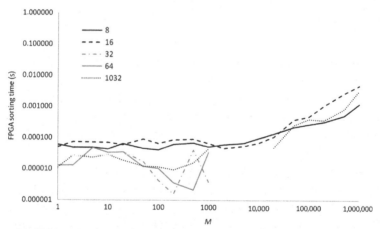

Figure 28 FPGA sorting times for the odd–even merge network sorting algorithm for different number formats and stream size M. The number formats are as follows: 8-, 16-, 32-, and 64- bit fixed point numbers and 32-bit floating point numbers (shown as entry 1032 in the legend). We used array sizes of $N = 8$. The results indicate that the FPGA sorting time is not dependent on the length and number format.

different algorithms behave identically with respect to the sorting time, which is partially confirmed in Fig. 29.

We selected the odd–even merge network sorting algorithm for speedup comparisons in the next section. Although this algorithm is not substantially

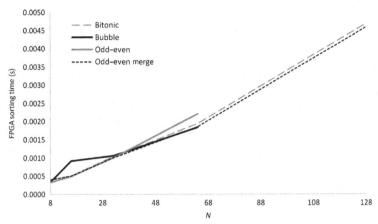

Figure 29 FPGA sorting times for different network sorting algorithms for different array sizes N. We sorted a stream of M = 50,000 arrays of 16-bit fixed point numbers. The sorting times do not substantially differ, and the odd–even merge algorithm is the fastest algorithm.

faster than the remaining network algorithms, it contains the least number of comparators, which makes it superior.

7.3. Comparison of Sorting Algorithms on the MAX2 Card and the Host CPU

One of the major questions of this study is as follows: does network sorting on dataflow computers offer any significant speedups over traditional sorting on control flow computers? Let us examine two simple results related to the two scenarios in Section 6.

In the first scenario, we sorted only one array at a time on the Maxeler card. The results for this scenario are shown in Fig. 30, which indicates that the control flow computers perform better than the Maxeler card.

Figure 31 shows the sorting times in the second scenario for a stream of M arrays of size $N = 128$. These results demonstrate a strong influence of the card starting time T_0. We can achieve a moderate speedup at $M \approx 20$, which increases with increasing M. The speedup S_2 for an identical test is shown in Fig. 32. We observe that the peak speedup of approximately 16 is achieved at $M > 1000$. The lower speedups at smaller M are due to the Maxeler card starting time T_0; with increasing M, the influence of T_0 decreases and becomes negligible at higher values of M, where the speedup curve flattens. At this point, only the ratio between $T_H(N)$ and $T_C(N)$ or between $T_H(N)$ and $T_S(N)$ is important (Eq. 10).

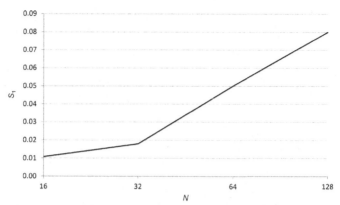

Figure 30 Scenario 1 (sending only one array at a time for sorting): using a bitonic network sorting algorithm on the MAX2 card versus the sequential quicksort algorithm on the host CPU. Speedup S_1 (Eq. 10) is given for array sizes ranging from $N = 16$ to $N = 128$. We observe that S_1 increases exponentially with N. Note that S_1 is substantially smaller than 1, which indicates that sorting one array at a time on a Maxeler system using a bitonic network sorting algorithm is slower than the sequential quicksort algorithm on a control flow machine.

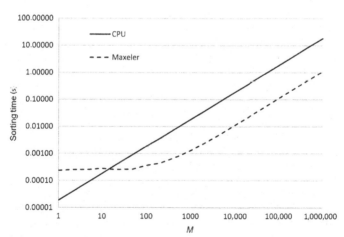

Figure 31 Scenario 2 (sending a stream of arrays for sorting): using the bitonic network sorting algorithm on the MAX2 card versus the sequential quicksort algorithm on the host CPU. We used array sizes of $N = 128$. For small M, the CPU performs better due to the constant time T_0 required to start the Maxeler card. With increasing M, the Maxeler performs better; above a specific M, the ratio between the CPU and the Maxeler sorting time S_2 (speedup) becomes constant.

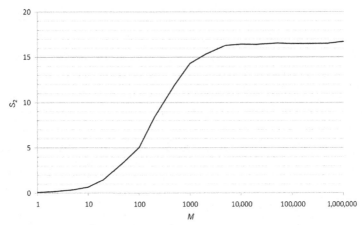

Figure 32 Scenario 2: the speedup S_2 for array size $N=128$. With increasing M the speedup increases to 16.

These results are both discouraging and encouraging and indicate that (a) network sorting on the MAX2 card is not suitable for occasional sorting episodes and (b) speedups can be significant when we sort several arrays as a stream. Both results reflect the properties of dataflow computing, which is more convenient for large amounts of streamed data than for small amounts of sporadic data.

Let us compare the best network sorting algorithms that run on the MAX2 card and the best sequential sorting algorithm that run on a host CPU. We use scenario 2 for all comparisons. In Section 3.1.1, we have shown that insertion sort and heap sort are the fastest sequential sorting algorithms for small array sizes. Insertion sort performs the best at $N \leq 64$, whereas heap sort performs better for $N \geq 128$. We selected heap sort for the majority of the comparisons because it will yield the most favorable results for sequential sorting algorithms, which execute on the host CPU for larger N. Consequently, a lower speedup is achieved by sorting networks on the MAX2 card.

We present the speedup S_2 for different array size N and stream size M. The results in Fig. 33 show that the odd–even merge network sorting algorithm on the MAX2 card is 11 times faster than the sequential heap sort algorithm on the host CPU. Regardless of M, the speedup is higher for a larger array size N.

Similar results are shown in Fig. 34 with the speedup S_2 for different operand formats. The results in Fig. 34 indicate that the highest speedups are achieved for shorter operands. We also observe that the speedup is

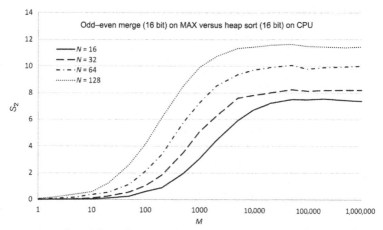

Figure 33 Speedup S_2 for different array size N. We use a 16-bit fixed point number format. The curves show the ratio between the sorting time of sequential heap sorting on the host CPU and odd–even merge network sorting on the MAX2 card.

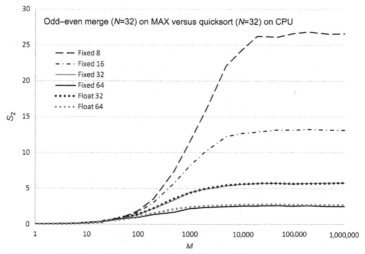

Figure 34 Speedup S_2 for different number formats with an array size $N = 32$. The curves show the ratio between the sorting time of the sequential quicksort algorithm on the host CPU and odd–even merge network sorting on the MAX2 card.

independent of operand representation. The speedup is dominated by the time required to transfer data between the host and the MAX2 card; a larger number format results in more communication time and lower speedup.

Using the MAX2 card, speedups are not significant. The limiting factor is the data transfer speed between the host and the MAX2 card. The results may be more attractive if we calculate the speedup from the net sorting time on the FPGA using Eqs. (12) and (14). By employing the results of the loopback tests, we can calculate the speedup S_{2L}.

Figure 35 shows the speedup S_{2L}, which is considerably higher than the speedup S_2. For example, the speedup S_{2L} is 150 at $N=128$, and the

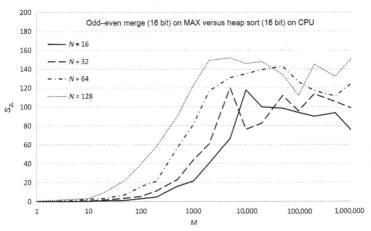

Figure 35 Speedup S_{2L} (considering the loopback) for different array size N using a 16-bit fixed point number format. The curves show the ratio between the sorting time of sequential heap sorting on the host CPU and odd–even merge network sorting on the FPGA ($T_S(N)$).

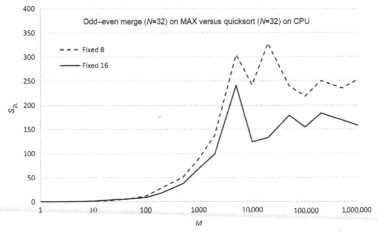

Figure 36 Speedup S_{2L} (considering the loopback) for different number formats and an array size $N=32$. The curves show the ratio between the sorting time for the sequential quicksort algorithm on the host CPU and odd–even merge network sorting on the FPGA ($T_S(N)$).

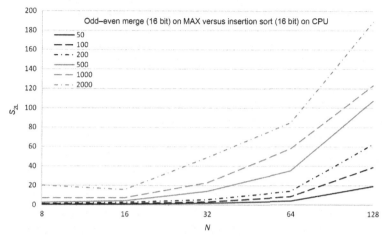

Figure 37 Speedup S_{2L} (considering the loopback) for different stream size M using the 16-bit fixed point numbers. The curves show the ratio between the sorting time of the sequential insertion sort algorithm on the host CPU and the odd–even merge network sorting on the FPGA ($T_S(N)$).

speedup S_{2L} remains 100 at $N=16$. Similarly, Fig. 36 shows speedups that attain a value of 250.

An additional interesting result is shown in Fig. 37, in which the speedup is shown for different stream sizes M. Higher values of N and M yield higher speedup S_{2L}.

The presented results indicate the potential for achieving high speedups by implementing sorting on Maxeler dataflow supercomputing systems. Although the sorting network that we implemented on our MAX2 system is small, we were able to achieve speedups S_2 above 10 and speedups S_{2L} above 200 using streaming multiple arrays.

8. CONCLUSION

Our study has demonstrated that nearly forgotten algorithms and solutions, which were previously impossible or impractical to implement, can re-emerge with advances in technology that enable their use. Sorting networks and their implementation on FPGAs are a natural match, whereas parallel execution of comparisons yields high sorting speedups. Speedups are demonstrated by our study and the extensive results in this chapter.

The limited number of comparators that can be realized on the FPGA chip presents limitations. This challenge restricts the size of the sorting network and the size of the array that can be sorted at a time. We sorted arrays with a maximum size of 128 values. We achieved the highest speedups of more than 10 (considering the communication times) and more than 200 (considering only the sorting time inside the FPGA). An additional challenge is the slow communication between the host and the Maxeler card, which increases the time for execution of the Maxeler portion of the application code. For sorting networks, the increased time is considerable.

Although these results may appear unimpressive and these challenges are significant, this study was performed using the least capable Maxeler system. With a more advanced Maxeler system, we plan to increase the array size, shorten the data transfer time, and improve the achieved speedup. Given the properties of sorting networks, we do not expect that this approach will produce high increases in array size; however, it may considerably improve the communication speed and directly affect the achieved speedup. The concept of a perfect shuffler is more promising. This concept requires future studies because it violates the sorting network principle of acyclic graphs. However, a successful solution of this idea may increase the array size by orders of magnitude.

An additional feasible improvement is the use of network sorting for the data that exists in the Maxeler system (for example, data used by other application processes or algorithms that run on the Maxeler system, which must be sorted).

By obtaining solutions to one or more of these problems and challenges, significant improvements in numerous applications that require sorting may be possible.

REFERENCES

[1] Donald E. Knuth, The art of computer programming, Sorting and Searching, vol. 3, Addison-Wesley, Boston, Massachusetts, USA, 2002.

[2] Robert Sedgewick, Algorithms in Java, third ed., Addison-Wesley, Boston, Massachusetts, USA, 2010, Parts 1–4.

[3] Thomas H. Cormen, Charles E. Leiserson, Ronald L. Rivest, Clifford Stein, Introduction to Algorithms, second ed., The MIT Press, Cambridge (MA), London, 2009.

[4] M.J. Flynn, O. Mencer, V. Milutinovic, G. Rakocevic, P. Stenstrom, R. Trobec, M. Valero, Moving from Petaflops to Petadata, Communications of the ACM 56 (5) (2013) 39–42.

[5] Yale Patt, Future Microprocessors: What Must We do Differently if We Are to Effectively Utilize Multi-Core and Many-Core Chips? vol. 5 (1), IPSI Bgd Internet Research Society, New York, Frankfurt, Tokyo, Belgrade, 2009.

[6] Sorting Algorithm, http://en.wikipedia.org/wiki/Sorting_algorithm (accessed 27.04.2013).

[7] Parallel Computing, http://en.wikipedia.org/wiki/Parallel_computing (accessed 27.04.2013).

[8] Veljko Milutinovic, Surviving the Design of Microprocessor and Multimicroprocessor Systems: Lessons Learned, John Wiley & Sons, Inc., New York, 2000.
[9] K.E. Batcher, Sorting networks and their applications, in: Proceedings of the AFIPS Spring Joint Computer Conference, 32, 1968, pp. 307–314.
[10] Sorting Network, http://en.wikipedia.org/wiki/Sorting_network (accessed 27.04.2013).
[11] Bitonic Sorter, http://en.wikipedia.org/wiki/Bitonic_sort (accessed 27.04.2013).
[12] H.W. Lang, Bitonic Sort, http://www.iti.fh-flensburg.de/lang/algorithmen/sortieren/bitonic/bitonicen.htm (accessed 27.04.2013).
[13] Ian Parberry, The pairwise sorting network, Parallel Process. Lett. 2 (2–3) (1992) 205–211.
[14] M. Ajtai, J. Komlós, E. Szemerédi, An O(n log n) sorting network, in: Proceedings 15th Annual ACM Symposium on Theory of Computing, 1983, pp. 1–9.
[15] Maxeler Technologies, MaxCompiler—Manager Compiler Tutorial, 2012, Version 2012.1, London.
[16] Maxeler Technologies, MaxCompiler—Kernel Compiler Tutorial, 2012, Version 2012.1, London.
[17] R. Mueller, J. Teubner, G. Alonso, Sorting networks on FPGAs, Int. J. Very Large Data Bases Arch. 21 (1) (2012) 1–23.
[18] V. Ranković, A. Kos, V. Milutinović, Bitonic merge sort implementation on the Maxeler dataflow supercomputing system, IPSI BGD Trans. Internet Res. 9(2) (2013) 5–10, Belgrade.
[19] http://www.maxeler.com/technology/dataflow-computing (accessed 27.04.2013).
[20] Maxeler Technologies, Dataflow Programming with MaxCompiler, 2012, Version 2012.1, London.

ABOUT THE AUTHORS

Anton Kos received his Ph.D. in electrical engineering from the University of Ljubljana, Slovenia, in 2006. He is a senior lecturer at the Faculty of Electrical Engineering, University of Ljubljana. He is a member of the Laboratory of Communication Devices at the Department of Telecommunications. His teaching and research work includes communication networks and protocols, quality of service, dataflow computing and applications, usage of inertial sensors in biofeedback applications, and information systems. He is the (co)author of eight papers that appeared in the international engineering journals and of more than thirty papers on international conferences.

Vukašin Ranković received his B.Sc. in electrical engineering and information theory from the University of Belgrade, Serbia, in 2014. He is a master student at the School of Electrical Engineering, University of Belgrade. He also works at the Microsoft Development Center Serbia as a Software engineer in Bing Local Classification team. His research and work includes machine learning and dataflow computing. He is the (co)author of one paper that appeared in the international engineering journal and of one paper on international conference.

Sašo Tomažič received his Ph.D. in Electrical Engineering from the University of Ljubljana, Slovenia, in 1991. He is a full professor at the Faculty of Electrical Engineering, University of Ljubljana. He is the head of the Laboratory of Communication Devices and the head of the Department of Telecommunications. He was the advisor for networking, teleworking, and telematics at the Ministry of Education of Slovenia; the advisor for Telecommunications at the Ministry of Defense; and the National Coordinator for telecommunications research of the Republic of Slovenia. He is the (co) author of more than fifty papers that appeared in the international engineering journals and of more than a hundred papers on international conferences.

CHAPTER FIVE

Dual Data Cache Systems: Architecture and Analysis

Zivojin Sustran*, Goran Rakocevic[†], Veljko Milutinovic*
*School of Electrical Engineering, University of Belgrade, Belgrade, Serbia
[†]Mathematical Institute of the Serbian Academy of Sciences and Arts, Belgrade, Serbia

Contents

Advances in Computers, Volume 96
ISSN 0065-2458
http://dx.doi.org/10.1016/bs.adcom.2014.11.001

Abstract

The last decade has demonstrated a substantial research effort concerning dual data cache (DDC) systems. DDC systems work in that way that they divide data according to their access patterns and then they use different caching algorithms on the divided data. One possible classification taxonomy is proposed in the first part of this chapter together with major examples thereof. After that, an analysis of the existing solutions is presented, emphasizing three most important issues: speed, complexity, and power consumption.

1. INTRODUCTION

This chapter has two major parts: one about the architecture and the other about its analysis. The architecture part sets the ground for the analysis part and prepares an interested reader to better understand the major research issues in this field.

As the performance difference between processor and main memory increases constantly, there have appeared many techniques that try to decrease the differences by hiding the latency of memory accesses. The dual data cache (DDC) system [1–3] is one of the proposed solutions. It tries to take advantage of different patterns in data accesses. The data is cashed into two cache subsystems that are physically and/or logically separated according to their access patterns. Similar access pattern data is stored in the same cache subsystem and organization of each subsystem is optimized accordingly. Separating data can be done at run time and/or compile time. It is possible to implement the system with or without ability to detect changes in the data access patterns. DDC systems have higher hit to miss ratio compared to classical cache systems. At the same time, they require smaller silicon die area, thus consuming less power. Additionally, when the data access pattern is predictable, DDC system can also reduce read hit latency by prefetching data intelligently.

The data access pattern is influenced by the type of locality that the data exhibits, the utilized data structure, the segment of the main memory where the data is stored, etc. Spatial and temporal types of localities are important for determining the data access pattern. When a particular memory location is referenced and it is likely that a nearby memory location will be referenced in the near future, the data item in that memory location exhibits spatial locality. When a particular memory location is referenced and there is a high probability that the same memory location will be referenced in the near future, the data in that memory location exhibits temporal locality. Knowing the type of data structure (scalar, vector, or complex) is useful in determining the data access pattern, as well. Accessing scalar data is similar to accessing data that exhibits temporal locality (for example, if the accesses happen in a loop); accessing vector data is similar to accessing data that expresses spatial locality. None of that applies to complex data, so such data cannot be predicted easily. In Table 1, several other terms that are important for determining the data access pattern are presented.

The most important issue in cache design is to maximize speed and performance, while minimizing complexity and power. This survey is focusing on comparing performances of different cashing solutions along the lines of the DDC paradigm. Cache memory uses about one-third of silicon die area in modern systems [4], but this area can be reduced considerably if a DDC approach is used, since it reduces the transistor count. Another important issue, especially for embedded and mobile systems, is power consumption and energy dissipation of DDC systems. This goal is also helped with a lower transistor count.

In the cases when the DDC paradigm reduces the transistor count by a factor of about 2, in multicore systems, the number of cores can be doubled 18 months ahead of time, compared to systems in which classical cache is used (this statement assumes that the transistor count of semiconductor chips doubles every 18 months). This fact proves the value of the DDC paradigm

Table 1 Definition of Terms Used

Term	Definition
Locality prediction table	A history table with information about the most recently executed load/store instructions; it is used to predict the type of locality of referenced data
2D spatial locality	If the data is stored in a matrix data type, it exhibits spatial locality, and there is a high probability that memory access to the neighboring element will happen in a near future
Neighboring and OBL algorithms	Algorithms used for prefetching data that exhibits 2D and spatial locality
Java processor	Java Virtual Machine implementation on an FPGA chip

in the ever-going effort of microprocessor manufacturers to be ahead of competition, as far as the number of cores on the chip.

The purpose of this chapter is to shortly present the research area of DDC. Several different approaches for splitting data cache in order to hide latency delays are presented. A taxonomy that defines possible classification criteria is suggested. In the context of these criteria, some of the existing solutions are described too.

2. A DDC SYSTEMS CLASSIFICATION PROPOSAL

In this section, possible criteria for classification of DDC systems are proposed with a goal to provide a broad and extensive view of the field of DDC. We tried to define classification criteria that are able to classify all existing systems into appropriate nonoverlapping subsets.

The type of the processor, for which the cache system is being designed, is the first criterion for classification. Types can be general or special purpose. Those processors designed for arbitrary types of applications and general-purpose computing are classified as general purpose, and the ones that produce better results for a specified type of application and/or for embedded computing are classified as special purpose. General-purpose systems have higher demands for performance and special-purpose systems have higher demand for reducing power consumption and for better usage of die space.

The second criterion depends on the usage of the processor—whether it will be a part of a uniprocessor or a multiprocessor system. The use of DDC system that provides the reduction in cache size brings a possibility to put more cores on a die in a multiprocessor system.

The placement of the mechanism for determining the type of locality that data exhibits is the third criterion for classification. There are two possibilities: (a) compiler-assisted when the type of locality is determined by compiler and/or profiler and (b) compiler-not-assisted when hardware or another system layer determines the type of locality. These possibilities indicate whether a DDC system can adapt to changes of data access patterns and how data, that does not follow the expected access pattern, is handled.

There may be other classification criteria, but the ones in this chapter were chosen to present the essence of the basic viewpoint of this research. Figure 1 depicts the classification tree that was obtained by successive application of aforementioned criteria. Section 3 of this chapter briefly elaborates the leaves of the classification tree as examples of research efforts.

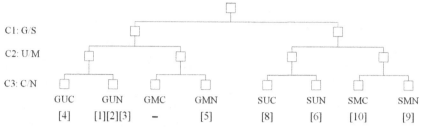

C1: G/S

C2: U/M

C3: C/N

GUC	GUN	GMC	GMN	SUC	SUN	SMC	SMN
[4]	[1][2][3]	–	[5]	[8]	[6]	[10]	[9]

Figure 1 The classification tree of dual data cache systems. *Legend*: G/S—general versus special purpose; U/M—uniprocessor versus multiprocessor; C/N—compiler assisted versus hardware assisted; GUC, GUN, GMC, GMN, SUC, SUN, SMC, and SMN—abbreviation for eight classes of DDC. *Description*: the classification tree obtained by successive application of the chosen criteria. *Implication*: the class of general uniprocessor compiler-assisted DDC system does not have known implementations. Listed are only the references of the most representative solutions in each class.

3. EXISTING DDC SYSTEMS

In this section, we present the existing implementations for each class of DDC systems (if existing).

3.1. General Uniprocessor Compiler-Not-Assisted

The general uniprocessor compiler-not-assisted (GUN) is a class of proposed solutions where solely hardware determines data localities and caching strategies. The help of a compiler is not necessary. For this class only, we present two solutions because they have an impact on every other solution. The first solution is the original DDC [1] and the second is split temporal/spatial (STS) data cache [2]. The major difference between the STS and the DDC is that the DDC, at run time, cannot move data between the temporal and the spatial parts, while STS can do that.

3.1.1 The DDC

Gonzalez *et al.* [1] proposed a novel data cache design for superscalar processors. Its goal was to resolve four main issues regarding the data cache design. These issues are large working sets, interferences when the stride and the number of sets are not co-prime, pollution due to nonunit strides, and prefetching. In this proposal, a DDC data cache is partitioned into two independent cache subsystems: one, named spatial sub-cache, which exploits both spatial and temporal localities, and the other, named temporal sub-cache, which exploits only temporal locality (Fig. 2).

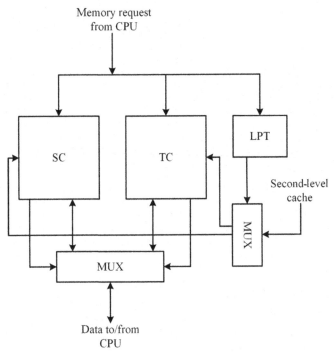

Figure 2 The dual data cache system. *Legend*: SC—spatial sub-cache; TC—temporal sub-cache; LPT—locality prediction table; MUX—multiplexer. *Description*: the cache is divided into two subsystems: the temporal sub-cache (TC) system and the spatial sub-cache (SC) system. *Explanation*: such a division allows the use of different caching strategies for different types of localities that data exhibits. Which sub-cache system the data block will be cached into is decided based on the associated locality in LPT. Previous accesses to a data block determine the associated locality of that data block. *Implication*: only when a cache miss occurs for a given data block, that block can change its sub-cache systems.

The DDC can be viewed as an attempt to accelerate the process of putting more processor cores onto a multicore chip. Actually, if the cache memory is split into two parts, the spatial part can exist only on the lowest levels of hierarchy, because the upper levels of hierarchy are not needed in the spatial part. Without the large upper level caches in the spatial part, the transistor count of the entire core with caches becomes much smaller. Consequently, conditions are created that permit a larger number of cores to fit onto a chip. In other words, a company that adopts the DDC approach can double the number of cores before the companies that follow the traditional approach to caching.

As depicted in Fig. 3, the locality prediction table (LPT) contains the information for determining the sub-cache system, where the missed data

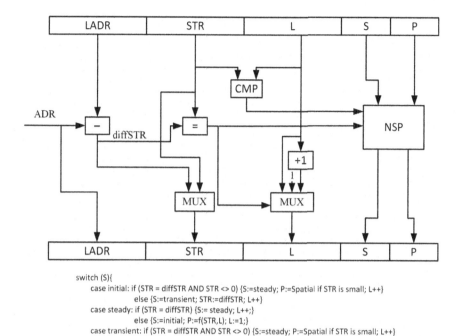

```
switch (S){
    case initial: if (STR = diffSTR AND STR <> 0) {S:=steady; P:=Spatial if STR is small; L++}
                  else {S:=transient; STR:=diffSTR; L++}
    case steady: if (STR = diffSTR) {S:= steady; L++;}
                 else {S:=initial; P:=f(STR,L); L:=1;}
    case transient: if (STR = diffSTR AND STR <> 0) {S:=steady; P:=Spatial if STR is small; L++}
                    else {S:=transient; STR:=diffSTR;}
}
```

Figure 3 Logic for tagging/retagging of data blocks against their locality. *Legend*: ADR—address of the referenced data; LADR—address of the previously referenced data; STR—stride, difference between the referenced address and the previously referenced address; diffSTR—the newly calculated stride; L—number of consecutive elements accessed with the current load/store instruction; S—state, information about the past behavior of the current load/store instruction; P—tag that determines locality of the data; NSP—unit that calculates new states and new tags; CMP—comparator; MUX—multiplexer; f(STR,L)—function that returns a temporal tag if STR is not small and L is not long, or returns a bypass tag if STR is not small and L is long. *Description*: there exists a row for each and every load/store instruction in the locality prediction table (LPT), and the schematic of this figure explains how it is changed by the hardware if and when a related instruction is executed. *Explanation*: the address of a load/store instruction determines the access to rows in LPT. Each time when a particular load/store instruction is executed, fields in a row are updated based on the presented algorithm (given above, under the schematic). When a row is initialized, the field STR is set to the zero value and the tag is set to temporal. *Implication*: when a cache miss occurs, the tag of the load/store instruction that is located in LPT determines which sub-cache system the fetched data should be placed into.

is cached or whether the missed data is not to be cached. The data is placed in the default sub-cache system when information for a particular instruction has not reached a "stable state" in LPT. The authors have evaluated a DDC system for three different types of benchmarks (synthetic benchmarks, kernels, and some benchmarks from the SPEC 92 suite). The results show that, for benchmarks that have memory references that exhibit both types of localities, DDC system has better performance than a conventional cache system of the same size. The research reported in Ref. [1] did not show reduction of power consumption and of transistor count compared to the conventional cache system. Still, the use of cache memory space could be reduced by not allowing duplication of data in both temporal and spatial sub-cache systems, which is an obvious improvement that could be utilized.

The example in Fig. 4 presents a code for calculating the sum of every kth element in an array. The values for summation are placed in the array a. After the execution of the code, the resulting sum is placed in the scalar variable *sum*. The code is executed on a system with a DDC system.

Initially all accessed data is dragged into the temporal sub-cache system, because initial tag is temporal. The state for every new row in LPT is set to initial, while the stride is set to zero. Every access to scalar data has the stride equal to zero and the state for each load/store instruction in LPT is set to

```
for i:=1 to M do begin
    sum:=0;
    j:=i;
    while (j < N) do begin
        sum:=sum + a[j];
        j:=j + k;
    end;
    p[i]:=sum;
end ;
```

Figure 4 An example that shows how a DDC system works. *Legend*: M, N—arbitrary constants; a—the array containing values that are being summed; k—stride; sum—the resulting sum; p—the array where partial sums are places. *Description*: algorithm that calculates a sum of every kth value in the array a. *Explanation*: the code is executed on a system based on a DDC approach. *Implication*: scalar variables are being cached in the temporal sub-cache system, because the stride for scalar variables, which are typically temporal data, is always zero and the state for that load/store instruction is always transient (meaning that the tag has a default value). Access to the fist element of the array a will result in placing the first element into the default temporal sub-cache system. Access to the next element of the array a will result in placing the next element into the default temporal sub-cache system and changing state to transient for that load/store instruction. The second element will also be cached into the default temporal sub-cache system and the state will change to "steady" for that load/store instruction. If stride is small, the rest of array blocks will be cached in the spatial sub-cache system, and if not, the rest of array blocks will be bypassed. Access to the first array block will result in placing data into the temporal sub-cache system if array is small, because the array cannot self-interfere; otherwise, the first block will be bypassed.

transient. It stays in the transient state until the end of the execution. If cache miss occurs for scalar data during the execution of a load/store instruction that is in the transient state, the data will be cached into the temporal sub-cache system. The second access to the array *a* will result in (a) placing the accessed element into the default temporal sub-cache system and (b) changing the state to transient (for that load/store instruction). The second element will also be cached into the default temporal sub-cache system and the state will change to steady for that load/store instruction. If a stride is small, the rest of array blocks will be cached in the spatial sub-cache system, and if not, the rest of the array block will be bypassed. Since the array cannot self-interfere, the access to the first array block will result in placing data into the temporal sub-cache system if the array is small; otherwise, the first block will be bypassed.

This example shows that data exhibiting only temporal and spatial locality with constant stride is correctly detected by this algorithm of a DDC system. Wrong decision is made only for the first accessed array block.

3.1.2 The STS Data Cache

Milutinovic *et al.* [2] present the STS cache system for effective utilization of different types of localities in data accesses. The goal of the research was to compare the performances of STS and conventional cache systems. In STS systems, data blocks are tagged as temporal or spatial based on the locality that data in them exhibits. The system is divided into temporal and spatial sub-cache systems, as illustrated in Fig. 5, and a data block is cached differently depending on its associated tag. Unlike DDC, where a large second-level cache is used for both sub-cache systems, in SST, the two-level temporal sub-cache system, used as second-level cache, is two times smaller. The spatial sub-cache system has only one level with hardware-implemented prefetching mechanism to the next level in memory hierarchy. For every cache miss, a run-time algorithm determines the sub-cache system where the missed data is cached, as illustrated in Fig. 6. This is implemented in hardware, which dynamically tags/retags blocks of data against their locality. In order to minimize the effects of a "cold-start" period, a compile-time algorithm (that tags blocks of data based on the data structure) and a profile-time algorithm (similar to the run-time algorithm) are used.

The performance evaluation was done without a compile-time algorithm for initial placement of data into one or the other sub-cache, and with ready-to-use traces (ATUM). It showed considerably better performance over a conventional cache system and a similar cache hit ratio. The same

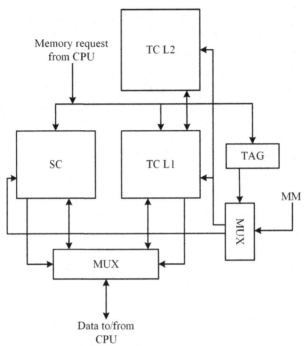

Memory request from CPU

Data to/from CPU

Figure 5 The split temporal spatial cache system. *Legend*: MM—main memory; SC—spatial sub-cache with prefetching mechanism; TAG—unit for dynamic tagging/retagging data; TC L1 and TC L2—the first and the second levels of the temporal sub-cache; MUX—multiplexer. *Description*: the cache organization is divided into two sub-cache systems: the spatial and the temporal sub-cache systems. The spatial sub-cache system has only one level with blocks of usual size and a hardware-implemented prefetching mechanism, while the temporal sub-cache system has two cache levels with one-word wide block. *Explanation*: the cache system is split into a "spatial" sub-cache system and a "temporal" sub-cache system, using different caching strategies for different types of localities that data exhibits. A data block is cached in a different sub-cache system based on an associated tag. The tag is determined for each data block based on the history of all previous accesses to that data block. *Implication*: only when a cache miss occurs for a given data block, that block can move to the other sub-cache system.

authors in Ref. [5] show that this method can also reduce the complexity of the die area occupied by the design and, consequently, decrease power consumption.

Further improvements of the proposed cache system can be made by adding a mechanism for detecting and not caching the data that does not express any type of locality and a mechanism for better utilization of vector data that has nonunit strides.

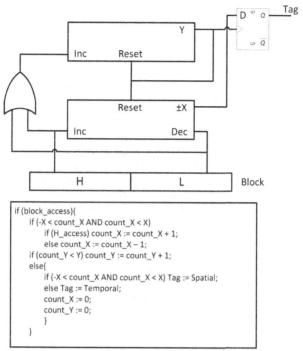

```
if (block_access){
    if (-X < count_X AND count_X < X)
        if (H_access) count_X := count_X + 1;
        else count_X := count_X – 1;
    if (count_Y < Y) count_Y := count_Y + 1;
    else{
        if (-X < count_X AND count_X < X) Tag := Spatial;
        else Tag := Temporal;
        count_X := 0;
        count_Y := 0;
    }
}
```

Figure 6 Dynamic tagging/retagging of data blocks against their locality. *Legend*: H—the upper half of the data block; L—the lower half of the data block. *Description*: every data block in cache has a two-counter logic associated with it. *Explanation*: the default tag for all data is spatial. Counters are initially set to zero. The value of the counter count_X is checked periodically. Period of count_X checking is controlled by the second counter count_Y, which counts the overall number of accesses to this block. When count_Y reaches some predefined value (Y), the value of the corresponding counter count_X is checked. The counter count_X is incremented after each access to the upper half of the block and is decremented after each access to the lower half of the block. If the count_X reaches maximum (X) or minimum (−X), further changes of the count_X are blocked until the next periodic check, when the count_X resets. Data in the block exhibits temporal locality if the count_X reaches X or −X after Y accesses to the block. If that happens, the tag for the block is tagged as temporal. Otherwise, the block is tagged as spatial. After the block is being evicted from the cache and accessed again, the block will be fetched in a different subsystem cache. *Implication*: the block can change its tag from spatial to temporal and back, arbitrary many times, even several times while being continuously cached. The predefined value Y has to be greater than the predefined value X, and X must be no less than a half of the block size (in words).

The example in Fig. 7 shows a code for calculating a table of values for a given polynomial function and for a given range of variable x. The coefficients of terms are placed in the array a. After the execution of code, the resulting table is placed in the array p. It is assumed that every scalar variable

```
for i := 1 to M do
begin
    p[i] := a[N+1];
    for j := N downto 0 do
        p[i] := p[i]*x + a[j];
    x := x + 1;
end;
```

Figure 7 An example that shows how the STS cache system works. *Legend*: M, N—arbitrary constants; *a*—the array containing coefficients of a polynomial function; *p*—the resulting array; *x*—the variable of the polynomial function; *i, j*—loop counters. *Description*: algorithm that calculates a table of values for a given polynomial function and for a given range of the variable *x*. *Explanation*: the code is executed on a system with an STS cache system and a transactional memory. After several iterations of the outer loop, an abort procedure restarts the outer loop. *Implication*: scalar variables are being cached in the temporal sub-cache system. The array *a* is being cached in the spatial sub-cache system. The array *p* is being cached in the temporal sub-cache system.

is placed in a different block of the main memory. The code is executed on a system with STS cache system and a transactional memory. Initially all accessed data is placed into the spatial sub-cache system. Since scalar data resides in the upper half of a memory block (and the lower half of the block does not contain data that is being accessed by the code), every access to a scalar data item is increasing the counter *count_X*, until it reaches the upper limit. When that happens, the block with the scalar data item is retagged as a temporal data block. Accesses to data in the array *a* are sequential with a unit stride. The counter *count_X* remains at value zero for all data blocks that contain the array *a*, except for the last block when it is not fully filled with data. If all parameters (X, Y) are set properly, the counter *count_X* for the last block will never reach the upper limit. Every element of the array *p* is accessed several times in the inner loop, depending on the number of terms in the polynomial function, while no other element is being referenced.

The presented access pattern increments or decrements the counter *count_X* until it reaches the upper or lower limit. All blocks that contain array *p* are retagged as temporal data blocks. After several iterations of the outer loop, when the retagging mechanism has reached the saturation point, an abort procedure restarts the outer loop and evicts all data from the cache. Execution of code will result in placing scalar variables and the array *p* in the temporal sub-cache system. The blocks containing the array *a* are placed in the spatial sub-cache system. This example shows that the run-time algorithm correctly detects data exhibiting only temporal or only spatial locality, while data exhibiting both types of localities is tagged as temporal.

The SST approach can be viewed as an attempt to address dynamicity in the behavior of data. Data characteristics are viewed dynamically, rather than statically. Data is allowed to change its characteristics in time, and a hardware mechanism is added that allow data to move between the spatial and the temporal parts. In other words, a company that adopts the SST approach could double the number of cores before the companies that follow the traditional approach to caching, and additionally will provide a better performance after the data changes its characteristics.

3.2. General Uniprocessor Compiler-Assisted

The general uniprocessor compiler-assisted (GUC) is a class of proposed solutions where both software and hardware determine data localities and caching strategies. Compiler help is necessary for these solutions.

3.2.1 The Northwestern Solution

Memik *et al.* [6] presented the Northwestern solution (NS) for improving cache performance using compiler and hardware techniques. The research was performed with the idea to investigate interaction between hardware and software techniques in optimizing data locality. In NS, for code areas that have regular data access pattern, compiler techniques are used, and for code areas with data that does not have regular access pattern, special instructions are used to selectively turn on/off the hardware-based technique. For caching data that does not exhibit spatial locality and has high access frequency, the system uses conventional cache system, and for caching data that exhibits spatial locality, it uses a small buffer, as illustrated in Fig. 8.

The proposed solution does not cache data that does not have high access frequency and does not exhibit spatial locality. Affine loop and data transformation compiler techniques are used to aggressively optimize temporal and spatial locality. When compiler techniques are used on data, it is cached as in a conventional cache system. The simulation results confirm that the NS, using the same die area and power consumption, has better performance than systems with pure-hardware, pure-software, or combined hardware/software nonselective techniques for optimizing data locality.

Examples for this solution are not provided because sufficient details for algorithms used for data manipulation were not available. However, adding details is relatively simple and is best left to the reader as a homework assignment.

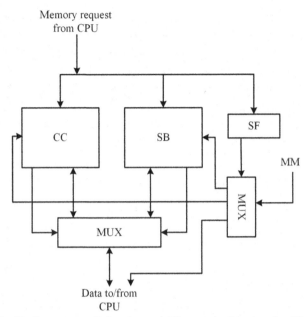

Memory request
from CPU

Data to/from
CPU

Figure 8 The Northwestern solution. *Legend*: CC—conventional cache; SB—small FIFO buffer; SF—unit that detects data access frequency and if data exhibits spatial locality; MM—main memory; MUX—multiplexer. *Description*: the cache system consists of a conventional cache and a small FIFO buffer. The SF unit controls into what subsystem the fetched data will be placed. *Explanation*: the CPU can turn on/off the SF. Software techniques for optimizing data locality are used when the SF is turned off and data is cached into the conventional cache. Hardware techniques for optimizing data locality are used when the SF is turned on and data is cached into the conventional cache or into the small buffer (if data has a high access frequency or it exhibits spatial locality). *Implication*: for turning on/off the SF, special instructions have to be added to the processor instruction set.

When working on the development of details for the NS approach, one should constantly keep in mind that the compiler can influence the behavior of data at the run time. If the data is placed in loops, the temporal aspect is augmented. If the data is placed in strides, the special aspect is augmented. Existence of efficient compiler technology is the major enabler for this approach to treatment of spatial and temporal localities in caches.

3.3. General Multiprocessor Compiler-Not-Assisted

The general multiprocessor compiler-not-assisted (GMN) is a class where solely hardware determines data localities and caching strategies and where the help of a compiler is not necessary. The cache system is created for processors used in a multiprocessor environment.

3.3.1 The Split Data Cache in Multiprocessor System

Sahuquillo and Pont [7] proposed a few extensions to the STS cache system, presented in Ref. [2], in order to adapt it for a shared memory multiprocessor environment. In GMN systems, a tag for data is kept until data eviction, and when the tag for data gets changed, the data is relocated to another sub-cache system. As depicted in Fig. 9, a snoop controller is added to the second-level temporal sub-cache system and to the spatial sub-cache system. In conjunction to the STS cache system, an extension of the Berkeley cache coherence protocol is used, as depicted in Fig. 10. When a hit occurs

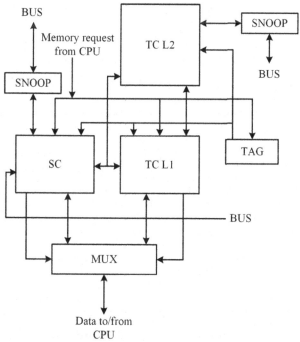

Figure 9 Split data cache system in a multiprocessor system environment. *Legend*: MUX—multiplexer; BUS—system bus; SC—spatial sub-cache with prefetching mechanism; TAG—unit for dynamic tagging/retagging of data; TC L1 and TC L2—the first and the second levels of the temporal sub-cache; SNOOP—snoop controller for the cache coherence protocol. *Description*: the cache organization is divided into spatial and temporal sub-cache systems. Each sub-cache system has an associated snoop controller. *Explanation*: the divided cache system allows the use of different caching strategies for different types of localities that data exhibits. A data block is cached into a specific sub-cache system based on the associated tag. The tag for each data block is determined by the history of the previous accesses to that data block, the ones that happened after the last time the block was fetched. *Implication*: data can change the sub-cache system in which it is stored. Only the spatial sub-cache system fetches data.

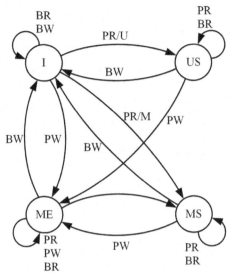

Figure 10 The modified Berkeley cache coherence protocol. *Legend*: I—invalid state; US—unmodified-shared state; MS—modified shared state; ME—modified exclusive state; PR—processor read; PW—processor write; BR—bus read; BW—bus write; U—requested block is unmodified; M—requested block is modified. *Description*: the shown cache coherence protocol must be used in the STS system, if it is deployed in a multi-processor environment. *Explanation*: read miss fetches a block in the US state or in the MS state, depending on whether the block is unmodified or modified in other parts of the memory system. Read hit does not change the state of a block. Write to a block changes the state of the block to ME and sends an invalidation signal to the bus. *Implication*: if the block is in the ME state when its eviction happens, the block is written back to the memory.

in one sub-cache system, it sends a signal to another one to stop it from accessing the bus and passes the requested data to the processor. When a miss occurs, the spatial sub-cache system requests the data on the bus and accepts the received data. Both sub-cache systems snoop into the bus for invalidation signal, and, when necessary, invalidate the data. Simulation shows that an STS system in a multiprocessor environment can achieve the same performance as a conventional cache, while occupying smaller space on the die. In order to avoid the "cold-start" period for data being read again after it has been evicted, it is possible to enable tag history, especially when eviction of shared block happened as a result of a write operation by another processor.

The example in Fig. 11 presents the code for calculating the sum of elements in an array. In a parallelized algorithm, each processor calculates a partial sum of elements for an unshared part of the array. The partial sum is saved

```
for i := 1 to N do
begin
    sum := sum + a[i];
end;
lock();
x = x + sum;
unlock();
```

Figure 11 An example of an STS cache in a multiprocessor system. *Legend*: *N*—arbitrary constant; *i*—loop counter; *a*—array; sum—unshared scalar variable; *x*—shared scalar variable; lock, unlock—synchronization primitives. *Description*: a parallel algorithm that calculates the sum of elements in an array. *Explanation*: the algorithm is executed on a system with an STS cache in a multiprocessor system, with the assumption that the array is relatively large. The loop is typically executed several times at execution time. *Implication*: the array is cached in the spatial sub-cache system and the scalar variables are cached in the temporal sub-cache system. Only the eviction of shared scalar variables is necessary, because the invalidation cycle is executed after every write.

in an unshared variable. When the partial sum is calculated, its value is added to global sum. The global sum is saved in a global variable for which the synchronization is necessary. When the calculation is over, each processor switches to another part of the array. An STS cache in a multiprocessor system is used in executing this code and the assumption is that the array is relatively large.

Initially, all accessed data is copied into the spatial sub-cache system. The counter *count_X* is increased with every access to scalar data (because scalar data resides in the upper half of the block and the lower half of the block does not contain data that is being accessed by the code) until it reaches the upper limit. The blocks with scalar data are retagged as temporal data blocks and transferred to the temporal sub-cache system. Accesses to data in the array are sequential with unit stride. The counter *count_X* contains the value zero for all data blocks that contain the array, and those blocks will stay in the spatial sub-cache system until evicted. The unshared scalar data will stay in the temporal sub-cache system during all iterations of the code, because blocks in the temporal sub-cache system have the size of one word and the invalidation of the unshared scalar data cannot happen. The shared data will be invalidated after every write. If the array is properly divided, the invalidation of blocks that contain parts of the array will not happen. This example shows that data exhibiting only temporal or only spatial locality is correctly detected by run-time algorithms. It also indicates that the number of invalidation cycles can be reduced, by overlapping some of the activities.

The essence of the approach of Sahuquillo *et al.* is to bring the SST approach into the multiprocessor environment, for utilization in the Shared Multiprocessors' systems and the Distributed Shared Memory systems. The most critical aspect of any concept extension research is to provide extensibility without jeopardizing on the performance issues that launched the concept in the first place. Sahuquillo *et al.* managed to solve this problem by applying an approach based on the efficient tagging of the history of data behavior.

3.4. General Multiprocessor Compiler-Assisted

The general multiprocessor compiler-assisted (GMC), to the best of our knowledge, is a class that does not have any existing implementations. Typically, such a scenario happens either when the technology is not yet ready for the solution, or when applications still do not need such a solution. Since the GMC class makes a lot of sense, its research might prove quite fruitful in the future [8].

The future research scenario induced by the introduction of the GMC approach is analogous the research scenario induced by the famous Russian chemist Mendeleyev. After the table of chemical elements was created by him, a set of missing elements came up as an obvious consequence of the classification effort of Mendelyeyev.

In the case of the GMC class, the outcome of the classification effort is a clear notion that the GMC approach makes full sense, and that the research in this direction is likely to lead to success. Hopefully, this chapter will induce creative research in this direction.

3.5. Special Uniprocessor Compiler-Not-Assisted

The special uniprocessor compiler-not-assisted (SUN) is a class of proposed solutions where data localities and caching strategies are determined solely in hardware, and where the help of a compiler is not necessary. The cache systems belonging to this group are optimized for special-purpose applications.

3.5.1 The Reconfigurable Split Data Cache

Naz *et al.* [9] present the reconfigurable split data cache (RSDC) architecture for embedded systems with the aim to accomplish better die area utilization. The RSDC detects spatial or temporal locality that data exhibits and fine-tunes cache policies in accordance with the detected type. As depicted in

Fig. 12, the cache is divided into an array cache, for exploiting spatial locality, a scalar cache, for exploiting temporal locality, and a victim cache, for lowering the associativity of the scalar cache. Every sub-cache system (Fig. 13) is further divided into multiple partitions [10]. These partitions can be used for purposes other than conventional caching (instruction reuse, as lookup tables, prefetching, etc.) or can be turned off to reduce power consumption. Reconfiguration of the cache partitions is used in applications that have lower memory requirements and can benefit from specialized

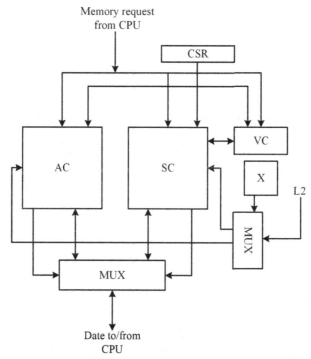

Figure 12 Reconfigurable split data cache. *Legend*: AC—array cache; SC—scalar cache; VC—victim cache; CSR—cache status register; X—unit for determining data type; L2—second-level cache; MUX—multiplexer. *Description*: the cache is divided into three sub-cache systems: the array cache, for exploiting spatial locality; the scalar cache, for exploring temporal locality; and the victim cache, for lowering the associativity level of the scalar cache. *Explanation*: the unit X determines the type of data that is being fetched and places the data into a proper sub-cache system (scalar or array cache). Data is placed in the victim cache only when the block containing that data is evicted from the scalar cache. In the CSR, there is information about which partition is used for conventional caching and which one is not. *Implication*: additional logic and wiring in sub-cache systems are needed if checking is performed to determine which partition is used for conventional caching. Such checking increases access time of a sub-cache system.

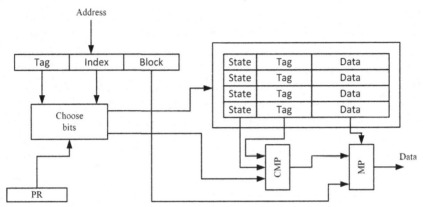

Figure 13 Reconfigurable cache organization. *Legend*: tag, index, block, state—information used to fetch data from the conventional cache; PR—register that holds information on which partition is used; CMP—comparator; MP—multiplexer. *Description*: one partition of the reconfigurable cache organization with multiple partitions and with overlapped wide-tag partitioning addressing scheme. *Explanation*: each cache partition size can be dynamically configured. Configuration is done by writing to PR register. Size of the partition depends on the application needs. The number of bits in a tag and index fields of the address will vary based on the size of the partition. Additional logic, based on the content of the PR register, is incorporated for choosing which bits in tag and index fields of the address will be used. *Implication*: a reconfigurable cache with N partitions must accept N addresses and generate N hit/miss signals.

hardware for nonstandard processor activity. Paper [10] concludes that only a small amount of additional logic and additional wiring is required for implementation of reconfigurable partitions. The cache access time is increased, but by a relatively small percentage. Since an array data can also exhibit temporal locality, it would not be good to induce data locality just based on the data types because it can generate misclassified data.

The example in Fig. 14 shows a code for calculating the table of values for a given polynomial function (for a given range of the variable x). The coefficients of terms are placed in array a. After the execution of the code, the resulting table is placed in array p. It is assumed that every scalar variable is placed in a different block in the main memory. The code is executed on a system with RSDC system.

It will be explained here what happens during execution of one iteration of the outer loop. The array sub-cache system uses prefetching mechanism, so when each element of the array p is accessed, a block that contains the element is fetched into the array sub-cache system along with two other neighboring blocks. The element that is accessed is exhibiting temporal

```
for i := 1 to M do
begin
  p[i] := a[N+1];
  for j := N downto 0 do
    p[i] := p[i]*x + a[j];
  x := x + 1;
end;
```

Figure 14 An example showing how the RSDC system works. *Legend*: *M, N*—arbitrary constants; *a*—an array containing coefficients of a polynomial function; *p*—the resulting array; *x*—the variable of the polynomial function; *i, j*—loop counters. *Description*: algorithm that calculates a table of values for a given polynomial function and for a given range of variable *x*. *Explanation*: the code is executed on a system with a RSDC system. *Implication*: scalar variables are being cached in the scalar sub-cache system. The arrays are being cached in the array sub-cache system. When the size of *a* is relatively large, there is a high possibility that accesses to the array *p* will generate a large number of misses.

locality because it is used during the execution of the inner loop. Data in the array *a* is accessed sequentially with a unit stride. Each miss that happens when accessing elements in the array *a* will fetch a block of data into the array sub-cache system. If the array *a* is relatively large, at some point in the inner loop, blocks with the array *p* data will be evicted. Access to the evicted element of the array *p* will happen very quickly and three blocks will be fetched into the array sub-cache system. Several misses will happen for the same element of the array *p* during one execution of the outer loop. Each time there is a miss; unnecessary blocks are fetched. This possible eviction of data that might be needed in a near future results in longer latency.

This example shows how an RSDC system works when some data in the array exhibits temporal locality and how prefetching mechanism can produce unhealthy latency.

Essentially, any effort related to reconfiguration can be viewed in the light of the work by Feynman [11], which states that, under specific conditions, arithmetic and logic can be performed at zero energy and typically with a negligibly small energy, while communications can never be done with zero energy and typically is performed with a nonnegligible energy. If a reconfigurable hardware is used, an obvious consequence is that the amount of communications needed for some computation is minimized. Actually, caching is an approach to minimize communications in computing [12]. An approach with the best potentials as far as the minimization of communications needed for computing is described in Ref. [13], but it carries with a number of other implementation problems.

3.6. Special Uniprocessor Compiler-Assisted

The special uniprocessor compiler-assisted (SUC) is a class of proposed solutions where data localities and caching strategies are determined in software and hardware. The cache systems belonging to this group are optimized for special-purpose applications.

3.6.1 The Data Type-Dependent Cache for MPEG Application

Cucchiara *et al.* [14] propose a data type-dependent cache for MPEG (DDM) applications and for effective use of two-dimensional (2D) spatial locality image data. The goal of the research was to achieve better performance for multimedia applications compared to cases that use conventional cache systems (Fig. 15). The first modification was to assign to the compiler the analysis of each memory reference and its classification as either addressing image or addressing nonimage data. Different prefetching algorithms are used to cache different types of data. In a dedicated memory table, using a special procedure call, information about each image data type, address range, and row size is stored. Every time when memory reference occurs, this information is used for deciding which prefetching mechanism will be used. New "neighbor-prefetching" (NP) algorithm (illustrated in Fig. 16) is proposed for exploiting 2D spatial locality and a standard

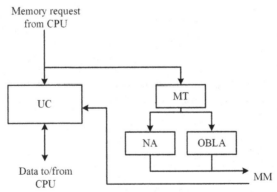

Figure 15 The data type-dependent cache for MPEG applications. *Legend*: UC—unified data cache; MT—memory table for image information; NA—unit for prefetching data by the neighbor algorithm; OBLA—unit for prefetching data by the OBL algorithm; MM—main memory. *Description*: different prefetching units handle different data types. The cache organization is not divided into sub-cache systems. *Explanation*: in order to exploit 2D spatial locality, image data is prefetched using NA. In order to exploit standard spatial locality, nonimage data is prefetched using the OBLA unit. The information created by the compiler about the type of locality exhibited by data is stored in the MT unit. *Implication*: a specialized instruction set is necessary to change content of the MT.

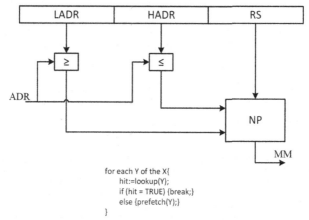

for each Y of the X{
    hit:=lookup(Y);
    if (hit = TRUE) {break;}
    else {prefetch(Y);}
}

Figure 16 Run-time logic for prefetching data that exhibits 2D spatial locality. *Legend*: ADR—address of the referenced data; MM—main memory; LADR—the lowest address of the image data; HADR—the highest address of the image data; RS—row size of the image data; NP—unit that implements the neighbor-prefetching algorithm; X—currently referenced memory block; Y—all neighbors of X; lookup()—checks whether the block is in the cache; prefetch()—prefetches the block into the cache. *Description*: a row in a dedicated memory for keeping track of the address range for an image data item and algorithm for the NP. Every image variable has one row in a dedicated memory. *Explanation*: each time an image variable is allocated, its address range and row size are stored in a dedicated memory by a procedure call. At each memory reference, the memory address is compared with those stored in the table, in order to state whether this is an image reference or not, and its row size is forwarded to the NP. When memory block with image element is accessed, the NP finds all neighbors of that block based on the row size. The NP checks whether all neighbors are in the cache; if some of them are not, it prefetches only one neighbor. The rest of the noncached neighbors are prefetched during future memory references. *Implication*: the address range check is done for all allocated rows in the dedicated memory for each memory reference. The NP checks in parallel whether the neighbors are cached using dedicated adders and a multiported tag directory.

One-Block-Lookahead (OBL) prefetching algorithm is proposed for exploiting spatial locality of nonimage data. The DDM is useful for applications that handle a substantial amount of image and video data. The compiler classifies data based on the variable declarations generated by a programmer. Thus, if a programmer uses a nonappropriate programming style, this approach can miss-classify data. The compiler requires a specialized instruction set to access the memory table.

It may be possible to improve the overall performance of the DDM approach by inclusion of another sub-cache system for exploiting temporal locality of scalar data.

The example in Fig. 17 shows code for an algorithm that processes image data. Each image element gets changed based on its neighboring elements. The image data and the resulting image data are given in matrix forms. It is assumed that both nonimage and image data are placed into different blocks of the main memory. The compiler inserts a special procedure call to store (into a dedicated memory) the information about image address range and row size. The code is executed on a system with DDM cache system.

Initially, all data is initialized. The cache is flushed afterward. Every access to nonimage data results in data prefetching from the main memory using the OBL algorithm. Every access to image data results in data prefetching from the main memory using the NP algorithm. When an element *image[i][j]* (the first element in a memory block) is accessed for the first time, all neighboring blocks are located and information about each of them (is it cached, computed blocks addresses, etc.) is stored into a multiported tag directory. If one of the lookups misses, the required missing neighboring block is fetched into the cache. If further lookups miss, their blocks will be fetched on the succeeding memory references. The rest of the elements in the same block that contains *image[i][j]* are accessed next, and for them (the neighbors of the next elements), there are no single cache misses in the most inner loop. Access to the first neighboring block of the block that contains the element *image[i][j]* will happen, while several neighboring blocks are

```
for i:=1 to N do begin
  for j:=1 to M do begin
    for each image[l][k] neighbor of image[i][j] do
      image[i][j]:= op(image[i][j],image[l][k])
  end;
end;
```

Figure 17 An example that shows how a DDM cache system works. *Legend*: M, N—arbitrary constants; image—a matrix containing image data; op—an arbitrary binary operation over two image elements; i, j—the loop counters; l, k—indices of neighboring elements. *Description*: algorithm that calculates a new value for each image element using its neighbors. *Explanation*: the code is executed on a system with DDM cache system. The compiler inserts a special procedure call that stores information about image address range and row size into dedicated memory. *Implication*: the cache initially does not contain image data. All nonimage data are prefetched using a standard One-Block-Lookahead algorithm. The image data is prefetched using the neighbor-prefetching algorithm. When the element *image[i][j]* (the first element in a memory block) is accessed several times, all neighboring blocks are fetched into the cache. The rest of the elements in the same block that contains *image[i][j]* are accessed next and for them there is not a single cache miss in the most inner loop.

already cached. This example shows that the run-time algorithm extensively uses 2D spatial locality.

One method to improve efficiency is to migrate a general concept onto a specific application domain. In that case, the complexity of the implementation may drop drastically, while the performance may increase drastically, due to the fact that generalized solutions always include redundancies that increase complexity and deteriorate performance (i.e., slow down the speed). The above explained is exactly the research philosophy behind the approach of Cucchiara *et al.*

3.7. Special Multiprocessor Compiler-Not-Assisted

The special multiprocessor compiler-not-assisted (SMN) is a class of proposed solutions where only hardware determines data localities and caching strategies and where the help of a compiler is not necessary. The cache systems belonging to this group are optimized for special-purpose applications in multiprocessor environment.

3.7.1 The Texas Solution

Adamo *et al.* present in Ref. [15] similar solution to the RSDC for use in embedded multiprocessor systems, named Texas solution (TS) cache system. Data is divided and placed into different sub-cache systems based on its type. The TS cache has two sub-cache systems: a system for storing array data (array sub-cache) and a system for storing scalar data (scalar sub-cache), as illustrated in Fig. 8. To enable hardware-based prefetching, a small fully associative first-in first-out (FIFO) buffer is associated with the array sub-cache system. When a miss occurs, the missed block is fetched into the array sub-cache system. Also, the next block is fetched into the buffer to avoid cache pollution that is possible when needed data is displaced in an untimely manner. The authors have shown that TS cache can deliver the same performance as a conventional cache. Because it is occupying less die area, it is a good choice for the first-level cache in embedded multiprocessor systems on chip—they leave more space for processor cores. Since the array data can exhibit temporal locality, it may be wrong to induce data locality based on the generated data type (what can generate misclassified data). The cache coherence protocol can greatly affect performance of the cache system, so it is important to select the best one.

An example for this solution is not provided, because the solution is similar to the uniprocessor RSDC. Paths of executions are expected to be similar. The structure from Fig. 10 is only slightly different from the structure of the TS and therefore the structure of that solution is not presented in this chapter.

If an interested reader is eager to develop details of the TS approach, the following should be kept in mind: (a) moving into the embedded environment is also an example of moving from global to specific (which enables smaller complexity and better performance), but the dimensions of the problem treated by TS are different from the case in which the movement from general to specific was related to one specific application; (b) embedded computing should be able to support a number of different applications and therefore could be treated as a middle way from the most general to the most specific; and (c) embedded systems can imply small data sets or very big data sets, and the philosophy of embedded system design depends a lot on the data characteristics.

3.8. Special Multiprocessor Compiler-Assisted

The special multiprocessor compiler-assisted (SMC) is a class of proposed solutions where both software and hardware determine data localities and caching strategies. These cache systems are optimized for special-purpose applications in a multiprocessor environment.

3.8.1 The Time-Predictable Data Cache

Schoeberl *et al.* proposed in Ref. [16] the time-predictable (TP) data cache for on-chip multiprocessor system, built from Java processor (JOP) cores. The goal of this research was to enable tight worst-case execution time analysis of real-time applications. Depending on the data memory access type, TP cache system stores scalar data in different sub-cache systems. Array data is being bypassed. The unit for determining memory access type is presented in Fig. 18. There are two sub-cache systems, as illustrated in Fig. 19. One is fully associative sub-cache system with last recently used (LRU) replacement and another is a direct-mapped (DM) cache. The compiler is in charge of dividing data into groups based on the data memory access type. Dynamic data (located on the heap) is cached in the associative cache and constant and static data is cached in the DM sub-cache system. According to the authors, splitting data cache simplifies the cache coherence protocol. In this way, its limiting factor on the multiprocessor system scalability is reduced, because it can detect shared data and, only when it is truly necessary, enforce data invalidation. Not exploiting spatial locality that array data exhibits (array data is skipped) can impact the performance.

The example in Fig. 20 shows code for implementing a FIFO buffer in a user-defined class X. Class X is designed using the Singleton design pattern.

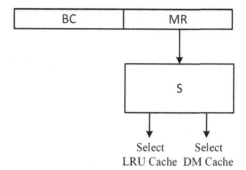

Select   Select
LRU Cache   DM Cache

Figure 18 The unit for determining memory access type in a time-predictable cache system. *Legend*: BC—operation bytecode; MR—operation data access type; S—unit for selecting destination sub-cache system; LRU—fully associative sub-cache system with LRU replacement; DM—direct-mapped sub-cache system. *Description*: data access types are classified as follows: CLINFO (accesses to type information, method dispatch table, and interface dispatch table), CONST (accesses to constant pool), STATIC (accesses to static fields), HEADER (accesses to dynamic type, array length, and fields for garbage collection), FIELD (accesses to object fields), and ARRAY (accesses to arrays). *Explanation*: an operation data access type is determined by the compiler. *Implication*: the unit for selection of the destination sub-cache system places data with CONST, CLINFO, and STATIC data access types into the direct-mapped sub-cache system; and data with FIELD and HEADER access types into the LRU sub-cache system. The data with ARRAY access type is not cached.

The data is placed in an array field buffer of the class X. The constant data *SIZE* determines the size of the array field. For getting data from the buffer and inserting data into the buffer, methods *get* and *set* are created. The code is executed in a multithreaded environment on a multiprocessor JOP system with TP cache system. Stack data is not conventionally cached in the JOP system so caching stack data is not performed.

Initially all data caches are empty. Using method getInstance an instance of the class X is created when the first thread accesses the FIFO buffer. The class info data, constant data *SIZE*, and static field instance are cached in the DM sub-cache system, the sub-cache system of the first thread. Subsequent accesses to the instance of class X, via method getInstance, by other thread, result in dragging the class info data and static field instance into their DM sub-cache systems. Since data in DM sub-cache systems will not be changed, cache coherence protocol will not be activated. When threads access data in the FIFO buffer, via methods *get* and *set*, fields head and tail are cached into LRU sub-cache systems, while data in the array buffer is cache bypassed. Every call to methods *get* and *set* results in changing field data head and tail, so the cache coherence protocol has to be activated.

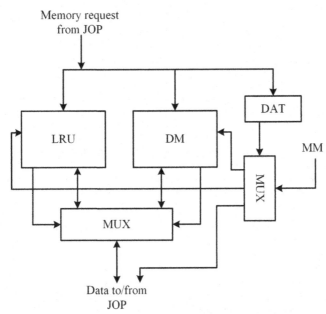

Figure 19 The time-predictable data cache. *Legend*: MM—main memory; JOP—Java processor; MUX—multiplexer; LRU—fully associative sub-cache system with LRU replacement; DM—direct-mapped sub-cache system; DAT—unit for determining data memory access type. *Description*: constant and static data is stored in the DM sub-cache system. Object headers and fields are stored in LRU. Array data is not cached. *Explanation*: different types of data compiler place into different memory areas. The DAT unit determines where and if to cache data. *Implication*: this simplified cache coherence protocol invalidates data only when a write to shared data occurs.

This example shows how TP cache system works within the JOP system, and how splitting of data cache for different data access types allows modularization of the cache analysis.

The TP cache research, conditionally speaking, belongs to a school of thought which argues for labeling of data, in time or in any other metrics of interest. Once this type of labeling is introduced, data can be classified by more criteria, and improvements can be looked at in combining the criteria and by doing some kind of multicriteria analysis. If the tagging is related to time of creation, data generations can be defined, and common characteristics of different data generations can be utilized.

3.9. A Comparison of the Existing Solutions

This section gives a table that compares the existing solutions, based on the data provided by original papers (Table 2). We transformed data from

```
class X {
        const int SIZE = ...;
        static X instance = null;
        int buffer[], head = 0, tail = 0;
        private X(){buffer = new int [SIZE];}
        public static synchronized X getInstance(){
                if (instance == null)
                        instance = new X();
                return instance;
        }
        public syncronized int get(){...}
        public syncronized void set(int product)
        {...}
}
```

Figure 20 An example that shows how the TP data cache system works. *Legend*: X—class type; SIZE—constant data; instance—static data; buffer—array data; head, tail—field data; getInstance—get method for only one instance of the class; get, set—methods for basic operation on the buffer. *Description*: class X represents a FIFO buffer, made using the Singleton design pattern. The class X is designed for a multi-threaded environment. *Explanation*: the instance of class X is created when the first time a thread calls the method getInstance. Every other call to method getInstance accesses the static class X instance. The set method is for inserting data into a buffer, and the get method is for getting data from a buffer. *Implication*: when the instance of the class X is created, data regarding class information, constant SIZE, and static field instance is cached into the DM sub-cache system. Data cached in the DM sub-cache system is not changed during execution, so a cache coherence protocol is not applied. Call to methods get and set results in changing field head and tail, that are cached in the LRU sub-caches system, and cache coherence protocol has to invalidate that data. Data in buffer arrays is never cached.

the original papers into comparison related conclusions, keeping in mind the characteristics of applications and run-time environments.

Of course, a much more useful type of comparison is when all surveyed approaches are compared under the same conditions, for a plethora of applications that span one entire domain of applications. This type of analysis implies that all the surveyed approaches are brought to a common "denominator," so complexities and performances can be compared under the same conditions. Such analysis is the subject of a follow-up research.

4. CONCLUSION OF THE SURVEY PART

The main goal of this survey was to extensively present different solutions of data access prediction patterns and utilization principles of hiding

Table 2 A Comparison of Selected Dual Cache Solutions with Traditional Cache

Solution	Performance	Size	Energy Consumption
Dual data cache	+	=	=
Split temporal/spatial data cache	+	+	?
The Northwestern solution	+	=	=
Split data cache in multiprocessor systems	=	+	?
Reconfigurable split data cache	=	=	+
Data type-dependent cache for MPEG applications	+	?	?
The Texas solution	=	+	?
Time-predictable data cache	?	+	+

+: The solution works better than traditional cache. −: The solution works worse than traditional cache. =: The solution works about equally well as traditional cache. ?: The comparison depends on the application and the environment.

memory access latency. The survey also shows that a lot of man–power and research efforts have been spent in developing cache systems based on the DDC approach. We tried to give a substantial overview of existing approaches in terms of targeted applications. With increasing number of domains, the processors are being used at, it is vital to ensure that cache systems, which use a significant portion of the on–chip transistors, are reduced in size as much as possible. Also, it is very important that the performances do not decrease, and if they do, the decrease is acceptably small. We pointed out which solutions have achieved this goal.

Also, for embedded computing, where power consumption is a limiting factor, we indicated designs with low power consumption.

The solutions for multiprocessor systems that we have analyzed offer possibilities for reducing power consumption and used die area. Some of them are uniprocessor solutions adapted for use in multiprocessor systems with a small change in cache coherence protocol (the one that is used for conventional cache systems). One of them, the TA data cache, designed specifically for use in multiprocessor systems, even simplifies the cache coherence protocol and thus reduces its limiting factor on multiprocessor system scalability.

We presented quite a few algorithms for determining data access patterns. Some of them are simple, some are more complex, but all of them have more or less difficulties in dealing with some specific data access patterns. We think that, through selective combination, some of these algorithms can achieve better results.

Besides using this survey for designing conventional computer systems, we believe that it can create new ideas for designing computer systems with transactional memory. Using a DDC system in systems with transactional memory might be able to reduce cost of abort procedures.

The rest of this text discusses a newly proposed solution that takes into consideration everything we mentioned earlier.

5. PROBLEM STATEMENT FOR THE ANALYSIS

Traditional cache memory architectures are based on the locality property of common memory reference patterns. This means that a part of the content of the main memory is replicated in smaller and faster memories closer to the processor. The processor can then access this data in a nearby fast cache, without suffering long penalties of waiting for main memory access.

Increasing the performance of a cache system is typically done by enlarging the cache. This has led to caches that consume an ever-growing part of modern microprocessor chips. However, bigger caches induce longer latencies. Thus, making a cache larger, beyond a certain point, becomes counterproductive. At that point, any further increasing of the performance of the cache represents a difficult problem, as indicated in Ref. [17].

6. CRITICAL ANALYSIS OF EXISTING SOLUTIONS

The use of multiple level cache hierarchies is the most common solution to the above stated problems. The problem of speed is solved using fast and small lower level caches that sit closer to the processor, while the need for capacity and hit ratio is solved with slower and much larger higher level caches closer to the memory [2]. On the other hand, these high-level caches occupy large portions of the chip inducing high latencies in the system.

As presented in the examples, some solutions include mechanisms that improve cache performance by adding some logic to caching, in order to avoid increase in cache size.

Some of these mechanisms have analyzed physical properties of cache memories and produced solutions that combine two or more cache memories of different characteristics on the same level (i.e., the victim and the assist caches). Mostly, these solutions use very fast DM cache memories with increasing associativity and do not incur long latencies of highly associative caches.

Other solutions try mostly to increase hit ratio, or to decrease complexity without compromising on hit ratio (by allowing smaller sized caches). They look at data access patterns in order to create a cache system that suits data characteristics better (i.e., DDC, STS cache, etc.). A much less detailed explanation of the taxonomy used in this paper can be found in Ref. [18], which is where this taxonomy was introduced for the first time.

Some of the concepts used in this chapter are taken from the STS cache, which was first introduced in a series of papers in the 1990s [1,2,19,20].

The modified STS cache fits into the second category, but the fact that the system also utilizes two cache memories of different characteristics on the same level puts it also in the first category.

Decreasing the overall access latency of the system is the major goal of the modified STS system. As improvement in hit ratio is not the primary interest, it will not be examined in detail.

The major idea behind STS is that it treats differently two different types of localities (spatial and temporal) in data access patterns [2].

If, after a given address is accessed, there is a relatively high probability that a neighboring address will be accessed, the data is exhibiting predominantly spatial locality. Thus, this data should be fetched in larger blocks. This, of course, means that some unnecessary data will also be brought into the cache, so a larger (and thus slower) cache should be used.

If there is relatively high probability of referencing a certain address again in the near future, the data is exhibiting temporal locality. This data is better to be fetched in smaller block sizes (i.e., one-word block size). Consequently, only frequently used data is fetched. Thus, a smaller and faster cache should be used.

7. GENERALIZED SOLUTION

In this section, we will explain the basic design behind this approach and analyze major improvements introduced by a modified STS system. Afterward we will examine some further issues concerning any STS system.

7.1. Basic Design of the Solution

The basic functioning model of this solution is splitting the cache into two parts, one handling data exhibiting temporal and the other handling data exhibiting spatial locality (as depicted in Fig. 21). Each part has a different organization and data handling, in style with data stored in it.

The spatial part is a larger cache and fetches data using usual block size. This part has latencies usual for similarly sized traditional caches.

The temporal part is organized as a small and fast DM cache and works with one-word-sized blocks. Smaller size and direct mapping bring lower access latencies.

To enable marking data locality (spatial or temporal), each memory word is augmented with one bit tag. A single tag can be used for an entire spatial block. A compiler should set those tags to an initial value and they will be changed at profile and run time. A default locality can be assumed, though it

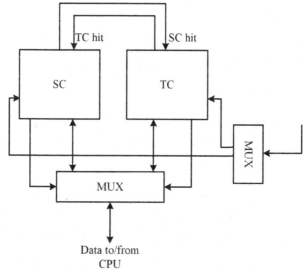

Figure 21 Organization of the STS cache. *Legend*: MM—main memory; SC—spatial part; TC—temporal part; MUX—multiplexer. *Description*: the novel cache organization—STS cache consists of two parts: the temporal and the spatial parts. Temporal part is organized as a small and fast direct-mapped cache with a one-word block size. Spatial part is a larger cache and has the usual block size. *Explanation*: the optimal cache structure (from the locality-related cache organization point of view) implies that the cache is split into a "temporal" part (with a smaller and faster cache) and a "spatial" part. Spatial data usually includes a temporal component which is symbolically indicated by including a larger block for the spatial part. *Implication*: correct dimensioning of the cache hierarchy levels is of crucial importance for the performance of the STS approach.

will later be clear that the default locality type should be set to spatial. During the run time, as the data is fetched, evicted, and later refetched, tags are updated and the system begins to function properly.

Created in this way, such a system can also be used with software compiled without STS support.

Processor sends a memory reference request simultaneously to both STS cache modules. When one STS part (temporal or spatial) detects a hit, a signal is sent to the other part to prevent its request to the main memory.

A memory fetch is initiated when requested data is not found in either of the STS modules. The data block length that is fetched from the memory depends upon its current locality tag. This tag determines whether the block is to be sent to the spatial or to the temporal STS part. The addressed STS part receives the data and responds to the CPU, while the other STS part cancels the request received from the CPU.

When a write-back to memory is performed, the cache also sends the information if the data has been retagged. For this purpose, the bus is widened by 1 bit to allow sending this new type of locality.

7.2. Expected Improvement Analysis

In this solution the main performance improvements come from the short access latency of the temporal part of the cache. The average memory access latency of the whole system is directly affected by this latency.

In a traditional cache system the average memory access latency (t) is

$$t = p \times t_c + (1 - p) \times t_m$$

where p stands for probability of a cache hit, t_c is the cache access latency, and t_m is the cache miss latency.

In a modified STS system, the average memory access latency (t) would be

$$t = p_s \times t_s + p_t \times t_t + (1 - (p_s + p_t)) \times t_m$$

where p_s and p_t stand for the probabilities of hits in the spatial and hits in the temporal part of the cache, t_s and t_t stand for access latencies of the spatial and the temporal parts of the cache, and t_m is the cache miss latency.

It is assumed that the hit probabilities for the whole modified STS system and the traditional cache system are the same. Since the hit probability of a modified STS system equals to the sum of probabilities of its both parts, it is easily shown that the overall average memory access latency is shorter for a modified STS system:

$$p_s \times t_s + p_t \times t_t < p_s \times t_s + p_t \times t_s = (p_s + p_t) \times t_s = p \times t_c$$

Also an improvement in hit ratio (also in hit probability) is shown in modified STS system. The data with poor spatial (and high temporal) locality goes to the temporal cache that leads to better cache utilization because temporal blocks are smaller and data from the same spatial block (as the temporal data being accessed) is not fetched. Thus, there is no eviction of potentially useful data. With less useless data being transferred, there is also less contention on the bus.

8. DETERMINING LOCALITY

Methods for resolving the data locality are basically the same as for the original STS system [2]. Determining the locality of data can be done at compile time, profile time, run time, or, preferably, as a combination of these methods.

8.1. Compile-Time Resolution

The simplest way to set the initial allocation is to assign T (temporal) to simple variables and constants and S (spatial) to elements of complex data structures.

It is possible to use more sophisticated algorithms, but one should bear in mind that proper labeling is vastly dependent on the (spatial) block size, as well as on the sizes of both parts of the cache.

Stronger spatial locality justifies use of larger blocks and subsequently more space the blocks occupy in the spatial cache. Thus, more data should be marked as temporal when large spatial blocks are used. Smaller spatial blocks generate less bus occupancy and less useless data is fetched, so the temporal cache can be reserved only for data exhibiting the highest temporal locality.

The cache size influences locality that data exhibits. Larger cache allows fetched data to reside longer in the cache (on average), so data that exhibits no spatial or temporal locality in a small cache might start to exhibit it in a larger cache.

The above means that, unless only a specific system with known block and cache size is targeted, it is difficult to perform a fine compile-time locality resolution.

The profile-time mechanism, which will be described in the following sections, can change the locality only from spatial to temporal. Therefore, for solutions where compile-time resolution is used in combination with profile-time mechanism, it is best to mark more data as spatial. The only data that should be marked as temporal is the one for which high temporal and low spatial locality can be anticipated with a high degree of certainty.

8.2. Profile-Time Resolution

All data blocks are initially regarded as spatial. Then, a profile-time algorithm, depicted in Fig. 22, is used for detecting and retagging to temporal those blocks that are found to exhibit temporal locality.

When a block is fetched into the cache, profile-time mechanism associates it with two counters (*Xcount* and *Ycount*). The *Xcount* value for a particular data block (initially zero) is incremented on each access to the upper half of the block, is decremented on the access to the lower half of the block, and resets on the replacement of the block. When the *Xcount* value reaches upper (x) or lower limit ($-x$), further counting is disabled. The *Xcount* value is checked periodically (because the density of accesses in a unit of time determines degree of temporal locality). Period of *Xcount* checking is controlled by *Ycount*, which counts overall number of accesses to this block. When this counter reaches some prespecified value (y), the value of corresponding *Xcount* is checked. If either limit (x or $-x$) is reached, the block is tagged as "temporal"; otherwise, it is tagged as "spatial." The block once tagged

```
if(hit.in.block)
   if(Tag=Spatial){
      if(-X<Xcount<X)
         if(Hi) Xcount=Xcount+1;
         else   Xcount=Xcount-1;
      if(Ycount<Y) Ycount=Ycount+1;
      else{
         if(-X<Xcount<X) Tag=Spatial;
         else Tag=Temporal;
            Xcount=0;
            Ycount=0;
         }
   }
```

Figure 22 The simple profile-time algorithm for tagging of data blocks against their locality. *Legend*: Xcount and Ycount—counters; X and Y—limits for Xcount and Ycount, respectively; Hi—flag which indicates the hit in an upper half of block. *Description*: the two counters are associated with each block in the data memory. *Explanation*: initially, it is assumed that all data is spatial and that the values of Xcount and Ycount are set to zero. This simple algorithm observes the overall access pattern for each block and retags to temporal the blocks with lower data block utilization.

as temporal cannot later be retagged to spatial (as it can be in the run-time algorithm).

The profile-time mechanism should give a better assessment of what data should be marked as spatial and what as temporal than the proposed compile-time mechanism (at the cost of running the profiler). However, the problem with temporal and spatial locality being relative to a block and cache sizes remains the same.

Application profiling, as already mentioned, is only applicable to selected applications and adds considerable overhead. With a large overhead, it becomes difficult to conclude what accuracy can be achieved.

8.3. Run-Time Resolution

The algorithm analogous to the profile-time algorithm can be easily implemented in hardware for run-time tagging/retagging of data according to the dynamically observed changing access pattern (Fig. 23). It works very similar to the profile-time algorithm, with two counters and the appropriate

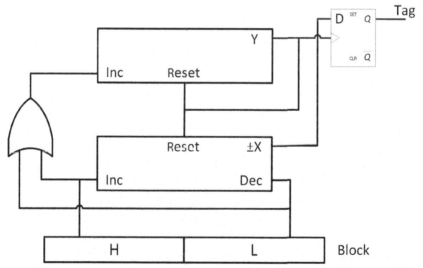

Figure 23 The simple run-time logic for dynamic tagging/retagging of data blocks against their locality. *Description*: the two-counter logic is associated with each block in data cache. *Explanation*: default tags of all data are spatial. Counters are initially set to zero. After each Xcount value checking, the proper tag is written in a D flip-flop, and both counters are reset. Even if a block changes its tag (it is retagged) on this occasion, it stays there until being evicted and is replaced in the memory with its new tag. On the next access to this block, a cache miss will be incurred, and the block will be fetched in the appropriate cache part according to the new tag.

control logic being implemented in hardware and attached to each block in the spatial part of the cache.

The run-time algorithm is implemented as a hardware part of the system. Therefore, the criteria for tagging can be adjusted to the parameters of the specific system. However, if only a run-time system is used, there will be a cold-start period during which all data is marked spatial. Therefore, it is best to use a conservative compile- or profile-time assessment to alleviate the cold-start and use the run-time mechanism for maximizing the performance.

It is necessary to note that overhead is incurred whatever approach is issued. A more complex cache system unavoidable adds to the memory access latency.

9. MODIFIED STS IN A MULTICORE SYSTEM

In a multicore chip, a problem of maintaining consistency within the chip might arise, if a modified STS system is used. There are several possible solutions to this problem.

One is to put an inclusive, nonshared L2 cache that would contain copies of 64 B blocks of all data in the L1 cache (disregarding the type of the block—spatial or temporal). Then, this L2 cache could implement any of consistency protocols used with regular caches (MESI, MOESI, etc.). However, this solution would eliminate any benefits that a modified STS brings in terms of reducing traffic on the memory bus. The fact is that a whole block is fetched from the memory, disregarding the type.

A second solution is to have both parts of the system snoop the bus independently and act as two separate caches. In this way, two or more temporal data, from what would be the same spatial block, might find themselves simultaneously in caches of different CPUs. This approach might have an additional benefit in reducing false-sharing,

This solution, as well as the whole topic of using a Modified STS in a multicore system, requires some further thought and is likely to be a topic of future research.

10. CONDITIONS AND ASSUMPTIONS OF THE ANALYSIS BELOW

The conditions and assumptions for the following simulations are described in this section.

Cache subsystems employed write-back policy in all the caches. The block size was eight 64-bit words for conventional two-level hierarchy and for the spatial part in STS variants and one word for temporal hierarchy in STS variants. Organizational parameters of the cache memory were four-way set associatively and LRU replacement algorithm.

The latency of conventional cache and the spatial part of the STS was three cycles, and the latency of the temporal part was 30% smaller (two cycles).

Only a run-time mechanism for determining data locality was used (no compile-time support and no profiling was done). Thus "the worst-case scenario" was examined.

Data bus was 32 bit wide. Cache memories were nonblocking. Simulated system had 512 MB of ram and a 2 GHz CPU based on Alpha ISA.

11. SIMULATION STRATEGY

Advantages and drawbacks of the simulation based approaches are well known: they do enable different scenarios to be compared under identical conditions, but they lack details on the implementation level.

The simulation of STS was done with an M5 Simulator System modified to work with STS. For comparisons, the same simulations were run under the standard M5, used as a traditional cache system.

M5 is a modular platform for computer system architecture research, encompassing processor microarchitecture as well as system-level architecture. Further information on M5 simulator is in Ref. [21].

All simulations were done under the syscall emulation mode using the Radix application with 262,144 keys and a 1024 radix. A Simple Timing model of the CPU was used.

Power consumption of the system was estimated using CACTI 4.2.

In the following sections, we will examine the results of the conducted simulations. We will look at overall system performance, as well as at the effects of several important parameters.

11.1. Overall Performance

Modified STS system showed shorter average memory access latency compared to a conventional cache system of a similar size. In some configurations, moreover, a modified STS manages to outperform substantially larger traditional cache systems. Figure 24 shows overall memory access latency.

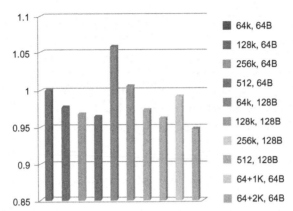

Figure 24 Normalized memory reference latency for the Radix application for different setups (lower is better). *Description*: modified STS system shows an improvement over the traditional system of a similar size.

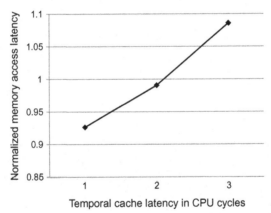

Figure 25 Effects of temporal cache part latency on the performance of a modified STS system (lower is better). *Description*: temporal cache part latency has a large effect on the system performance.

11.2. Effects of the Temporal Latency

A very important parameter of the modified STS system is the latency of the temporal part of the cache. Several simulations were done to get a clear view of how much this latency impacts the overall performance of the system.

Figure 25 shows the improvement in overall memory access latency. We compared a traditional system and a modified STS system both with the same amount of cache, but with different temporal latencies.

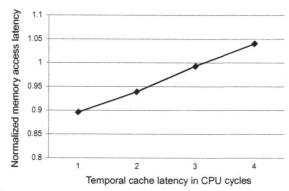

Figure 26 Effects of the temporal cache part latency on the performance of a modified STS system (lower is better). *Description*: temporal cache part latency has a large effect on the performance of the system.

When we used the same three-cycle latency for all cashes (temporal part of the cache, spatial part, and the traditional system), modified STS performed worse than the traditional system. As this latency was decreased, performances improved up to 7% for a single-cycle temporal latency.

Simulations were also done with latency of the spatial part and of the reference cache set to four cycles (Fig. 26).

Again, a similar pattern could be observed. The performances were worse compared to the reference system for the four-cycle temporal latency, and there was a linear improvement as the temporal part latency was being decreased. That improvement had up to a 10% increase for a single-cycle latency of the temporal part of the cache.

11.3. Effects of the Temporal Cache Associativity

Simulations proved that, for the performance of a modified STS system, the most crucial factor was the low latency of the temporal part of the cache. Also, it was shown that, at a certain point, it became difficult (if not impossible) to further decrease this latency.

At this point, we checked the possibility to increase the associativity without hurting the latency. We conducted several simulations in order to understand possible benefits of an increased associativity. An LRU replacement policy was assumed.

From Fig. 27, it is obvious that there was a significant improvement when going from a DM to a two-way associative temporal part of the cache. Increasing associativity beyond this point did not bring an improvement.

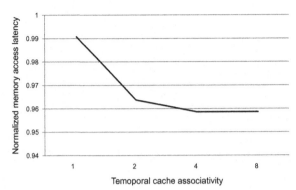

Temoporal cache associativity

Figure 27 Effects of the temporal cache part associativity on the performance of a modified STS system (lower is better). *Description*: increasing the temporal cache associativity from direct-mapped to two-way associative generates a substantial improvement in performances. Further increases in the associativity create much smaller improvements.

11.4. The X Limit Parameter

The X limit parameter determines what criteria data has to meet in order to be marked as temporal.

The lower the value of X limit is, the more data is marked as temporal.

If X limit is set too high, little or no data is marked as temporal, leading to temporal part of the cache not being used. If this value is set too low, there is too much temporal data, leading to a decrease in performance due to trashing.

For a system to function properly, X limit must be not less than a half of block size (in words); otherwise, all data might end up marked as temporal.

The results showed a maximum improvement in performances when X limit was 33.

One should note that the optimal value of the X limit parameter varies with the access patterns in the software, as well as with the size of the temporal part of the cache. Also, too small values of the X limit hurt the performances less than too large values. This is due to the fact that very limited amount of data can meet even relaxed criteria for strong temporal locality (Fig. 28).

11.5. Power Consumption

The power consumption of the system was estimated using CACTI.4.2. The results, with some reference values, are shown in Fig. 29. The modified STS system dissipated around 10% more power than the traditional cache system used for reference.

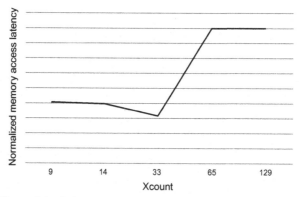

Figure 28 Effects of the "X limit" parameter on the performance of a modified STS system (lower is better). *Description*: with 1 kB of temporal and 64 kB of spatial cache and a block size of eight 64 bit words, a modified STS system shows maximum performance when "X limit" is set to 33. For smaller values of "X limit" the temporal cache is overburdened, and for higher values it is underutilized.

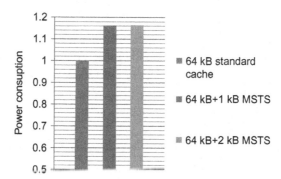

Figure 29 Power consumption of modified STS systems. *Description*: a modified STS system dissipates around 10% more power than the traditional cache system used for reference.

We used CACTI tool also to verify that temporal cache latency could be at least 30% shorter than that of the spatial cache.

Results show an estimated access latency of 0.96 (ns) for the 64K spatial part of the cache, and 0.631 and 0.64 (ns) for 1K and 2K direct caches, respectively. The latter ones would be used for the temporal cache part.

The power consumption in most recent efforts [22] was considered with highest priority. This research exploits memory region semantics to partition data cache.

12. CONCLUSIONS OF THE ANALYSIS PART

This chapter shows that the STS approach manages to outperform traditional cache systems of similar size, and, in many cases, matches the performance of substantially larger traditional caches. STS implementation can achieve a reduction of transistor count consumed by the cache, as well as better return from invested transistors.

The fact that an increase in cache size leads to an increase in latency might give the possibility to improve performances beyond those that can be achieved by a traditional single-level hierarchy, regardless of the size.

It is important to stress that the implementation of STS does not affect possible higher level caches. It is still possible to add a traditional level cache to the system, in order to further increase the performance.

The cache subsystem has not been changed drastically, so conventional techniques for device fault detection and diagnosis circuitry can be used (we mean detection of VLSI fabrication faults and on-line detection and recovery from hard failures).

There are indications that incorporation of modified STS cache may help in system applications like treatment of abort procedures in transactional memory systems, which is the subject of the follow-up chapter.

The results of simulations are based on a system with only a run-time locality resolution. Further improvements can be expected if compile- or profile-time support is added.

Finally, in the simulations, we have concentrated on average memory access latency as an important parameter for performance evaluation. A modified STS system should also bring improvements in terms of reducing bus contention, as the unnecessary data is not fetched (the data that would be in the same block with some temporal data that is being fetched). It remains yet to be studied how the DDC concept would behave in the context of multicore and many-core systems [23,24].

13. THE TABLE OF ABBREVIATIONS

Table 3 includes only the abbreviations used in the text. Those used only in figures and explained in their captions are not listed here.

Table 3 Abbreviations

Abbreviations	Meaning
2D	Two-dimensional space
CACTI	An integrated cache and memory access time, cycle time, area, leakage, and dynamic power model
DDC	Dual data cache
DDM	The data type-dependent cache for MPEG application
DM	Direct-mapped sub-cache system
FIFO	First-in first-out
FPGA	Field programmable gate array
GMC	General multiprocessor compiler-assisted
GMN	General multiprocessor compiler-not-assisted
GUC	General uniprocessor compiler-assisted
GUN	General uniprocessor compiler-not-assisted
ISA	Instruction set architecture
JOP	Java processor
LPT	Locality prediction table
LRU	Last recently used
M5	General-purpose architecture simulator
MESI	Full cache coherency protocol
MOESI	Full cache coherency protocol
MPEG	Standard for lossy compression of video and audio
NP	Neighbor prefetching
OBL	One-Block-Lookahead
RSDC	Reconfigurable split data cache
SMC	Special multiprocessor compiler-assisted
SMN	Special multiprocessor compiler-not-assisted
STS	Split temporal/spatial
SUC	Special uniprocessor compiler-assisted
SUN	Special uniprocessor compiler-not-assisted
TP	Time-predictable data cache
TS	The Texas solution

ACKNOWLEDGMENTS

The results of this research were generated under the project of the Serbian Ministry of Sciences, III 44006.

REFERENCES

[1] A. Gonzalez, C. Aliagas, M. Mateo, Data cache with multiple caching strategies tuned to different types of locality, in: Proceedings of the International Conference on Supercomputing, 1995, pp. 338–347.

[2] V. Milutinovic, M. Tomasevic, B. Markovic, M. Tremblay, The split temporal/spatial cache: initial performance analysis, in: Proceedings of the SCIzzL-5, Santa Clara, California, USA, 1996, pp. 72–78.

[3] M. Valero, The DDC cache, in: Invited Lecture at the UPC, Barcelona, Spain, 1994.

[4] D.A. Patterson, J.L. Hennessy, Computer Organization and Design: The Hardware/Software Interface, fourth ed., The Morgan Kaufmann Series in Computer Architecture and Design, Morgan Kaufmann Publishers Inc., San Francisco, CA, 2008.

[5] V. Milutinovic, M. Tomasevic, B. Markovic, M. Tremblay, The split temporal/spatial cache: initial complexity analysis, in: Proceedings of the SCIzzL-6, Santa Clara, California, USA, 1996, pp. 89–96.

[6] G. Memik, M. Kandemir, M. Haldar, A. Choudhary, A Selective Hardware/Compiler Approach for Improving Cache Locality: Technical Report CPDC-TR-9909-016, Northwestern University, Evanston, IL, 1999.

[7] J. Sahuquillo, A. Pont, The split data cache in multiprocessor systems: an initial hit ratio analysis, in: Proceedings of the Seventh Euromicron Workshop on Parallel and Distributed Processing, 1999, pp. 27–34.

[8] Z. Sustran, Comparing Two Multiprocessor Oriented Compiler-Assisted Approaches to General Purpose Processing: The Case of Abort in Transactional Memory System: Technical Report of FP7 BalCon Project, Thessaloniki, Greece, September, 2011 (Ph.D. Thesis in Preparation).

[9] A. Naz, K.M. Kavi, J. Oh, P. Foglia, Reconfigurable split data caches: a novel scheme for embedded systems, in: Proceedings of the 2007 ACM Symposium on Applied Computing (SAC), 2007, pp. 707–712.

[10] P. Ranganathan, S. Adve, N.P. Jouppi, Reconfigurable caches and their application to media processing, in: Proceedings of the 27th International Symposium on Computer Architecture, 2000, pp. 214–224.

[11] R.P. Feynman, Lectures on Computation, Addison-Wesley, Boston, MA, 1998.

[12] A.J. Smith, Cache memories, ACM Comput. Surv. 14 (3) (1982) 473–530.

[13] M.J. Flynn, O. Mencer, V. Milutinovic, et al., Moving from PetaFlops to PetaData, Commun. ACM 56 (5) (2013) 39–42.

[14] R. Cucchiara, A. Prati, M. Piccardi, Data-type dependent cache prefetching for MPEG applications, in: 21st IEEE International Performance, Computing, and Communications Conference, 2002, pp. 115–122.

[15] O. Adamo, A. Naz, T. Janjusic, K.M. Kavi, C. Chung, Smaller split L-1 data caches for multi-core processing systems, in: Proceedings of the ISPAN, 2009, pp. 74–79.

[16] M. Schoeberl, W. Puffitsch, B. Huber, Towards time-predictable data caches for chip-multiprocessors, in: Proceedings of the SEUS, 2009, pp. 180–191.

[17] G. Rakocevic, Z. Sustran, V. Milutinovic, A modified split temporal/spatial cache, in: Proceedings of the IEEE Multi-Conference on Systems and Control (MSC), IEEE, Dubrovnik, Croatia, 2012.

[18] Z. Sustran, S. Stojanovic, G. Rakocevic, V. Milutinovic, M. Valero, A survey of dual data caches, in: Proceedings of the IEEE International Conference on Industrial Technology, Athena, 2012.
[19] V. Milutinovic, The STS Cache: Technical Report #35/95, University of Belgrade, Belgrade, Serbia, Yugoslavia, 1995.
[20] V. Milutinovic, M. Tomasevic, B. Markovi, M. Tremblay, A new cache architecture concept: the split temporal/spatial cache, in: Electrotechnical Conference, 1996. MELECON '96., 8th Mediterranean, vol. 2, 13–16 May 1996, pp. 1108–1111.
[21] N. Binkert, R. Dreslinski, L. Hsu, K. Lim, A. Saidi, S. Reinhardt, The M5 simulator: modeling networked systems, IEEE Micro 26 (4) (2006) 52–60.
[22] Z. Fang, L. Zhao, X. Jiang, S. Lu, R. Iyer, T. Li, S.-E. Lee, Reducing L1 caches power by exploiting software semantics, in: Proceedings of the 2012 ACM/IEEE International Symposium on Low Power Electronics and Design (ISLPED'12), New York, NY, USA, 2012, pp. 391–396.
[23] M.J. Flynn, Interview: development of microprocessors, IPSI Trans. Internet Res. 5 (2) (2009) 2–3.
[24] Y. Patt, Future microprocessors: what must we do differently if we are to effectively utilize multi-core and many-core chips? IPSI Trans. Internet Res. 5 (1) (2009) 5–9.

ABOUT THE AUTHORS

Zivojin Sustran, Ph.D. student, received his B.Sc. and M.Sc. in Computer Engineering at the University of Belgrade, Serbia, in 2010 and 2012. He is currently a teaching assistant at the School of Electrical Engineering, University of Belgrade, Serbia. His research interests are mainly in computer architecture and they are focused on heterogeneous architectures and memory systems.

Goran Rakocevic, Ph.D. student, received his B.Sc in Electrical Engineering at the University of Belgrade, Serbia, in 2007. He currently works at Seven Bridges Genomics at building genomics analyses pipelines around peer-reviewed tools and the IGOR platform. He was previously with the Mathematical Institute of the Serbian Academy of Sciences and Arts, Belgrade, Serbia where he was a research assistant.

Veljko Milutinović, received a Ph.D. degree in Electrical Engineering from the University of Belgrade in 1982. During the 1980s, for about a decade, he was on the faculty of Purdue University in the USA, where he coauthored the architecture and design of the world's first DARPA GaAs microprocessor. He is a professor at the School of Electrical Engineering, University of Belgrade, Serbia. Dr. Milutinovic is a Fellow of the IEEE and a Member of Academia Europaea.

AUTHOR INDEX

Note: Page numbers followed by "*f*" indicate figures and "*t*" indicate tables.

SUBJECT INDEX

Note: Page numbers followed by "*f*" indicate figures and "*t*" indicate tables.

CONTENTS OF VOLUMES IN THIS SERIES

247

Volume 82

Volume 83

Volume 84

Volume 94

Volume 95

Printed in the United States
By Bookmasters